The Great Confrontation

The Great Confrontation

EUROPE AND ISLAM
THROUGH THE CENTURIES

Ilya V. Gaiduk

IVAN R. DEE

Chicago 2003

Library of Congress Cataloging-in-Publication Data:

Gaiduk, I. V. (Il'ia V.), 1961–
   The great confrontation : Europe and Islam through the centuries /
Ilya V. Gaiduk.
     p. cm.
   Includes bibliographical references and index.
   ISBN 1-56663-535-7 (alk. paper)
   1. Europe—Relations—Islamic countries. 2. Islamic countries—
Relations—Europe. 3. Civilization, Islamic—Western influences. 4.
Europe—Civilization—Islamic influences. 5. Christianity and other
religions—Islam. I. Title.

D34.I85G35 2003
303.48'24017671—dc21

                                       2003055292

To My Friends of Youth

Contents

Preface

THE IDEA FOR THIS BOOK occurred to me long before the terrorist attacks of Osama bin Laden's Islamic extremists against the United States on September 11, 2001, and the ensuing war in Afghanistan that brought the world to consider the nature of terrorism and its connections with Islam as a religion and a civilization. Nor was the book inspired by the debate in the West throughout the 1990s about the "roots of Muslim rage."[1] At the time some observers attempted to locate the causes of Islamic terrorism in the civilization's incompatibility with modern society, its undemocratic nature, its historical enmity toward the followers of other faiths, and the Prophet Muhammad's direction to wage "holy war" (*jihad*) against the infidels until Islam's complete victory. Others pointed to poverty; the uneven distribution of wealth in the Muslim world; the resentment of Western domination; double standards in Western policies toward Middle Eastern regimes; discrimination against Muslim communities in Western countries; the Israeli-Palestinian conflict; and the legacy of cold war rivalries over Afghanistan. All these factors were presumed to provoke Muslim aggressiveness and the radicalization of opposition movements in Islamic domains. Those who found problems within Islam itself were mostly people of non-Muslim and even non-Asian origin, whereas those who saw Western treatment at fault had some connection with the Muslim or third world, either directly or through ancestors and relatives. The conflict of civilizations, it seems, found its way into the pages of books and articles. Debate often degenerated into mutual accusation.[2]

Meanwhile, with the formation of a broad alliance of world powers in the struggle against terrorism after September 11, the thesis of "the clash of civilizations" ceased to be fashionable. Even its propagator, Samuel Huntington, had to retreat, in the pages of a French magazine, from his earlier certain position on the issue.[3] The concept nevertheless appears to be strongly entrenched in the minds of most people, including academics and politicians, chiefly because it provides a ready explanation for many phenomena in contemporary East-West relations.

In fact the idea for this book initially had purely academic foundations: it grew out of my interest in the history of medieval Europe. One of the salient features of this history was a long and, at first glance, incessant war between European powers and the world of Islam. The Byzantine Empire, Spain and Italy, then Greece and other countries of the Balkan peninsula, finally Russia and the countries of the Caucasus—all of them at various times became targets of attack by the Muslim world and were forced to defend themselves. At the same time the European powers were not averse to armed encroachments upon Islamic possessions when the moment seemed opportune for such undertakings. The Crusades, the audacious expeditions of the Emperor Charles V in North Africa, and Russian conquests of the Tatar khanates in Kazan and Astrakhan are only a few examples of European incursions into the regions of Islam over the centuries. All these military offensives and counteroffensives were clothed in religious phraseology. Each side presented its actions as sanctioned by God and undertaken for the purpose of disseminating the proper religion and eradicating heresy. Both worlds, it seems, were involved in a permanent "holy war," a consequence of hatred and enmity whose roots lay in their incompatibility. Is this impression correct? In this book I hope to answer this question.

World events that occurred just before my beginning work on this book continue to shock the West in particular. Cruel terrorist attacks in New York, Washington, and Moscow by people who called themselves or were called by others Muslims, Islamists, fundamentalists, *mujahedin*, or *shahids*, and who killed or took as hostages thousands of innocent people with a cry of "Allahu Akbar," seemed to prove that after the end of the cold war the world had entered upon a new conflict, one that might threaten the very foundations of the world community. It appears to be an inherited confrontation between two civilizations.

Under these circumstances, the history of relations between European and Islamic civilizations becomes more than a purely academic undertaking. It strikes chords of ongoing contemporary passion, and it may help us understand ongoing political and social dynamics. Civilizations are living organisms, continuously changing under the influence of internal developments and outside events; relations between them must be considered in light of different historical periods and contexts. But history as well as religion may also become the propaganda tools of terrorists. And discussions in the West about the nature of Islam and its relationship to the outside world are often "abstract, static, and ahistorical,"[4] which may make them appear shallow.

A detailed history of fourteen centuries of Europe-Islam relations is beyond the ability of any single author. Such a formidable undertaking would require the joint effort of a group of scholars from various countries and would fill several volumes. It would provide an exhaustive account accompanied by a thorough analysis and a suggestion of the implications for our lives. But in the very size of such a work the reader may find himself lost in an overabundance of facts and arguments.

A shorter book on such a large subject is unavoidably neglectful of some aspects of the subject at hand. But I hope to present my ideas, hypotheses, arguments, and suggestions while stimulating the reader's interest and his desire to make further inquiries. It is an introduction rather than a complete study. And the bibliography at the end of the book may serve as a guide for interested readers.

In the course of writing this book I have therefore been aware of the shortcomings as well as the advantages of the undertaking. This work differs from the earlier works of, for example, Franco Gardini[5] or Bernard Lewis[6] on the same subject because of its greater emphasis on Russia as a part of European civilization and on Russian relations with Islam. It also attempts to present a more detailed picture of developments in the Muslim world in the twentieth century and their implications for relations between Europe and Islam.

The title of the book suggests that it is limited chiefly to the history of contacts between Europe and Islam that occurred in a zone between the two civilizations. Although the configuration of this zone changed over time as a result of conquests and demographic developments, it is possible to identify it as beginning in the Mediterranean and traveling northward through the Balkans and the Black Sea regions and northeastward into the Volga basin. Of course Europe touched Islamic civilization in other parts of the globe, especially during the era of European discoveries and expansion, but European relations with Islam beyond the principal region just outlined are different in character and scope and deserve special study. The only exclusion from this rule is the interaction of Russia and Muslims in Central Asia, because for a long time Central Asian lands formed a part of first the Russian Empire and then the Soviet Union. Even today Russia exerts an important influence on that region.

Finally, a point on the English transliteration of Arabic and Persian names. As one author has noted, it is a messy business. I found as many types of transliteration as I did books and studies. Generally I have followed the styles of the sources I have used, but I have tried to avoid diacritical marks that often hamper the reading of a book by nonspecialists. Those names that appear frequently in English literature, such as Muhammad, Nasser, etc., I have spelled as they appear in common usage, though variants exist in these cases as well.

While writing this book I continued to enjoy the cooperation and encouragement of many colleagues in the Woodrow Wilson

International Center for Scholars in Washington, D.C., where most of the basic work was done, and in Moscow. Among them I wish to express my appreciation to the Wilson Center's library staff, who helped me immensely in locating books and other source materials from libraries in the United States and from various databases on the Internet. I am also greatly indebted to the Center's visiting scholars from Russia and other countries of the Commonwealth of Independent States (CIS), who were with me for six months at the Kennan Institute for Advanced Russian Studies, for their enthusiasm for and interest in my work. Among this group I am especially grateful to Yelena Morozova from Belarus and Vyacheslav Kozliakov from Russia, with whom I spent hours discussing various aspects of this book. I also wish to thank Ivan Dee, my publisher. This is our second book together, and, as with the first one, he proved to be not only a skillful editor of my English but an attentive and intelligent reader of the manuscript. He made it much better; whatever deficiencies remain are mine. The book is dedicated to my friends from Turkmenistan—Turkmens, Russians, Armenians, Kazakhs, and others—who shared my youth and early career.

Antonio

Mark you this, Bassanio,

The devil can cite scripture for his purpose.

An evil soul producing holy witness

Is like a villain with a smiling cheek—

A goodly apple rotten at the heart:

O, what a goodly outside falsehood hath!

—Shakespeare, *The Merchant of Venice*

The Great Confrontation

ONE

Setting the Stage

With the September 11, 2001, attacks on New York and Washington, and the discovery that all the hijacked planes had been seized by Muslim radicals, it seemed that the most somber predictions of a war between the civilizations had begun to be realized. Such predictions first appeared in the early 1990s when a wave of terrorist acts organized by Islamic activists shook the world. These acts differed from those of the Palestinians in the 1970s and 1980s. In the nineties the participants included representatives from various countries whose official or dominant religion was Islam. They also differed in their targets: the United States and other countries that fell within the category of Christendom. And the scope of the terrorists' objectives and means was much wider and more ambitious.

Although this campaign of violence, according to some observers, had been initiated as early as 1983,[1] the first spectacular assault occurred on February 26, 1993. A terrorist bombing attack at the World Trade Center in New York left six people dead and more than a thousand injured. On August 7, 1998, terrorist bombings of the U.S. embassies in Nairobi, Kenya, and Dar es Salaam, Tanzania, resulted in 224 deaths of American and African citizens. In the interim there had been several attempted terrorist attacks in the United States and other countries that had been prevented or foiled by police and security forces.[2]

All these events were accompanied by declarations from militant Islamic leaders that left no doubt about the purpose of their actions and its ideological context. On February 23, 1998, *Al-Quds al-Arabi*, an Arabic newspaper published in London, printed a "Declaration of the World Islamic Front for Jihad Against the Jews and the Crusaders." The text was signed by Osama bin Laden, head of the Al Qaeda international terrorist organization, later to become infamous in connection with the events of September 11, and other leaders of militant Islamist groups in Egypt, Pakistan, and Bangladesh. The statement accused the United States of waging war "against God, his Prophet, and Muslims," and, in turn, declared war against the United States and its allies. "To kill Americans and their allies, both civil and military, is an individual duty of every Muslim who is able, in any country where this is possible," read the *fatwa*, or religious ruling, "until the Aqsa Mosque [in Jerusalem] and the Haram Mosque [in Mecca, Saudi Arabia] are freed from their grip and until their armies, shattered and broken-winged, depart from all the lands of Islam, incapable of threatening any Muslim." And further: "By God's leave, we call on every Muslim who believes in God and hopes for reward to obey God's command to kill the Americans and plunder their possessions wherever he finds them and whenever he can. Likewise we call on the Muslim *ulema* [religious leaders] and leaders and youth and soldiers to launch attacks against the armies of the American devils and against those who are allied with them from among the helpers of Satan."[3] After the September 11 attacks, in a message recorded on videotape, bin Laden was explicit that the attacks represented a war for Islam and against infidels. He noted the "humiliation and disgrace" that Islam had suffered for "more than eighty years"—that is, since the final defeat of the Ottoman Empire and the occupation of its capital, Constantinople, by the Western powers.[4]

Thus, while President George W. Bush spoke about "evil-doers" or "evil ones" and insisted that they were neither Afghans nor Muslims, and while most world leaders openly refused to make war against Islam or Muslims, and while Pope John Paul II expressed the Catholic church's respect for Islam and condemned fanaticism and terrorism as a profanation of God,[5] leaders of Islamic radical organizations openly declared *jihad*, a holy war against Western civilization and its allies. And many Muslims, radical or not, supported this declaration. According to a poll taken in Morocco in late September 2001, for example, although a majority of Moroccans condemned the September 11 bombings, 41 percent sympathized with bin Laden's message.[6]

THE CLASH OF CIVILIZATIONS

Not only Arabs and other Muslims viewed the September 11 attacks as a war between civilizations. A significant segment of public opinion in countries with predominantly Christian populations tended to agree. In Western Europe the expression of this point of view appeared in an article (and later a book) written soon after the tragic events by the renowned journalist Oriana Fallaci. In the Italian daily *Il Carriere della Sera*, she passionately aired her views on the events in New York and Washington and their implications. The very title of the article, "The Rage and the Pride," reveals the feelings of this woman who had reported from the battlefields of the Vietnam War, interviewed the Ayatollah Khomeini soon after the 1979 revolution in Iran, visited Palestine to interview Yassir Arafat, and for years had lived in New York, where she had now witnessed the tragedy in Manhattan. For Fallaci there was no doubt that this attack was part of a religious war, one "which is not aimed at the conquest of our territory, perhaps, but which certainly pursues the goal of the conquest of our soul, of the death of our liberty and of our civilization."[7] She accused the "sons of Allah" of seeking to "destroy our culture, our art, our science, our morale, our values, our joy of life. . . ." She appealed to European leaders to become worthy of Richard the Lion-Hearted and rally around the United States against the menace of Islam. She insisted on the superiority of Western culture over Islamic and, on that ground, called for a defense of this culture with all possible means.

That her opinion found many supporters was demonstrated by the demand for Fallaci's book. Published in December 2001, *The Rage and the Pride* quickly sold a million copies.[8] But not only ordinary people seemed to share Fallaci's view of a conflict between civilizations. Italian Prime Minister Silvio Berlusconi, during a visit to Berlin soon after September 11, spoke of the superiority of Western civilization compared with that of Islam: "We have respect for human rights, religious and political, which certainly does not exist in Islamic countries. We have understanding of diversity and tolerance." Western society, he declared, had values, such as "love for liberty per se, for liberty of the people and the individual," that were "certainly not a property of other civilizations, for example, Islamic."[9] The conclusion to be derived from these pronouncements was the same: the incompatibility of the two civilizations and the inevitability of their conflict. Although Berlusconi later cautioned against the "criminalization of Islam" and endorsed a "meeting and dialogue between people and religions,"[10] scarcely anyone believed in the sincerity of these statements.

Surprisingly, the articles and observations of well-known experts on Islam, in magazines and on talk shows, did not help ease the anxiety of many people who feared other, more deadly terrorist attacks in various European countries as well as on the American continent. Assertions that the enemy was only a faction—a "militant Islam"—not Islam as a religion or culture or even a civilization, seemed not to accord with facts. Even before September 11, the mass media had supplied plenty of evidence of terrorist acts conducted by Muslims; why were the adherents of Islam, not of other religions, involved in terrorist plots around the world? People knew about terrorist activities in Ireland, where encounters between Catholics and Protestants had been accompanied by bloody clashes. They had heard about the conflict between Buddhist Sinhalese and Hindu Tamils in Sri Lanka and the many victims of terrorism of the Tigers of Tamil Eelam. They had shuddered at the news from Japan about poisonous gas attacks in the subway by the religious sect Aum Shinrikyo. Yet all these terrorist acts, while seemingly of a religious nature, were local phenomena. Although inhuman and in many cases monstrous, they had been aimed only at people in one country. Islamic terrorism, on the other hand, seemed to represent a danger to a larger community of nations and peoples.

Nor were people's concerns alleviated by explanations of the true nature of the Islamist threat. While drawing attention to the fact that there is no monolithic "Islamintern" (a coined analogy with the Communist International's Comintern[11]), and that Islam embraces "a mosaic of many national, ethnic and religious groups competing for power and influence; a multinational phenomenon ranging from Malaysia to France,"[12] expert observers emphasized the "ideological fervency" of militant Islam, "its reach, its ambitiousness, and its staying power."[13] Moreover they demonstrated, in the words of Daniel Pipes, that "militant Islam has proved itself to be the only truly vital totalitarian movement in the world today. As one after another of its leaders have made clear, *it regards itself as the only rival, and the inevitable successor, to Western civilization.*"[14]

Such assertions about the totalitarian character of Islamist movements are absorbed by Western peoples who have already heard the experts predict a "clash of civilizations." They know that most, if not all, countries in which Islam occupies a dominant position have failed to establish a democratic regime; that "Western-style parties and parliaments almost invariably ended in corrupt tyrannies, maintained by repression and indoctrination";[15] that for many years Saudi Arabia and Pakistan gave moral, material, and financial support to the Taliban hosts of bin Laden and Al Qaeda.[16] As a result, the image of a militant or radical Islam—only one of many trends within Islamic discourse—has grown to overshadow all others. It stirs alarmist feelings in the man in the street, who fails to see the difference between Islamists and undemocratic Islamic regimes. He becomes ever more ready to believe in the "clash of civilizations."

FROM LEWIS TO HUNTINGTON

The idea of a clash of civilizations between Islam and the West appeared initially in the article "The Roots of Muslim Rage," written by Bernard Lewis, a renowned authority on the Middle East, and published in September 1990 in the *Atlantic Monthly*. In it Lewis, after providing a thoughtful and substantial explanation of the resentment that so many Muslims feel toward the West, concluded: "It should by now be clear that we are facing a mood and a movement far transcending the level of issues and policies and the governments that pursue them. *This is no less than a clash of civilizations*—the perhaps irrational but surely historic reaction of an ancient rival against our Judeo-Christian heritage, our secular present, and the worldwide expansion of both. It is crucially important that we on our side should not be provoked into an equally historic but also equally irrational reaction against that rival."[17] Lewis appeared to blame only Islam for the clash of civilizations, hence his admonishment to the West to be vigilant and avoid being provoked into "irrational" reaction by the challenge of an ancient rival.

This argument acquired worldwide popularity after the publication in *Foreign Affairs* of an article by Samuel Huntington, "The Clash of Civilizations?" Almost from the outset, Huntington declared his belief that in the years ahead the "clash of civilizations will dominate global politics. The fault lines between civilizations will be battle lines of the future." He tried to prove that in place of the battles between princes, nations, and ideologies that have characterized the modern world, including the post–World War II period better known as the cold war, a conflict of civilizations would involve the "highest cultural grouping of people and the broadest level of cultural identity people have short of that which distinguishes humans from other species." In his words, "the Velvet Curtain of culture has replaced the Iron Curtain of ideology as the most significant dividing line in Europe."[18]

Several years later Huntington published a book in which he developed these ideas.[19] There he stated in no uncertain terms: "In this new world local politics is the politics of ethnicity; global politics is the politics of civilizations. The rivalry of the superpowers is replaced by the clash of civilizations." The Iron Curtain that had divided Europe during the cold war, separating Western from Communist countries, now became a line that separated the peoples of Western Christianity from Muslims and the Orthodox.[20]

Of the two, Huntington pays most attention to Islam. He is convinced that conflict between Islam and the West, which "on both sides" is seen as a clash of civilizations, will continue and grow more virulent.[21] He rejects the assertions of American political leaders that the West is opposed not by Islam as a whole civilization but only by violent Islamist extremists. "Fourteen hundred years of history demonstrate otherwise," Huntington says. In his vision, Islam is an implacable rival not only of Western civilization but of Christianity: "The relations between Islam and Christianity, both Orthodox and Western, have often been stormy. Each has been the other's Other. The twentieth-century conflict between liberal democracy and Marxism-Leninism is only a fleeting and superficial historical phenomenon compared to the continuing and deeply conflictual relation between Islam and Christianity. At times, peaceful coexistence has prevailed; more often the relation has been one of intense rivalry and of varying degrees of hot war."[22]

Christianity, however, is not the only object of Muslim hatred. Other civilizations also have strained relations with Islam: "In Eurasia the great historic fault lines between civilizations are once more aflame. This is particularly true along the boundaries of the crescent-shaped Islamic bloc of nations from the bulge of Africa to central Asia. Violence also occurs between Muslims, on the one hand, and Orthodox Serbs in the Balkans, Jews in Israel, Hindus in India, Buddhists in Burma and Catholics in the Philippines." Huntington's conclusion is dreary: "Islam has bloody borders."[23]

Huntington's article and book have stirred heated debates among intellectuals in the United States and other countries. But rarely do the participants in these debates attempt to understand what is meant historically by a "clash of civilizations."

THE CLASH OF CONCEPTS

The very term "civilization" presents difficulties of definition. As scholars have tried to define the meaning of the word, they have produced as many definitions and interpretations of "civilization" as there are philosophers, historians, ethnologists, anthropologists, sociologists, and other thinkers. There remains no consensus among them. Later generations criticize the definitions of their predecessors and are not satisfied with the interpretations of their contemporaries. Thus when we enter the world of civilizations we set foot on a slippery slope of generalizations, contradictions, oversimplifications, and exaggerations. We must admit, following the historian Fernand Braudel, that for most social scientists "civilization" is a "means—legitimate or not—to reduce History to grand perspectives—*their* perspectives. Hence we have choices, arbitrary approaches that may be justifiable in themselves but that divide the concept of civilization, each time reducing it to just one of its sectors. From one author to another the sector changes, according to choice or intention, making it more difficult to resolve, finally, the usefulness of the history of civilization for our understanding of the present world."[24]

According to this view, Huntington's approach to the problem of civilization is no less subjective than those of Oswald Spengler, Arnold Toynbee, Philip Bagby, or any other author who writes or speaks of civilizations. Huntington defines a civilization as "the highest cultural grouping of people and the broadest level of cultural identity people have short of that which distinguishes humans from other species. It is defined both by common objective elements, such as language, history, religion, customs, institutions, and by the subjective self-identification of people. . . . Civilizations are the biggest 'we' within which we feel culturally at home, as distinguished from all the other 'thems' out there." And he adds that his study is concerned with the "major civilizations" in human history,[25] including Western, Confucian, Japanese, Islamic, Hindu, Slavic-Orthodox, Latin American, and "possibly" African.

This listing prompts many questions. Why, for example, do the countries in Central and South America form a distinct Latin American civilization, not considered like the United States and Canada as part of Western civilization? After all, they have much in common with their northern neighbors. Like them, they were colonized by Europeans who not only implanted their religion, in the form of Western Christianity, but also their culture. Like the United States and Canada, the Latin American countries liberated themselves relatively early. While the nations of North America (and some former British and French colonies in Latin America) retained close relations with Great Britain and France after liberation, most countries in Latin America developed relations with Spain and Portugal and share with their former mother countries many of the characteristics of their political institutions and cultural and spiritual traditions. Why, on the other hand, do Spain and Portugal, according to Huntington, belong to Western civilization while Brazil, Argentina, and Mexico, to name just three, are part of a distinctive cultural entity? Would it not be worthwhile to unite Spain and Portugal with most of the countries located in Central and South America and call this new civilization, say, Ibero-American? Undoubtedly Spain and Portugal have much more in common with Argentina and Brazil than with Germany and Sweden.

Although most of Huntington's explanations[26] are convincing, similar explanations may be advanced to justify, for example, the division of the world into not eight but a greater number of civilizations, among them British, French, German, Italian, American, Russian, and Chinese, each with its peculiarities and sense of identity, history and culture, customs and traditions, even prejudices and phobias.[27] In this light, the chain of identifications suggested by Huntington for a resident of Rome (a Roman, an Italian, a Catholic, a Christian, a European, a Westerner)[28] appears questionable. The sequence is neither strict nor wholly inclusive.

Difficulties only multiply if one moves from the concept of civilizations to the problem of their clash. What are its forms? Is it a military conflict or a cultural and ideological competition? Nowhere in the writings of those authors who support the idea of clashing civilizations can a substantial explanation of the phenomenon be found. Dictionaries define the word "clash" as a conflict or skirmish, as of views or interests. Using this word with the word "civilization" thus presupposes that civilization is a highly coherent, homogeneous entity with clear-cut boundaries; that it has nothing or very little in common with another civilization in any sphere of life; and that, as a whole, it may be in a state of war with another civilization during a more or less definite period of time. No civilization that clearly satisfies these conditions exists in the real world. Whatever their number and territory, Braudel writes, they are not "closed worlds, independent, as each of them stands as an island in the middle of an ocean, but their convergences, their dialogues are essential, and more and more they share all, or almost all, rich common funds."[29] Any civilization embraces at least one nation, at best many nations with different, often contradictory, aspirations, perceptions, interests, and desires. And however much people who belong to one civilization share in terms of heritage, they differ in many ways. They act not uniformly and very often contrary to the patterns expected by common blood, religion, and way of life. History is filled with examples of such "deviations."

Thus the idea of a clash of civilizations, though attractive in the present circumstances, should be viewed with suspicion. Most students of the history of civilizations prefer other terms for describing the interaction between them. One of them is "encounter," even in referring to the situation between the Islamic world and the West.[30] Perhaps no less ambiguous, it nonetheless does not exclude forms of contact besides conflict and opposition.

That relations between civilizations involve more than conflict and opposition becomes clear if one turns to the history of relations between Europe and Islam. At first glance there may appear some inconsistency in placing Europe, largely a geographical concept, and Islam, a religion, on the same plane. But since the idea of civilization, as we have seen, can be abstract and subjective, Europe and Islam may justifiably be regarded in civilizational terms.

Historically, European civilization, notwithstanding a broad variety of peoples, cultures, traditions, and even races,[31] has developed a unity characterized by the common features of a dominant majority of people who inhabit the continent. Most of them are Caucasian; their religion is Christianity; they have drawn most of their rich heritage from ancient Greece and Rome, the cradle of European civilization. All peoples of Europe have lived through similar historical experiences—barbaric invasions, the Middle Ages, the Industrial Revolution, imperialism, two world wars, and the technological era. To divide Europe into parts, as some writers do, because of the local particulars of historical development, religion, political and economic institutions, or other grounds seems specious. Is it not paradoxical when Greece, which gave the rest of Europe democracy and politics, science and literature, Aristotle and Plato, is placed in another civilization, a rival to the one that unites Britain, France, and Italy, only on the grounds that its dominant religion is Orthodox Christianity? Does it seem logical to exaggerate one aspect that is different while neglecting many other aspects that are held in common? Even if one accepts religion as the primary characteristic in distinguishing among civilizations on the European continent, one must admit that both Catholics and Orthodox Christians have many more common features than those that separate them. Besides, Byzantium, which is considered a spiritual ancestor of Orthodox Christianity, until the

Great Schism of 1054 was also a spiritual leader of the Western church. In other words, eleven centuries of common history of Western and Eastern churches can scarcely be outweighed by nine centuries of separation, especially considering the rise of secularism in modern times.

It is not religion but other factors that have contributed to the distinctions among different parts of European civilization. Geography is of prime importance. Braudel draws attention to the so-called core of each civilization and its border areas, its frontiers, its "edges."[32] If we acknowledge that civilizations are not closed worlds and are in constant contact with one another, it is on these border areas that the influence of other worlds is most powerful. There new features or tensions appear that are yet unknown to the core of the civilizations. The stronger the influence—or, following Toynbee, the radiation of the neighboring civilization[33]—the more durable, salient, and ingrained into the fabric of society in the border areas are the traits that distinguish its culture, traditions, and institutions from other parts of the home civilization. The countries of the Balkan peninsula, such as Greece, Bulgaria, Romania, Serbia, as well as Croatia and Slovenia, have for many centuries experienced the powerful influence of Islam.

Russia, in addition, has occupied a unique position on the borders of at least three civilizations: Islamic to the south, Chinese and Japanese to the east. It also relates to those countries in Europe with a distinctively Western or Catholic-Protestant civilization. The three great civilizations of Asia have for centuries exerted their influence on the Russian culture, mentality, and way of life. This fact helps explain the "Russian enigma" that often puzzles other Europeans. Nevertheless, in its origins, its historic roots, and its cultural and spiritual ties, Russia is a part of European civilization, though its relationship with other parts of this civilization has never been without contradictions. Another peculiarity that distinguishes Russia especially from Western Europe is that it embraced a Muslim population earlier than any other European country save for Spain and Italy. But while these Mediterranean powers expelled or converted adherents of Islam soon after the Christian reconquest of Muslim possessions, in Russia Christians and Muslims have coexisted successfully, though not without friction and conflict. In a sense, Russia's unique position is similar to the United States, which not only borders a Latin American civilization, whose influence has led to the emergence of Spanish as a second official language in America, but, being a nation of immigrants, has embraced many features of such distinct cultures as African and Chinese.

Thus Europe, despite many evident differences of geography, history, and cultural heritage, may be regarded as a "smallest intelligible field of historical study"[34] called civilization. And one must remember that Europe was once known as Christendom, that is, a part of the world where inhabitants professed Christianity. This label has now become misleading because Christianity is professed in many other countries and on other continents. But Christianity has been an element of European unity in relation to other cultures and religions, such as Islam.

Unlike Europe, Islam is not a place, not a continent or a part of the world. It is a religion. If we criticize the division of Europe into different civilizations on grounds of religion, why should we accept the existence of a distinct civilization of Islam? First, because Islam is in fact something more than a religion, more than a system of belief and worship. It is also a way of life, endowing people with an identity and social and cultural distinctiveness. At the same time it is a community (*ummah*) that unites Muslims around the world, regardless of their race or nationality. Indeed, races and nationalities often fade in relation to the *ummah*. Islam is also a political identity and allegiance; for centuries the world of Islam was one polity ruled by one sovereign, the caliph, however fictitious and ephemeral his real power over the faithful. Thus religion has been only one aspect of Islamic civilization—though the most important one, for this civilization grew under the aegis of that religion.

Most of the countries with a predominantly Muslim population occupy a compact area in the Middle East, Central Asia, and North Africa. It forms a belt stretching from the Atlantic Ocean in the west to China and Southeast Asia in the east. Its core consists of the lands conquered by Arabs, followers of the Prophet Muhammad in the seventh and eighth centuries, which had belonged to the Byzantine and Persian Sassanian empires. Later these acquisitions were consolidated by the Seljuk and Ottoman Turks while their kinsmen from Central Asia spread Muslim power to the Indian subcontinent.[35] This compactness of territory, which nonetheless includes a great many diverse peoples, may serve as another argument in support of viewing Islam as a distinct civilization.

Thus there would appear to be no inconsistency in approaching Europe and Islam as two civilizations. According to Bernard Lewis, both "represent a primary civilizational self-definition of the entities which they designate, and may be seen as counterparts, whose association is not inappropriate. A discussion of the relations between them and of their reciprocal perceptions and attitudes need not therefore be seen as asymmetrical."[36]

THE EUROPE-ISLAM FRONTIER: THE MEDITERRANEAN

For centuries these two civilizations have lived side by side, competing with each other for territory, spheres of influence, people's allegiance, and the possession of divine rights. It has always been difficult to draw a sharp line between European and Islamic civilizations because of Muslims who live in Europe and Europeans who have founded their communities on lands that were a part of Islam's realm. But a careful look at the history of the two civilizations reveals that the frontier between Europe and Islam lies in the basin of the Mediterranean, extending through the Balkans and the Black Sea region. This frontier has been far from "metaphorical," though it has not been easy to define and delimit.[37] At times each civilization has regarded the other's encroachment across the border with alarm—at the same time making plans itself for further conquests. The liberation of lands on either side has been celebrated, defeats in the struggle for liberation deplored. Participants in such struggles have become heroes or martyrs, glorified in *chansons de geste* like Roland, or in Arabic sagas like Saladin.

The Mediterranean, separating two civilizations, divides two geographic zones, different in their physical characteristics. North of the Mediterranean lie the mountain chains of southern Europe with their thick forests. Both have served as an effective barrier to Arab, and later Muslim, invasion and expansion.[38] South of the Mediterranean are vast plains with scarce water resources and vegetation, with dry and often hot climates—survived with difficulty by Europeans used to a mild and humid climate. Geography influences ways of life on both sides of the sea. While the inhabitants of the lands of Islam have been nomads and cattle breeders since ancient times, peoples on the European continent founded sedentary cultures, cultivating plants and domesticating animals. The barbarian nomads who invaded Europe in prehistoric times and during the *Völkerwanderung* of the Christian era were either assimilated or quickly adapted to a settled way of life, becoming peasants whose principal wealth was in land and its fruits.

To say that geography explains all the differences between the two civilizations would be an exaggeration. But it is worth noting that Islam, this "child of deserts,"[39] though having its origins in sedentary Mecca and Medina, spread rapidly among nomads, those people best adapted for life in an arid zone. Meanwhile a very small percentage of the European population became adherents of Islam, mostly those who lived under Muslim rule and were motivated by reasons other than purely spiritual. South of the Mediterranean, the only country where Christians can claim to be a majority of the population is small Lebanon. To the north, only tiny Albania has a Muslim majority, though in other European countries, such as the former Yugoslavian republics and Bulgaria, Greece, and Romania, the number of Muslims is matched by Christian minorities in Egypt, Syria, Turkey, Iraq, and Jordan.[40]

Being a border between two civilizations, the Mediterranean basin has also been a vast zone "of interaction and flux."[41]

Contacts between Europe and Islam have occurred in many spheres of human activity. For centuries the Mediterranean was an arena of warfare in which each side sought to encroach on the other's territory and to spread its influence beyond the boundaries determined by geography and history. The Muslim conquest of Spain and Sicily, the Balkans and Cyprus, was balanced by European conquests in the Levant and North Africa and, later, by European imperial domination over almost all of Islam's possessions. But even in periods of acute military struggle, countries continued to exchange embassies and delegations, form political and military alliances, sign treaties, and declare their assurances of amity and friendship.

Economic activity has been another prime area of interaction between the two civilizations. In a sense the Mediterranean comprises an economic unity, overcoming geographic and political barriers. The exchange of raw materials and manufactures has continued during times of peace or war. While some countries fought with each other, others were trading and even profiting from the state of war, selling the warriors arms and materials needed on the battlefields. After a war ended, former enemies resumed trade relations as if no conflict had occurred between them.

Not only material goods were transported across the border that divided the Christian and Islamic worlds. Ideas, scientific discoveries, and cultural achievements overcame barriers and became the property of people on both sides of the border. Even religious divergence could not block this exchange of cultural and spiritual values. Thus the Mediterranean not only divided the two civilizations but also drew them together, serving as a vehicle of communication. Across the sea, as in a mirror, each saw itself reflected.

TWO WORLDS, TWO RELIGIONS

Contrary to conventional wisdom, Christianity and Islam have much in common. Both faiths originated in the Middle East and share a common heritage. Both inherited from Judaism, their predecessor, ideas about monotheism, prophecy, revelation, and scripture. Both borrowed heavily from Greek philosophy and science, from Roman law and government. Both are universalistic in their aspirations and goals, and claim to be a unique possessor of God's truth.[42] These similarities often became a source of conflict between the two faiths. In the words of Bernard Lewis, only in Christendom did Muslims "encounter a rival and in many respects a similar religio-political power, challenging their claim to both universal truth and universal authority."[43] Besides, the two had been neighbors from the very beginnings of Islam in the seventh century. In itself this circumstance presupposed their constant contacts and communication as rivals, enemies, or partners. However paradoxical it may seem, Europe and Islam have helped each other to define themselves, their difference from their neighbor, their distinctiveness.[44] The discovery of the Other leads to a better understanding of ourselves.

The perceived threat from Islam dictated to Europeans the need to study their rival, chiefly its religious precepts. Hence the desire in Europe over time, but especially in the twelfth and thirteenth centuries, to learn Arabic and to translate the Koran and other Muslim texts, the sole purpose being to save Christians from conversion to Islam and to convert Muslims to Christianity. It was soon discovered that Arabic was not only the language of the sacred texts but also the language of an extensive culture. The greatest examples of the wisdom of Ancient Greece had been translated into Arabic and accompanied with thoughtful commentaries by Arabic translators and scholars. Works on medicine, mathematics, philosophy, and geography, some translated from the Greek, some written by such Arabic scholars as Avicenna (Ibn Sina) and Averroës (Ibn Rushd), drew the attention of European scholars. Beyond these cultural and intellectual interests, many details of dress and taste were imported from the Middle East and from Muslim Spain, "a testimony to the scale of Europe's debt to the Islamic world."[45] From the time of the Renaissance onward, this interest developed into an infatuation with the rich culture of the Orient, which led to the phenomenon of orientalism in the European world.

None of this interest denied the otherness of Islamic civilization. Quite to the contrary, it only intensified a sense of competition as the talents and achievements of the Other became a stimulus to greater power and well-being, a search for inner resources and for new ways and methods of outdoing a rival. Viewed in this light, it seems justified that a "weak, divided, and irresolute" Christian Europe, instead of concentrating its efforts on the expulsion of the infidels from its territory, turned to "seeking the Indies and the Antipodes across vast fields of ocean, in search of gold," as one sixteenth-century observer complained to his contemporaries.[46] These complaints proved to be shortsighted because, as a result of discoveries by Vasco da Gama, Christopher Columbus, and other adventurers, a new age of world history was inaugurated, one of European domination. The roots of this age can be found in the European struggle for supremacy with Islam.

European success in spreading its influence around the world, and later achievements in science and technology, changed Muslim attitudes toward this rival civilization. Initially the Muslim world showed remarkably little interest in Christendom because it saw nothing of value in its culture and way of life, nothing worthy of borrowing or imitation.[47] But in the wake of European success beginning in the early nineteenth century, the Muslims found it useful to acquire, buy, copy, or adopt weaponry, naval construction, the practice of medicine, and technology such as clocks and watches, eyeglasses and telescopes.[48] As Europe continued to achieve and modernize, and to expand its domination in the world, the perception of Islam's backwardness grew amidst its failures to compete with European imperialism. Islamic countries thus became more and more willing to follow European examples in spheres of government, administration, and the secularization of political life. Dramatic reform programs were aimed at meeting the challenge of European superiority and domination.[49]

From Mohammed Ali of Egypt and Mahmud II, the reforming Ottoman sultan of the nineteenth century, to Gamal Abdel

Nasser and Mustafa Kemal Atatürk, as well as Ahmad Ben Bella in Algeria, Sékou Touré in Guinea, and Sukarno in Indonesia in the twentieth century, Islamic reformers sought to copy European political models and accept European ideas in order to solve problems of backwardness in the Muslim world and increase the dynamism of Islamic civilization. It was soon clear, however, that European liberalism could not cure all the vices of modern society. Furthermore, regimes created by the reformers, based on ideas of secularism, liberalism, or socialism, became vehicles for corruption and oppression while undermining Muslim identity—those values and traditions that for centuries had been cherished by the Islamic community. The result of these failed initiatives was a return, toward the end of the twentieth century, to Islamic tradition and an increasing desire to use Islam, rather than imported ideology, as the basis for reforming society. According to John Voll, an authority on Islam and Islamic society, this reappraisal of values "does not mean an abandonment of transformation efforts or attempts to revert to a premodern social order; it means an attempt to build a postmodern society utilizing traditions that are deeply rooted within society as well as in modern experience."[50] Nevertheless it has become clear for Muslims—as well as for Europeans (and their American allies) who had regarded their values as universal—that the distinctiveness of the two civilizations dictates specific solutions in each society.

One may conclude that the relationship between Europe and Islam is much richer and diverse than is described by such terms as "clash" or even "encounter." It includes all the range of contacts and interaction that characterize the life of human communities, from military confrontation to the borrowing of ideas, from opposition to cooperation. And by no means has religion played the dominant role in this relationship. To emphasize the "Muslim propensity to violence" on the grounds of Islamic religion is to neglect so many other factors in the centuries-long history of the European and Islamic civilizations.[51] Let us now recount this history at greater length.

TWO

Islam Confronts Europe

Confrontation would appear to be the salient feature of the history of relations between Europe and Islam. From its earliest days Islam embarked on military campaigns aimed at conquering the lands belonging to Christian powers and inhabited mostly by people whose creed was Christianity: Byzantium and the lands of Armenia and Georgia, then Spain and attempts to penetrate the possessions of the Carolingians in Europe, later the Ottoman drive into the Balkan peninsula and its threat to Austria and Italy. Over centuries these incursions created an image of an implacable Muslim menace to Christian Europe. On the other hand, the Crusades, *La Reconquista* in Spain, the overthrow of the "Mongol yoke" by Moscow and the subsequent conquest of the Islamic Kazan and Astrakhan remnants of the Golden Horde, and, in the modern period, the "Eastern Question" and general expansion into the lands of Islam marked stages in the European counteroffensive. It seems that throughout history Europe and Islam have confronted each other in seeking land, wealth, and people's souls—a situation of permanent war that has consumed their energies and abilities.

Although this picture is in many respects true, one must remember that all of mankind's history is permeated with wars, invasions, and conquests. If powers were not always at war, they were often preparing for it. The Peloponnesian War in ancient Greece and the struggle of Athens and its allies against the Persians; the military campaigns of ancient Rome and its conquest of almost all of Europe; the Hundred Years War; the Thirty Years War; the Mongol conquests; the two world wars of our age—why should Islam be outside this sad page of human history? Why should it bear more responsibility for the victims of these wars? Is it legitimate to speak of Islam's "bloody borders" when world history is replete with examples of such bloody borders extended across Europe, Asia, Latin America, and Africa?[1] Indeed, if we consider the history of just the last century, it was Europe where the bloodiest wars resulted in millions of deaths. To this should be added those wars waged by Europeans in India, Africa, and other parts of the world.

RELIGION AND VIOLENCE

What makes Muslims appear more militant than the representatives of other religions is the doctrine of the *jihad*, an essential element of Islam. The most conspicuous feature of the *jihad* is the holy war against the infidels for the extension of Islam over the world. The *jihad* is often interpreted as a permanent state of hostility of Islam against the rest of the world, as an imperialist war aimed at territorial conquests, as "part of the normal functioning of the Muslim world."[2] This interpretation finds strong confirmation in the Koran, the Muslim holy book, in the sayings of the Prophet and his associates, and, of course, in the history of Islamic conquests. The most frequently cited lines of the Koran order Muslims to slay unbelievers wherever they find them,[3] to strike off their heads "and strike off from them every fingertip,"[4] to kill those who join other gods "and seize them, besiege them, and lay in wait for them with every kind of ambush."[5] But even a superficial reading of the Koran reveals many other injunctions that contradict those exhortations to violence. For example, Sura 4 contains an injunction to slay infidels but excludes those "who shall seek an asylum" among the

Muslims' allies and "those who come over to you—their hearts forbidding them to make war on you." "If they depart from you," the Koran reads, "and make not war against you and offer you peace, then God alloweth you no occasion against them."[6] The Koran also prescribes retaliation for bloodshed and instructs Muslims to fight for the cause of God only against those who are already fighting, not to "commit the injustice of attacking them first."[7] Thus whoever wishes to find in Muhammad's teachings proof of the peace-loving character of Islam and its justice will not lack examples in the Muslim holy book.

The same is true of Christianity. If one reads the Bible in its entirety, one finds many events that testify to the militant character of this religion, especially in the Old Testament that Christians accept. Yahweh, the God of the Old Testament, is far from the image of a loving and merciful God that we see in Jesus Christ. The most frequently cited passage in this regard is from the fifth book of Moses, called Deuteronomy: "When thou comest nigh unto a city to fight against it, then proclaim peace unto it. And it shall be, if it make thee answer of peace, and open unto thee, then it shall be, that all the people that is found therein shall be tributaries unto thee, and they shall serve thee. And if it will make no peace with thee, but will make war against thee, then thou shalt besiege it: And when the Lord thy God hath delivered it unto thine hands, thou shalt smite every male thereof with the edge of the sword." While for faraway cities it was permissible to spare women and children, in those cities which were given by God as an inheritance for his "chosen people" (among others, the cities of the Hittites and the Amorites), all people should be utterly destroyed, lest their sins divert the followers of the true God from their rightful path.[8]

Thus when some authors write that "Muslims who kill are following the commands of Muhammad, but Christians who kill . . . are ignoring the words of Christ," and that therein lies "the basic philosophical" as well as "one of the basic ethical differences between Islam and Christianity,"[9] they offer only part of the truth. Muslims follow not only the commands of their

Prophet but mostly the word of God, conveyed to Muhammad directly from Allah through the angel Gabriel. Since most of the instructions for punishing unbelievers are taken from the Koran, they are God's commandments—the same God who speaks in the Christian Bible. The Bible must also be regarded as God's word because the book is sacred for Christians, conveyed to humans by divine authority. Thus its commandments are no less obligatory for the adherents of Christ. Considered in this light, there is little difference between the sayings of the Koran and the Bible.

The striking similarity between the Koran and the Bible in their attitude toward unbelievers is a consequence of many circumstances that existed at the time these books were written. Among them was the need for any nascent religion to establish itself firmly and to win the greatest possible number of adherents; contemporary attitudes toward crime and punishment; and the demands of defending the faith against rival religions. For Islam these demands were especially strong, because it had sought a foothold in the struggle against a serious rival, Christianity, with its claim to universality, its inclination to proselytism, and its attraction to the poor, oppressed, and unfortunate. The apparent militancy of Islam is thus the result of the need to establish a more prominent position vis-à-vis other creeds, to prove that the Prophet Muhammad's teaching was truer and more responsive to people's aspirations than that of Jesus Christ. Why otherwise would the Koran include a short history of God's revelations to the people, beginning with Judaic law and ending with the "Book of the Koran with truth, confirmatory of previous Scriptures, and their safeguard"?[10] Why also did Muhammad seek to present himself as Jesus' equal by lowering him from a divine position to that of simply one of the apostles who had suffered for God?

Jihad may be regarded as part of Muhammad's efforts. It was aimed not only at outsiders without but also within. Its goal was not just to suppress the followers of rival religions who doubted the divinity of the word of Allah, but to strengthen the belief of those who accepted this divinity and Muhammad's role as the Prophet. The common translation of *jihad* as "holy war" is inaccurate and even deluding, since it associates *jihad* with the Crusades and all other wars waged for the faith and in the name of the faith. In fact, the Arabic word literally means striving, and is usually followed by the words "in the path of God."[11] This meaning broadens the notion of *jihad*: not only an external struggle against unbelievers, and the propagation of Islam or its defense ("minor" *jihad*), but an internal struggle for the perfection of the soul, the betterment of behavior so as to become worthy of God's grace ("major" *jihad*). While Islam consolidated its position in the world, minor *jihad* played a dominant role among its adherents; only later did major *jihad*, the individual duty of the faithful, gain preeminence.

This brief discussion of theology should demonstrate that it is misleading to approach any religious doctrine without recognizing the conditions under which it was founded and to which it responded. Religious doctrines are complex phenomena. They include not only ideas of the moment but, if they aspire to be of universal value, contain many tenets that respond to people's basic needs—their desires for justice, well-being, and a better life. As a result, there are many inconsistencies in the texts of the Bible, the Koran, and other sacred books, which demand that an attentive reader distinguish between what was momentary and what is eternal. Thus the many interpretations of the Bible and the Koran. The argument that Muslims blindly followed the commandments of Muhammad because they were conveyed to him by God[12] is false; the Koran has always been subject to interpretation, no less than the Bible, and remains so. Since the Koran is the primary source of holy law, the response to its injunctions always depends upon the clarity of its statements. The more elliptic or allusive, the greater need for interpretation. Over time this became a responsibility of those learned in Islamic knowledge, the *ulema* ("learned people"), who have become associated with different schools of jurisprudence. Four of them—the Maliki, Shafii, Hanafi, and Hanbali—have survived to the present day.

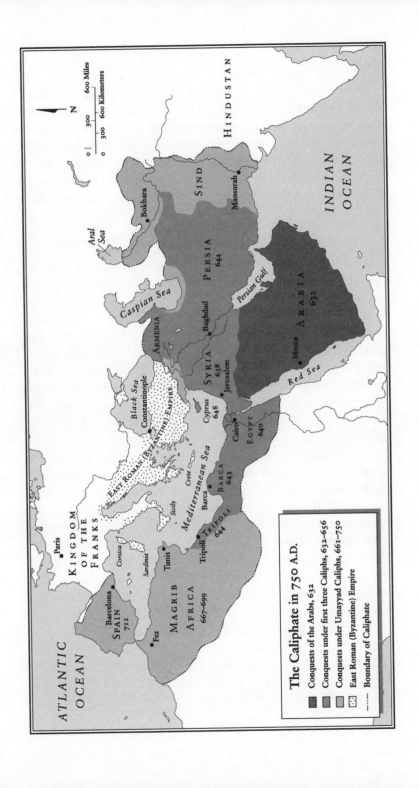

The Caliphate in 750 A.D.

Conquests of the Arabs, 632
Conquests under first three Caliphs, 632–656
Conquests under Umayyad Caliphs, 661–750
East Roman (Byzantine) Empire
Boundary of Caliphate

ATLANTIC OCEAN

N

600 Miles
300
0
600 Kilometers
300
0

KINGDOM OF THE FRANKS

Paris

Barcelona

SPAIN 711

Fez

Corsica

Sardinia

Tunis

MAGRIB

AFRICA 667–699

Sicily

Tripoli

TRIPOLI 644

Crete

Mediterranean Sea

Barca

BARCA 643

Black Sea

Constantinople

EAST ROMAN (BYZANTINE) EMPIRE

Cyprus 648

Jerusalem

SYRIA 638

Cairo

EGYPT 640

Red Sea

Mecca

ARABIA 632

ARMENIA

Baghdad

Caspian Sea

Aral Sea

Bokhara

PERSIA 644

SIND

Mansurah

Persian Gulf

HINDUSTAN

INDIAN OCEAN

To see the history of relations between Europe and Islam only in terms of religion leaves many aspects of this chronicle inadequately explained. However appealing it may be to locate the roots of confrontation between Christians and Muslims solely in Islam with its powerful weapon of *jihad*, this approach would be simplistic. Specific events will show that many factors other than religion have played a role in this centuries-long confrontation.

ARAB CONQUESTS AND CHRISTIAN EUROPE

Islam announced its birth with sweeping conquests, overrunning vast territories from the Indian Ocean to the Atlantic. Muslim Arabs erupted from their Middle Eastern peninsula in the 630s and during the next hundred years invaded the Near and Middle East and North Africa, capturing Jerusalem, Babylon, Alexandria, and the islands of Rhodes and Cyprus; landed in Sicily; laid siege to Constantinople; and reached Sind and the Indus River valley in the east, and the Iberian peninsula in the west. What accounted for the astounding success of these Arabic invasions? Undoubtedly religious fervor played a role in stimulating and uniting Arab tribes in their offensive. But the question arises, why has nothing similar occurred in later centuries? Why did this Arab *élan* fade before completing the conquest of the Byzantine Empire? Why did the Arabs not penetrate deeper into Europe and complete their war against the infidels by conquering the south of France, Italy, and Greece, thus transforming the Mediterranean Sea into an "Arabic Lake"? It seems unlikely that the *jihad* had lost its motive power for the victorious successors of Muhammad. We need to look for reasons other than *jihad* to explain the initial successes of the Arabs and their subsequent decline.

Although a theory about the deterioration of climatic conditions in the period preceding the Arab conquests deserves attention,[13] it too fails to explain the absence of similar eruptions in later years. Material interests, however, were important. The prospect of captured treasure was no less a stimulus for the

Muslim Arabs than the aspiration to spread Islam into new territories. In combination with Islam's religion it became a powerful force that made the Bedouins invincible. Thus religion served as an ideology for conquest and justified earthly motives. In addition, Islam was a powerful organizer of formerly independent tribes. The religion not only united these disparate forces, it submitted them to a single authority and armed them with a feeling of invincibility and the idea of the righteousness of their cause.[14] It is worth noting that Islam's role in this regard was determined not by religion per se nor by its inherent militancy. In the period of the Arab conquests, Islam was still in the process of formation. The idea of a holy war for the faith was as much a motive force as a product of the Arab's stunning successes.[15]

The triumph of Muslim armies in those years was also due to Arab military prowess. Arab cavalry was more effective than that of its foes. For tactical reasons, the Arabs chose to fight on flat, level ground, the most propitious for horses and camels. They frightened their enemies with battle cries and often used retreat as a tactic to delude an opponent and then surprise him with an unexpected attack.

The religious fervor and military strength of the Arab armies in the seventh and eighth centuries proved to be quite effective, especially compared with the weakness and instability that characterized the camps of their foes. The speed with which the Arabs conquered vast territories can be explained largely by the fact that they encountered not strong and consolidated powers, resolute in their struggle, but countries weakened by internal strife, economic problems, civil disorders, and incessant wars with their neighbors. Christian Byzantium was the telling example. The situation in this empire on the eve of the Arab conquests was precarious. The Byzantines were exhausted by extended Persian invasions and by the need to contain the Avaro-Slavic threat in the Balkans. The empire had lost its possessions on the Iberian peninsula, and its African provinces were threatened by warlike tribes of Berbers and other indigenous peoples. In Italy, Byzantium was unable to recover the lands it had lost to the

Lombards in early years of the seventh century. In sum, although the empire was not on the verge of collapse at the moment of the first Islamic raids and invasions, "it was fiscally, psychologically, and militarily unstable and potentially volatile. Decline and disintegration were not inevitable, but there was a potential for things to go either way, for better or worse."[16]

While the Arab invaders were strongly motivated by their religious beliefs, nothing comparable existed in the Byzantine Empire. Moreover, the friction that existed in Byzantium among Monophysites, Monothelites (who were officially recognized by Emperor Heraclius), and the followers of the Chalcedonian creed did not help promote a coordinated and effective resistance against the Muslims. In some instances, tensions between these different creeds in various areas of the empire led to the purchase of separate truces with the Arabs or even the defection of local leaders to the Muslim side, which eroded the empire's ability to withstand the invasion. In Egypt the initiative in negotiating a truce with the conquerors was assumed by the Monothelitic patriarch Cyrus, who sought to use it partly to gain time in order to suppress the Monophysites.[17] The emperor's ecclesiastical policies aroused considerable opposition in Armenia as well, which made it impossible to organize an effective defense against the Arabs. Some Armenians, such as Theodore Reshtuni, commander-in-chief of the Armenian forces, found it in their interest to ally themselves with the invaders and even to help them defeat Armenian resisters.[18]

To the internal disunity of the Byzantine Empire and its general weakness must be added its commanders' failure to develop an effective military strategy and to gain the initiative from the very start of the Muslim invasions; their inability to organize the local population for defense against the invasion; and the emperor's passivity in converting the state's economic resources, which initially exceeded those of the Muslims, into a decisive military advantage. The Byzantines may also have underestimated their foe and his ability to use the techniques of war. They generally dismissed the hitherto disunited elements of Arabian society, initially regarding attacks by armies of the new Islamic society as nothing more than the Bedouin raids they had experienced for centuries.

After their early victories over the Byzantine army at Ajnadayn in July 634 in southern Palestine and, more important, in the battle of Yarmuk in August 636, the Arabs flooded the lands of the empire in Syria and Palestine. Some cities, such as Damascus, fell rapidly. Others held out for a while. In 637 the Muslims occupied Antioch, Aleppo, and Hierapolis without encountering further resistance. In the same year Jerusalem yielded to the Muslim invaders.[19]

The capture of the Holy City, equally revered by Christians and Muslims (the latter still call it al-Quds, "the Sacred"), had a symbolic significance for both conquerors and vanquished. It was therefore not unusual that Caliph Umar himself decided to visit the city, though the true circumstances of his sojourn remain obscure.[20] Descriptions of Umar's stay in Jerusalem, found in Arabic and Christian sources, sometimes blend with legends. But some details are important for an understanding of the Arab motives in their conquests in Byzantium. They demonstrate that however important the role of religion, it alone did not determine the behavior of the conquerors. Umar entered the city in the company of the Christian patriarch Sophronius, after having given him assurances that the lives and property of the Christian population would be respected and their holy places left intact. As if to confirm this promise, he prayed outside the Church of the Holy Sepulchre in order to prevent the Muslims from claiming ownership of the church. He also visited the holy places of Judaism and Islam, the Temple and the sacred rock of Mount Moriah.[21] From Umar's behavior it becomes evident that the Muslims firmly intended to respect the rights of the Jews and Christians for whom Jerusalem was likewise the Holy City.

From the seventh to the early eleventh century, Jerusalem was a place where representatives of the three religions coexisted peacefully. Its division into quarters, each for every creed, was respected, and Christian pilgrims continued to visit it undisturbed.

How strikingly this behavior of the Arab conquerors differed from that of the later Crusaders! After their conquest of the city on June 15, 1099, the Christian bearers of the Cross spent a week massacring Muslims and Jews, and burning mosques and synagogues. Not even their coreligionists were spared. One of the first measures taken by the Crusaders was to expel from the Church of the Holy Sepulchre all the priests of oriental rites— Greeks, Georgians, Armenians, Copts, and Syrians. They then tortured these priests to make them reveal where they had hidden the True Cross on which Christ died.[22]

Not even the Byzantines perceived the Arab invasion of their empire as religiously motivated. For them, these were Saracen, not Muslim, conquests. "For them," Walter Kaegi writes, "there was no implicit concession that the religion of Islam was responsible for the success of these conquests, let alone any desire to leave open the related possibility that such events indicated the possibility that there was any truth or power in Islam."[23] Although many people, following the Arab invasion, were converted to Islam, especially among Christian Arab tribesmen, there is relatively little evidence of conversion by Byzantine troops, voluntary or forced. Nor did the conquerors force the civilian population to convert. Instead they allowed those non-Muslims who wished to evacuate conquered regions to do so, in some cases with movable property. One of the purposes of this strategy was to seize and redistribute landholdings in the countryside and in the towns—which testifies to the material aims of the Arabs rather than their desire to augment the followers of the Prophet Muhammad.[24]

Arab attempts to seize Constantinople in 668 and in 717–718 were similarly aimed at the capture of the riches of that splendid city, the center of Byzantine civilization that had always attracted the Arab conquerors and inspired their respect. But all their attempts to crush the resistance of Constantinople's defenders led to failure. The geographic position of the city, advanced military techniques (including the use of "Greek fire," a burning liquid made from naphtha, sulphur, and pitch, which could not be extinguished even by water), and the genius of such military leaders as Leo the Isaurian proved to be serious obstacles to the Arabs. But the most important factor was finally the power of the empire which, though shattered, had not been undermined by Arab conquests. Seven centuries later, when most of the Byzantines' strength and cohesion had been bled away by the incessant assaults of the peoples of the steppe, Constantinople, the proud creation of the ancient Romans, fell to the most ferocious and successful besiegers, the Ottoman Turks.

Meanwhile, Muslim invaders under the banner of the Prophet continued their conquests. They invaded and overcame the Christian powers of Armenia and Georgia, where disunity, religious confusion, and the perfidy of rulers and commanders led to easy conquests. But the Arab successes there can also be explained by their policy of tolerance and the introduction of a clever system of taxation. In Armenia there is little doubt that Muslims initially placed no high priority on converting the inhabitants of the country. The Armenians did not welcome the conquerors, and the conquest was violent and destructive.[25] Nevertheless the caliph granted the Armenians, at least temporarily, the most favorable autonomy. Armenia's population generally did not convert to Islam or become assimilated to Islamic and Arabic civilizations. Although later the Muslims did press for conversion and for the imposition of higher taxes, the resistance of the people and the role of the Armenian church, as well as the country's situation at the edge of the two empires—Byzantine and Caliphate—prevented its complete subjugation.[26]

A similar situation occurred in Georgia. When the Arabs began their campaign against Kartli-Iberia in 642–643, they met little resistance. On the contrary, the local prince sent his ambassador to meet the Arab commander, Khabib ibn Maslamah, and to offer him gifts in exchange for peace. Khabib was pleased with such a demonstration of peaceful intentions and later granted Kartli a kind of "Charter of Immunity," which laid out the conditions of submission of the Georgians to the authority of the caliph.[27] Later, as in the case of Armenia, Georgian principalities became contested ground between the Byzantine Empire, which strove to recapture its former possessions, and the Arab caliphate. This competition probably brought more damage to the Christian population of these two countries than their conquest by the Arabs.

Arab raids were directed not only to the east and north; they also spread westerly, in 639 toward Egypt. In 647 an Arab army penetrated Ifriqiya (present-day Libya, Tunisia, and most of Algeria), and its conquest was completed by about 705. In 649 Cyprus became the first European island invaded by the armies of the Prophet's followers. Sicily, in 668, was the next major Mediterranean island to be attacked by Arab sea forces. But the most important event, marking the beginning of a direct assault on the European continent by the army of the caliph, was the landing of an expeditionary force sent by the governor of Ifriqiya, Musa ibn Nusair, under the command of a Berber, Tariq ibn Ziyad, on the Iberian peninsula. This event took place sometime in April or May of 711. Within a few years Arab armies had occupied the whole of the peninsula and posed a serious threat to the possessions of the Franks.

This sudden eruption into the Iberian peninsula, from the Pillars of Hercules to the spurs of the Pyrenees, filled Christian Europe with amazement and fear. For many years this catastrophe, which delivered to Islam not lands in Africa or Asia but a portion of Europe itself, appeared to some as an incredible event, a sort of "historical miracle."[28] But there was nothing miraculous in the Arab conquest of Spain. As in Byzantium, here the conquerors encountered a power weakened by internal strife, religious discontent, and the passivity of the population. As in the Middle East, the Arabs found in Spain willing collaborators.

The idea for the invasion is said to have come to the Arabs from such a collaborator—Count Julian, governor of the city of Ceuta, who sought vengeance on the Visigoth king Rodrigo for the dishonor of his daughter, Florinda. Although this story may well be more legend than fact, it reflects the precarious situation in the Visigothic kingdom ruled by the usurper who drove the country into misery. An infuriated Count Julian supposedly visited the governor of Ifriqiya, Musa ibn Nusair, and tried to persuade him how easy it would be to conquer the Iberian peninsula. He even agreed to a reconnaissance operation of sorts, which landed in a bay near Algeciras, captured rich booty, and returned to Ceuta. This raid strongly impressed the Arabs and convinced them that their campaign against the Visigoths would indeed go smoothly.[29] But they probably did not anticipate how easily they would overrun the country. They not only rallied the support of the sons of King Witiza, who hated the usurper of the throne Rodrigo, but also the majority of the population, including the Jews, who had been denied (by the decisions of the Council of Toledo in 702) the right to marry and were turned into slaves and forced to convert to Christianity.[30] As a result, many cities yielded to the conquerors without a struggle. Even the capital of the kingdom, Toledo, offered no resistance. When the Arabs approached the city, they discovered that almost all its inhabitants had fled, leaving behind—if one believes Arab chroniclers—countless riches.[31]

In Spain, as in other countries won by the Arabs, the success of the conquest was assured by their flexibility and tolerance. Since most of the cities in Spain yielded to the Arabs without resistance, they were spared pillage and the murder of civilians. But some cities were razed and disappeared from the map. There is no need to idealize the followers of the Prophet who invaded the Iberian peninsula, nor their opponents. Still, according to many observers, the eighth-century occupation of Spain proceeded under more civilized conditions than was usually the case in that age.

News of the Arab invasion of the Iberian peninsula had not yet reached the ruling houses of Christian Europe when advanced detachments of the Muslim army appeared on the other side of the Pyrenees and penetrated the territory of Frankish Gaul. In the following years the Muslims threatened Toulouse and Bordeaux, and reached the outskirts of Avignon and Lyon. These forays frightened Europe, which imagined Islam establishing its realm in the heart of the continent—its armies occupying Rome and transforming St. Peter's into a mosque, converting the people and thus realizing the dream of the Prophet about the Dar al-Islam extended over the whole known world. Many centuries later, in our own time, this vision still finds its supporters who, for example, attribute such a design to Musa ibn Nusair.[32]

If such plans ever existed, they might have been realized at least in Gaul. The Merovingian monarchy was struggling. After the death of Pepin of Herstal in late 714, Gaul suffered through an anarchy similar to the one that led to the fatal downfall of the kingdom of the Visigoths in Spain. Thus it presented an easy prey for invaders. The Arabs needed only to be numerous enough to occupy effectively the vast territories that lay before them; but the forces that had invaded Spain had neither the material nor, more important, the human resources to realize these ambitious plans. Considering the level of knowledge of the people of the eighth century about the outside world, whether in Europe or in the Middle East, Arab commanders probably had no clear idea of the distances they would have to cover in pursuing their plans for conquest. They also possessed imprecise information about the local populations in the countries they planned to conquer—that is, the people's attitude toward invaders and their ability to resist. Besides, the Arabs had recently conquered the vast territory in the Iberian peninsula that they now had to "digest": to suppress pockets of resistance that appeared here and there in Spain, to establish an effective power structure, and to build an effective defense against future invaders.

Considering these shortcomings, what pushed the Muslims to undertake a campaign across the Pyrenees was cupidity and an adventurous spirit, to which should be added, of course, the desire to destroy the infidels.[33] Their penetrations into Gaul should be regarded not as parts of a greater plan but as uncoordinated raids, something similar to the *sa'ifas* against Christian possessions in Asturias, which involved a strong craving for booty.

If this is the case, the battle of Tours loses much of its symbolic, almost apocalyptic significance as a decisive encounter between the two worlds, in which Christianity stopped Islam on its way to world domination.[34] Yet the importance of this battle should not be minimized simply because Arab chroniclers scarcely mention it.[35] Its significance lies in the fact that for the first time since their triumphant invasion of Spain, the Muslims suffered a serious defeat, at the hands of the Christian army led by Pepin's son, Charles Martel ("The Hammer"). Despite the scarcity of information we have about the melee that took place somewhere between Poitiers and Tours (even the exact location of the battle is uncertain) in October 732, historians do know that the Muslims lost many soldiers and that their commander, Abd al-Rahman al-Ghafiki, was killed. Nevertheless, two years after the battle, the Arab governor of Narbonne, Yusuf ibn Abd al-Rahman, again advanced into the valley of the Rhone. He crossed the river, captured Arles without encountering resistance, took Saint-Rémy-de-Provence and the outskirts of Avignon, and proceeded along the valley of the Durance. The Muslims remained on Frankish territory for four years and might have stayed longer if not for a new intervention of Charles Martel.[36] For many years territory on both sides of the Pyrenees continued to be an area of heated contest between Christians and Muslims. Here the pendulum of success continued to swing without advantage to either side, until the son of Charles Martel, Pepin the Short, recaptured Narbonne in 751, and his son Charlemagne, in turn launched his military expeditions across the Pyrenees.

PIRENNE'S THESIS

However disastrous in Christian eyes were the Saracen incursions into the heart of Europe, the Arab offensive may have had an even more profound impact on the course of the continent's history. The famous historian Henri Pirenne, in his celebrated book *Mohammed and Charlemagne*, argued that because of the Arab conquests, the unity of Mediterranean civilization was shattered and Europe entered the Middle Ages. He based his argument on the many facts of European economic life that changed significantly after the Arabs had transformed the Western Mediterranean into a "Muslim lake," thus interrupting long-standing economic ties that even the barbarian invasions of earlier centuries had not damaged.[37] The consequences were numerous: the decline of commerce in European cities, such as Marseilles, which had been principal emporia of Western trade with the Levant; the general stagnation of the economy and its increasing ruralization;[38] the weakening of the king's authority and the rise of a landed aristocracy;[39] the rapid growth of the church's influence over the affairs of the state and intellectual life.[40] Drawing together these observations, Pirenne concluded: "All the consequences of this change became glaringly apparent after Charlemagne. Europe, dominated by the Church and the feudality, assumed a new physiognomy, differing slightly in different regions. The Middle Ages—to retain the traditional term—were beginning."[41]

Pirenne's thesis is attractive because it explains many trends in European development in that period. But history turns out to be more complicated than the schemes of even the most renowned historians. As has been demonstrated by scholars who have studied the development of feudalism in Europe, Pirenne exaggerated the consequences and extent of the first Arab victories. Despite Arab successes on land and at sea, their ascendancy was quite gradual. The followers of the Prophet did not establish their indisputable naval superiority at the time Pirenne investigates. Arab raids on Sicily before 700 drew a vigorous naval response from the Greeks, who were confident enough of their Aegean position to conduct operations against Egypt and North Africa and in the West. Moreover, the two most powerful caliphs, Muawiya and Abdul Malik, had to pay tribute to the Greeks to preserve the Syrian ports from attack, proving that in the seventh century the Arabs were still unable to break the Greek lines of communication and thus cut off Western Europe from the Byzantine Empire. Indeed, the Byzantine fleet was master of the Aegean and the eastern Mediterranean not only in the seventh century but at least until the end of the eleventh century. Pirenne's assertion that "navigation with the Orient ceased about 650 as regards the regions situated eastward of Sicily, while in the second half of the 7th century it came to an end in the whole of the Western Mediterranean"[42] cannot be accepted.[43]

On land, serious Arab threats to trade routes arose only after Charlemagne's death, when in 848 the Arabs raided Marseilles for the first time and then established a pirate base at Fraxinetum and pushed into Switzerland. Thus nothing could seriously have prevented the Mediterranean from remaining an area of trade between East and West in the very years when, according to Pirenne, the Arabs ruptured all economic ties between the two parts of the "Romania." In fact, historians have comparatively full records of commerce between the Arabs, on one side, and Naples, Amalfi, Sorrento, Gaeta, and Venice, on the other. This commerce prospered despite all the efforts of the authorities to suppress it. Papyrus, the shortage of which in Europe was, in Pirenne's view, one of the marks of the interruption of economic ties, continued to be produced in Egypt and delivered to the West until the competition of paper finally destroyed the industry in the middle of the eleventh century. The last Western document to use papyrus, a bull of Pope Victor II, is dated 1057 and coincides with the end of production in Egypt.[44] Gaul continued to import spices and silks from the countries that were engaged in commerce with the East—Italy in the south and the Scandinavian countries in the north, the latter having maintained an active intercourse with Persia via the water routes of Russia.[45]

Thus the general decline of economic life in Western Europe and the advent of the Middle Ages cannot be attributed solely to the Arabs' offensive and their dominance in the Mediterranean, at least in the seventh and early eighth centuries. As archeological excavations have revealed, this decline had begun earlier, between 400 and 600, when massive and far-reaching developments led to the disintegration of the Mediterranean world.[46] When the Muslims began their offensive they were conquering an already decaying civilization. Islamic expansion was a symptom of the decline of the Roman world, not a cause. Still, Pirenne's thesis, though questionable, helps uncover the complexity of relationships between civilizations, and the influence one civilization may exert upon another. In other words, although many of Pirenne's arguments should be rejected, his general approach to the history of relations between Europe and Islam—as not limited solely to military confrontation but involving trade, ideology, culture, and other spheres of human activity—deserves recognition.

THE NEW WAVE OF CONQUESTS: SELJUKS

No sooner had Christian powers succeeded in repulsing Muslim penetrations into the heart of the European continent and containing the Saracens to Spain and Sicily than a new threat took shape at the faraway borders of Christendom. Turkish tribes of nomadic pastoralists, called collectively Seljuks, after their enterprising leading family, the Seljukids, from 1037 on seized the principal cities of Khurasan, to the south of the Oxus-Jaxartes basin, then occupied the chief provinces of western Iran and replaced the Buyid power at Baghdad (1055). Soon they entered the well-watered mountainous areas south of the Caucasus and took up lands there. In the Armenian highlands they began to infiltrate into the possessions of the Byzantine Empire.[47] The new invaders were mostly Muslims. Islam had spread among them when they had served as auxiliaries to Turkic rulers beyond Oxus.

Again, as in the time of the Arab conquests, Byzantium was torn to pieces by internecine upheavals. After a brief period of revival and unity, when the empire had been able to recover some of its territories lost to the Arabs, violent struggles in the highest circles of the Byzantine ruling class pushed the empire into convulsions. The clash occurred between the representatives of the civil bureaucracy in the capital and the military magnates in the provinces, generals who were large landholders. As leaders of armies conscripted in Anatolia and the Balkans, they plunged the empire into a long civil war which threatened the territorial integrity of the state. In thirty-two years of this struggle, sources record thirty major rebellions, or about one each year.[48] In order to undermine the position of the generals, the bureaucrats in Constantinople undertook efforts to dismantle the military apparatus. This included the dismissal of competent generals, the dissolution of entire military corps, and the cutting off of financial support for local, indigenous troops. These troops were now replaced by foreign mercenaries, among them Normans, English, Russians, Georgians, Alans, Armenians, Patzinaks/Pechenegs and even Turks and Arabs. Their loyalty was questionable, for any dissatisfaction with salaries or an expected reward led to desertion. This was precisely what happened in 1057 when the Norman chief Herve Frankopoulus, disappointed with his failure to obtain a promotion, deserted to the Turk Samuh who was then raiding the eastern borders of the empire. In 1063, after having returned to the services of the emperor, Frankopoulus betrayed the Byzantine commander of Edessa to the enemy.[49] Considering this sort of behavior, it is not unusual to find that the Byzantine Empire collapsed before the Seljuks. Rather, it seems miraculous that it did not disappear altogether but survived for another three and a half centuries.

The Seljuk invasion of Byzantium was not a sudden catastrophe. The Turkish conquest of the empire's possessions was a long process. After the first appearance of the Turkish raiders on the Byzantine borders in 1016–1017, more than fifty years passed before the fateful battle of Manzikert in 1071, in Armenia near Lake Van. During these years Turkish raids into Byzantine territory increased in audacity, frequency, and scope. Turkish tribesmen penetrated deeper into imperial territory; they plundered, destroyed, and burned cities, desecrated churches, massacred inhabitants, and took prisoners. They met little or no resistance from Byzantine forces: the system of local defense had collapsed. The battle of Manzikert confirmed the disastrous state of the empire's army. The desertion of most of the Emperor Romanus IV Diogenes' troops on the eve of the battle, and the discord among the Byzantine nobility, predetermined the outcome. Panic spread among the Byzantine troops. The emperor, finding himself abandoned on the field by much of his army, fought bravely until he was wounded in the arm and his horse shot out from under him. The Turks, under the command of their sultan Alp Arslan, gained a resounding victory. They flooded into Asia Minor and eventually occupied the towns and cities.

The defeat of the Byzantine army at Manzikert profoundly influenced conditions in the Byzantine Empire. Central authority in Asia Minor was seriously threatened. The weakening of the state and the successive blows it received from Balkan peoples and then from the Crusaders made it impossible to halt the gradual Turkish westward infiltration, a process aided by Byzantine rebels in western Anatolia. What remained of the Byzantine armed forces were occupied with civil strife. When the rebels asked the sultans and Turkmen chiefs for aid, they gladly assisted in a process that could benefit them.

But the Seljuk Turks were not able to establish a stable empire in their conquered territories. For almost a century, power in the region was divided among ten or eleven chieftains and many lesser ones who claimed some relation to Seljuk authority. The invasion of the Crusader army from Europe only added to the general confusion and resulted in a further weakening of Turkish power. The final blows to the unity of the Seljuk state were dealt by Turkmen rebellions and Mongol conquests during the late thirteenth and the early fourteenth centuries. The decline of the Seljuks did not, however, bring an automatic reassertion of Byzantine power. Although the emperors had regained some lost territories and even returned Constantinople as their capital after its loss to the Crusaders in 1204, the empire after 1261 displayed only a shadow of its former valor. For centuries it had served as the shield of Europe against the threats of Asian peoples, most of whom were adherents of Islam; now the Byzantine Empire crumbled before the strength of a new and mighty power, the Ottoman Turks.

THE OTTOMAN MENACE

The Ottomans were descendants of Othman, a chief of one of the Turkish tribes that had invaded the territory of the Byzantine Empire and settled in western Anatolia. In 1299–1308 Othman established himself as the local *amir* (military leader) and a serious threat to Byzantium; he captured territory around Bursa and reached the Bosporus. In 1326 his forces captured Bursa, which became the first capital of the growing Ottoman state.

By this time the Ottomans had become strong enough to interfere in the internecine struggle in the Byzantine Empire, which now held little more than the area nearest Constantinople on the Anatolian side. In civil wars the Ottomans offered their help to rival imperial parties, which gladly used the Muslims in their disputes for control of the decaying empire. The Greeks employed the Ottomans as mercenaries, and Orkhan, son of Othman, used the situation to extend his own possessions well into the other side of the Bosporus. In a new contest for the imperial throne in 1352, Ottoman troops crossed the straits and penetrated European territory as far as Adrianople. Soon, probably with one of the Byzantine claimants' consent, a Turkish settlement or military colony was established at Tzympe on the Gallipoli peninsula. Here was a springboard for further Ottoman conquests in Europe.

These conquests continued for more than three centuries, during which the Ottomans became a nightmare for Christian Europe by controlling an important area of the continent. They eliminated the Byzantine Empire and captured its splendid and glorious capital, Constantinople; they subjugated or placed under their authority most of the Balkan peninsula; they put Austrian emperors, Polish kings, Russian tsars, and Roman popes on the defensive, constantly threatening their possessions and declaring their aim to extend the power of Islam throughout Europe. For centuries the European Christians lived under constant threat from the Ottoman Empire; a prayer, "From the fury of the Mahomedan, spare us, O Lord," was heard in all the churches of central and southern Europe.

Never during this period were the European powers able to counter the Ottoman threat with sustained and united action. Lack of cohesiveness and glaring contradictions were constant features of European policy toward the Ottomans. When Orkhan and his successors began their conquests on the continent in the fourteenth century, the situation in Europe was precarious. The Hundred Years War between England and France had erupted on the eve of the first appearance of the Turks on European soil. The War of the Roses in England, and the opposition of the semi-independent duchies—such as Brittany, Burgundy, and Provence—to the king's power in France, weighed heavily on those countries' attention to the situation on the eastern borders of the continent. The Holy Roman Empire was also weak. It represented a loose conglomerate of duchies, princedoms, margravates, electorates, and free cities, under the nominal authority of the Bohemian king as Emperor Charles IV, whose interest in the inherited kingdom was much greater than in the needs of the empire itself. Italy, like Germany, was a ground of rivalry and competition between various dynasties and independent cities. Venice and Genoa, the principal seapowers of the day, were consumed by a race for supremacy, while Rome lacked the presence of the popes, the only rallying force behind the struggle against infidels. The prelates had moved to Avignon on the French border and were preoccupied with the war in Italy rather than with building a defense against the Turks.

Leadership in the campaign against the Ottoman offensive might have come from Hungary and Poland, but they too were engaged with internal demands and ambitious schemes aimed at enhancing their rulers' power. Louis the Great of Hungary was more interested in using the Turkish peril as a convenient excuse for sparing the church in his kingdoms from the excessive taxation of the pope. He also used the Turks as a pretext for renewed territorial expansion at the expense of the schismatic Christians of the Balkans, the Serbs, Walachians, and Bulgarians.[50] Poland's rulers effected a matrimonial and political alliance with the prince of Lithuania, which extended Polish interests to the

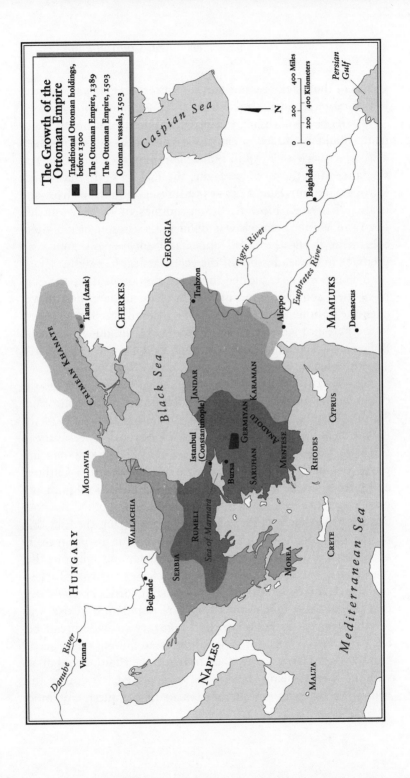

shores of the Black Sea and to more easterly regions, to the neglect of more pressing needs on Poland's southern borders.

To the political disarray that reigned on the European continent should be added social upheavals—peasant revolts such as the Jacquerie of 1358 in France and of Wat Tyler in 1381 in England—and the terrible plague, the Black Death, that struck European countries in 1347–1350, taking millions of lives and dealing a serious blow to the economies of many countries. Even the Western church was divided, as a result of the Great Schism in 1378–1417, and popes and anti-popes claimed supremacy in the leadership of the ecclesiastical hierarchy.

The Ottomans exploited this condition of weakness to augment their acquisitions in Europe and consolidate their power over the conquered territories. They routed the Serbian army in the battle of Kosovo Polje in June 1389, subdued Walachia, Bulgaria, Macedonia, and Thessaly, and in 1394 conquered Thessalonica.

The Turkish conquests were often aided by volunteers in the threatened countries. Contesting ambitions of noble factions in Serbia, Albania, Bosnia, Romania, and other territories of the Balkan peninsula; the willingness of the oppressed peasantry to trade the yoke of local magnates for a lighter tax system imposed by the Ottomans; religious strife between the Catholic and Orthodox churches as well as between the official faith and numerous heresies—all these circumstances smoothed the conquerors' path into southern Europe. Considering the fact that the Turkish offensive coincided with such great disturbances in all spheres of European political, economic, and religious life, one can see why many in the exploited classes regarded Turkish rule as no worse than that of their Christian lords. The only fear that might have given the Christian population pause was forcible conversion to Islam. But, contrary to widespread beliefs, conversion was not generally pressed among the peaceful populations. Those who wished to retain their faith could do so without fear of being slaughtered or enslaved. Of course this benefit varied with the circumstances of conquest, but more frequently the conquerors trusted the church hierarchy, which sometimes remained the sole authority amidst general chaos and turmoil, with administrative functions making them partly responsible for the conduct of their flock.

As a consequence, throughout the period of Turkish invasions in Europe one can find Christian princes fighting against their coreligionists on the side of the Ottomans, or assisting them in battles against European alliances. For example, in the battle of Nicopolis, in Bulgaria in 1396, an army of several thousand Serbs fought for the sultan against the Hungarians and their allies. A Hungarian, Janos Hunyadi, "one of the gigantic figures of the war against Islam,"[51] sent a gunnery expert to Sultan Mehmed to teach the Turk artillerymen how to break down the defense of Constantinople, the very city whose capture was deplored by the whole Christian world.

The fall of Constantinople and, with this city, the Byzantine Empire, occurred on May 29, 1453. It was preceded by several decades of agony during which the possessions of the empire shrunk to the territory in the immediate vicinity of the city. Appeals of the Byzantine emperors to Europe for help remained unanswered. Even the union of the Greek and Latin churches proclaimed at the Council of Florence in 1439 did not alter the situation. In fact it provoked strong opposition among the inhabitants of the city, who declared: Rather the turban of Mahomet than the pope's tiara![52] This "fifth column" inside Constantinople aided the capture of the city by the armies of Mehmed II the Conqueror (1451–1481).

The capture of Constantinople was not only a significant defeat for Christendom; it also became an important victory for the Ottoman state, which now became a durable empire, "supported by much the same constellation of political interests on the geographic and economic level as had supported the Byzantine empire, and by cultural and religious interests analogous to those of the Byzantines."[53] Istanbul, as Constantinople was renamed after its fall, allowed the Turks to concentrate in their hands the trade between the Black Sea and the eastern

Mediterranean, and the resources of the conquered lands in
Anatolia and Rumelia. Its capture also gave the Ottomans prestige in the world of Islam as legitimate heirs of the Arab
caliphate: the Ottoman sultan could rightfully assume the title
of Caliph of the Faithful. At the same time the Ottoman Empire inherited the other two great empires of the past, those of
Alexander the Great and of the Romans. In addition to obvious political and moral advantages, the capture of Constantinople gave the sultans important tactical advantages. By taking the imperial city, seat of the ecumenical patriarchate, the
Turks ensured their control over the Christian hierarchy of the
conquered European countries and strengthened the ties between the Ottoman state and the Orthodox church.

After the fall of the Byzantine Empire, the Ottomans' pressure on Christendom increased. They captured Belgrade and
Buda, raided the Italian coast, and laid siege to Otranto. They
penetrated as deep into the European continent as Vienna,
which they attempted to capture twice, in 1529 and 1683. More
than once it seemed that the fate of Christendom hung by a
thread. Only toward the close of the seventeenth century did the
Ottoman threat subside, with the peace treaty of Carlowitz,
signed on January 26, 1699, marking the turning point in the
confrontation between Europeans and Turks[54] and, perhaps
more generally, between Europe and Islam.

THE MONGOL INVASION OF
RUSSIA AND ITS CONSEQUENCES

While Western Europe was shuddering at news of the Ottoman
onslaught, and *Türkenglocken* (Turk bells) were ringing daily in
European cities, Russian lands were being devastated by hordes
of nomads from the Far East, known at the time as Mongol-
Tatars. These were a conglomerate of tribes and clans in which
the Mongols actually occupied a rather modest place. A considerable number of soldiers in the Mongol armies that invaded
Russia were Turks under Mongol leadership, but the name
"Tatars" was eventually used to refer to the invaders.

Contrary to a widely held view,[55] the Mongol hordes were not Muslim at the time of their invasion of Russia and incursions into Europe. Among them were shamanists, primarily worshipers of the sky, as well as Buddhists and even Nestorian Christians.[56] Some among the conquerors did adhere to the religion of the Prophet, but they were few. In any case, not long after the Mongols conquered Russian duchies and made them part of their khanate of Kypchak, later known as the Golden Horde, their khans adopted Islam. Within a century of its emergence as a distinctive political and administrative unit, this khanate became firmly a part of Dar al-Islam.

The adoption of Islam as a state religion by the Golden Horde was predetermined by many factors. First, the heartlands of the state that Batu, a grandson of Genghis Khan, established in the Volga valley, with its capital in Saray, had a rich Islamic heritage. By the time of the Mongol conquest, the people who inhabited this region were already well acquainted with Islam. Most prominent among them were the Volga Bulgars, who were converted to Islam as early as the tenth century. The Bulgar state played an important role in the political, economic, and cultural relations of the region. It was a center of transit trade which linked the countries of Central Asia, Persia, India, and China with Kievan Rus and Scandinavia and, eventually, with western Europe. The list of goods exchanged at the markets of the Bulgars included furs, wax, fish, amber, honey, and cattle imported from the countries to the west, as well as carpets, brocade, and precious stones brought from the Orient.[57]

Trade promoted Bulgar relations with the outside world. Muslim merchants were seen in Bulgar cities as often as Christian artisans and pagan cattle breeders. But the adoption of Islam was a function of the Bulgar rulers to free themselves from a dependence on the Khazar khanate, whose official religion was Judaism. As a result, Tsar Almush, whom Arab chroniclers have credited as the initiator of the conversion to Islam, asked Caliph Muctadir in 922 to help him build a fortress to enhance the prestige of his state and defend it against the Khazars. This request led to the arrival of the caliph's envoys to Volga Bulgaria and the building of a mosque in its capital. In all probability, however, the process of Islamization began earlier than these events; some scholars insist that it was initiated as early as the first Arab campaign against the Khazar khanate in the early ninth century.[58] In any event, having conquered the state of the Bulgars, the Mongols inherited a rich Islamic tradition which had flourished there well before their arrival.

Islam spread not only among the inhabitants of the Bulgar state. Chroniclers also registered a sizable Muslim population in the Khazar khanate and noted the influence of Islam among the nomads of the steppe between the north Caucasus and the Black Sea, such as the Pechenegs. This influence was augmented by the Golden Horde's commercial and cultural ties with its neighbors. The geographic location of the khanate of Kypchak between the steppes and forestry area of North Russia, with the variety of resources in each of these regions that encouraged a lively trade between them, made it the focal point of commerce. With the destruction of the Bulgar cities that played a role as intermediaries in this trade, commercial supremacy passed to the Muslim merchants of Central Asia. The latter had been placed under the protection of the Mongol rulers and played an important role in the finances of the Golden Horde. They were even commissioned to gather taxes from the conquered lands of Russia, which led to uprisings and hatred toward them among the oppressed Russian population. This privileged position of the Muslim merchants had evidently smoothed the penetration of the Islamic faith among the ruling classes of the Golden Horde.

This weight of cultural and commercial links between the khanate of Kypchak and parts of the Islamic world helped to bring about an early royal conversion there with the accession of Berke in 1257. "From then on in coinage and diplomacy, the Golden Horde belongs to the Muslim world, despite the 'unconverted' status of most of Berke's successors down to the time of Özbek Khan."[59] It was in the reign of Özbek (Uzbek) Khan, in the first quarter of the fourteenth century, that Islam was effectively and definitively established at the Mongol court. But the khan's decisive turn toward Islam hardly entailed an overnight transformation of the Golden Horde into an Islamic state. Among the people the process probably took much longer, and Islamization continued well after Özbek's time. Nor did the conversion to Islam lead to considerable changes in the relationship between the Golden Horde and Russia.

The nature of these relations differed importantly from the usual pattern between conquerors and the defeated. After their devastating raid across Russia from north to south, the Mongols withdrew to the lower Volga, leaving most administrative functions to local princes, sometimes under the supervision of the khan's agents. Only in a few areas of Russia did the Mongols remove the Russian princely administration, replacing it with their own direct control. It was a symbiosis of sorts, in which both parties played their roles, which were essential for the functioning of the whole. While the Mongols were interested in the Russian lands as a source of recruits for the army and of the material means necessary to maintain the state and the imperial family, the Russian princes saw the Mongols as a counterweight to the attempts of their Western neighbors to extend their power over Russian territories. This was especially important at a time of active papal policy aimed at the unification of the Catholic and Orthodox churches, which did not exclude a forcible extermination of the Eastern "Orthodox heresy" by means of crusades.[60] This strategy manifested itself most clearly during the reign of Prince Alexander Nevsky, who had chosen a looser and, in many respects, informal rule of the Mongols instead of renouncing Orthodox Christianity and submitting to the authority of the Teutonic Knights.[61]

The Mongols maintained the territorial integrity of the Russian duchies and did not attempt to change the religion of their subjects. On the contrary, they issued immunity charters, or yarlyks, for the Russian church that confirmed the privileges of the clergy as a social group, including their families: the landed estates of the churches and monasteries were exempt from taxation; all the "church people" were exempt from military service; and death was decreed for anyone guilty of defaming or vilifying the Greek Orthodox faith.[62] These yarlyks remained in force even after the spread of Islam in the Golden Horde, and the position of the Russian church was further consolidated. The first Muslim khan of the Horde, Berke, approved the proposal of Alexander Nevsky and Metropolitan Cyril to establish a Russian bishopric at the Mongol capital of Saray. Khan Özbek, who had made Islam the official religion of his state, continued to extend favors to Christian communities in his realm, issuing yarlyks that confirmed privileges to the church granted by his predecessors. Özbek even married his own sister to Moscow prince Yuri, allowing her conversion to Christianity and baptism.[63] During Özbek's reign the Moscow region under Prince Ivan Kalita (the Money Bag) acquired prominence among Russian principalities. Thanks to good relations between Ivan and Özbek, life in Moscow became more secure than elsewhere, and its population grew rapidly.[64]

This Mongol policy benefited both sides. The protection of the church by the khans of the Golden Horde secured for them the loyalty of the best-educated social group in Russia, which enjoyed a high moral standing among the people. And the Mongols used Russian clergy as intermediaries in their relations with Byzantium. On the other hand, the church was preserved as a great unifying force which played an important role in the process of consolidating the Russian state and, eventually, in the struggle for the liberation of the Russian people during the reign of Grand Duke Ivan III in 1480. When cooperation with the Mongols succeeded in protecting Russian lands against outside interference, and when Russia became strong enough to need protection from a Mongol state weakened by internal disorders, Moscow ruptured the alliance and entered the arena of European politics as an independent player.

The fall of the Golden Horde did not eliminate for Russia the problem of relations with Islam. Three states appeared out of the debris of the Golden Horde: the khanates of Kazan and

Astrakhan in the Volga basin, and the Crimean khanate. In the Crimea the Russian state waged a long and exhausting struggle for many years.

The Crimean khans considered themselves rightful heirs of Genghis Khan and his successors, and on this ground they claimed their authority over the Russian state. They demanded tribute from the Moscow tsars. The Crimean Tatars continued their devastating raids against Russian possessions, plundering cities and villages, taking peasants and artisans, women and children into captivity, and thus inflicting substantial damage on Russia's economy and culture. Almost every year the Crimean Tatars made incursions into Russia, reaching even the outskirts of Moscow in 1591.[65]

In addition to material damage, Russia found political and diplomatic disadvantages in having such a hostile neighbor. The Crimeans were used by other European countries as a tool against the rising Moscow state. Poland, Lithuania, and Sweden often resorted to the Tatars for help in undermining the Russian position, blocking Moscow's expansion, and generally weakening Russia so as to eliminate that country as a rival. To justify these actions, which stained the reputation of the Polish kings as good Catholics and fervent fighters against the infidels, King Stephen Bathory (1576–1586) put forward a whole theory of the conquest of Muscovy for the purpose of converting it to Catholicism and uniting all forces against the Turks and Tatars under the aegis of the Pope.[66] During twenty-four years of Russian war in Livonia, twenty-one years were marked by Tatar raids against the Moscow state.[67] During the civil war in Russia and the Polish intervention in the early seventeenth century, the Tatars often acted concurrently with the movements of the armies of the False Demetrius. With the general weakening of the Russian state, they reached the Moscow region, pillaging and burning towns and villages and taking thousands of people into captivity. The damage was so great that the Persian shah Abbas, at a reception of Russian envoys, expressed his amazement that people still remained in Russia after these raids.[68] According to figures on the number of captives during the Tatar raids, based on incomplete data, in 1632–1637 the Crimean Tatars captured and led to their khanate some 18,000 people, while in the period 1641–1645 this number rose to 25,000.[69] Considering that several centuries ago the population of Russia was much less than it is today, these numbers are stunning. Most of the captives were later sold at slave markets at Kaffa and in Istanbul and Alexandria.

In 1475 the Crimean khanate came under the protection of the Ottomans and joined in the aggressive schemes of the sultans against Europe. In 1593–1606 the Turks used Tatar troops in their war in Hungary. They frequently stirred up the Crimeans against Poland. The Tatars also served as a useful tool of Ottoman policy toward Russia. One of the most famous Turkish campaigns was a 1569 attempt to retake Astrakhan from Muscovy as part of a project to open a water route between the Black Sea and the Caspian. Although this campaign was chiefly aimed at Safavid Persia, the Ottomans were also alarmed by Russia's growing influence in the Caucasus, particularly as the Circassians sought Moscow's protection against the Crimean Tatars in 1552, and the Kalmyks and Kabardinians followed suit in 1557.[70] Among other aims, the Turks sought to capture Kazan, which Ivan the Terrible had conquered in 1552, and to secure ties with Muslim countries in Central Asia.[71] For this the Turks planned to dig a canal between the Don and Volga Rivers. But all these plans failed because the Tatars were not at all enthusiastic about the establishment of a Turkish stronghold in the Volga basin, and attempts to take Astrakhan by storm proved futile. Under pressure from the rank and file, the Turkish commander was forced to order a withdrawal.

In addition to losses inflicted by the Tatars when they raided Russian territory, Moscow had to pay great amounts of money to Crimean khans, who regarded these payments as a tribute to the heirs of the Golden Horde. For the tsars, however, this was a way perhaps to buy a respite from the raids against their country. The tribute to the khans included not only money but also various goods, including furs, coats, and dresses for the khan's wives. It drained Russian financial resources, for the Tatars demanded ever-growing amounts of tribute. During the first half of the seventeenth century Moscow spent about one million rubles for payments to the Crimean khanate, not including clothes and other goods. By comparison, for the building of two new towns in 1640 the Russian treasury allocated only 13,532 rubles.[72]

Russian envoys who delivered the tribute to Crimea suffered humiliation and even met with danger to their lives. They disseminated money and goods not only among the khans and their wives but also among the khan's retinue, who often extorted money and furs by means of violence. The envoys were thrown into jail, beaten and tortured, and often had to borrow additional funds from local merchants in order to satisfy the demands of the Tatar nobility.[73] With the strengthening of the Russian state, the size of the tributes declined. Nevertheless, not until after the conquest of the Crimean khanate in the late eighteenth century did Moscow free itself completely from this burden.

Another means of saving Russian lands from Tatar raids was the creation of a system of defense. For many years Moscow built fortresses on its southern borders, placed army units there, and populated the area with peasants whom the tsars had freed from serfdom. But the most frightening force opposing the Tatars was the Cossacks. Some historians believe they were descendants of those who had served in the army of the Mongols and whom the khans of the Golden Horde used as messengers in the postal system they created in conquered lands.[74] After the fall of the Golden Horde, they settled in the free and unpopulated lands of the steppe in the Don River basin and on the Black Sea coast, and soon were involved by the Russian tsars in the defense of the country against the Tatar raids.

The Cossacks pursued a state of permanent war with the Crimean khanate and Ottoman Turkey. They made forays into the Crimea, attacked the Ottoman fleet in the Black Sea, raided the Turkish coast, and even reached Constantinople.[75] Russian tsars enlisted the Cossacks' help in defending the country as early as 1570. That year Ivan the Terrible wrote to the Don Cossacks requesting their services, for which they would be paid. In 1571 an agreement between Moscow and the Don called for "gunpowder, lead, and money" to be sent regularly from Moscow in return for the Cossacks' freeing of prisoners captured by the Tatars during their incursions into Russia. This agreement was renewed in 1584 and 1592. One of the Don Cossacks' main tasks was to roam the steppe and provide Moscow with early warning of Azov, Crimean, or Nogai Tatar intention.[76] Although relations between the tsars and the Cossacks were not always harmonious (the Cossacks often acted independently, in disregard of Russian foreign policy priorities[77]), the Cossack role in defending the southern borders of Muscovy against the Tatars was crucial. The Cossacks also represented a real threat to Ottoman possessions on the northern coast of the Black Sea. In 1637 the Cossacks seized the Turkish outpost at Azov and held it for five years, repulsing numerous attacks by Turkish forces. After Moscow's decision in 1642 to leave the fortress, the Cossacks blew up its walls and towers and retreated into the steppe. This event enhanced Russian prestige, and Moscow began to deal with the Turks and Tatars with greater assertiveness.

Thus for ten centuries after the appearance of Islam on the Arabian peninsula, Europe faced an enemy that threatened the very foundations of its civilization. This threat was all the more real after the Muslim conquest of vast European territories and the open declaration of their desire to overthrow Christianity and impose their own faith among Europeans. Europe's response to the threat, however, was often disconcerted and contradictory.

THREE

The European Response

From the first Arab invasions of the European continent until well into the seventeenth century, Christendom found itself on the defensive against the advance of Islam. The principal task of the European princes seemed to be to halt the further penetration of the Muslims. For this purpose they created a system of buffer states whose aim was to contain the invaders. They would occupy them with local defense and slow their movement while a counterattack was being prepared by Christian armies. These functions were assumed, for example, by the kingdom of Aquitaine, created by Charlemagne in the late eighth century in the interior of his empire of the West. It controlled the movements of the armies of the caliphate of Cordoba by intervening at proper moments in order to divert Arab attacks.[1] Likewise the Danubian Hapsburg Empire later became a shield against the advance of the victorious Ottomans.[2] Hidden behind natural walls of mountains and man-made defenses, the Europeans nurtured plans for counterattack.

From time to time Christians probed their adversary with expeditions into the territories occupied by Islam. One was prepared by Charlemagne in 778. He crossed the Pyrenees and laid siege to Saragossa in the north of the caliphate of Cordoba. The attempt to capture the city failed, however, when Saragossa refused to open its gates to Charlemagne's army, which was not prepared for a long siege. In addition, news arrived of a revolt in Saxony, in the heartland of the Frankish empire, and Charlemagne was forced to retreat. His unsuccessful expedition nonetheless remained memorable because of the legendary feats of Roland, a member of Charlemagne's royal entourage and Count of the Marches of Brittany. When the rear guard of the retreating Frankish army was ambushed, Roland died in the fight against the attackers. Although the Basques who formed the main attacking force were certainly Christians, and the presence of Muslims among them was doubtful,[3] Roland and his comrades-in-arms who perished in this battle became heroes of the legendary struggle against the infidels.[4]

The 778 expedition became the first in Charlemagne's campaign against the Moors, as the Muslim conquerors of Spain were called in medieval Europe. They led eventually to the capture of Barcelona in 801 and to the formation of the Spanish March on the other side of the Pyrenees. Charlemagne's advance may be seen as part of a greater process known as *La Reconquista*, the liberation of Christian lands conquered by Muslims, waged from the mountainous area of the Asturias by the remnants of the Visigoths who had found a refuge there from the advancing Arabs.[5] The kingdom of the Asturias was founded by Pelagius the Goth, but the real founder of the state that became a vanguard in the struggle against the Muslims on European soil was Alphonse I, the Catholic (*el Católico*) whose reign (739–757) marked the beginning of the *Reconquista*. Although Alphonse's followers were more concerned with the capture of booty and additional lands,[6] his raids were undertaken in the name of Christianity, and his patron saint became St. James of Compostela (Santiago). Gradually, by 754, Alphonse had occupied the whole of Galicia and the north of today's Portugal. When, under Alphonse the Great (866–910), the capital of the Asturias was transferred to Léon, the policy of expanding boundaries southward became explicit.

It was impossible to wage a large offensive against the Spanish caliphate, whose forces were far greater, but lightning raids were common. In their turn, the caliphs of Cordoba led razzias (forays) against the territories of the Asturias and the Spanish March. Almost every year they organized expeditions (*sa'ifa*) which became a form of holy war against the Christians. The Muslims enjoyed initial success, but they were never able to overwhelm the Christian possessions. With the decline of the caliphate and growing internal disorder, however, the Moors began to yield. The last spectacular Muslim victory in the war against the *Reconquista* was the capture of Santiago by the army of al-Mansur (Almanzor of the Christian chronicles and of *Romancero*) in August 997. The Moors plundered and set fire to this city that was sacred for Spanish Christians. This was a deliberate insult to the rivals of the caliphate, though the Tomb of the Apostle was respected and the monk who looked for it was not harmed.[7]

With the collapse of the caliphate of Cordoba and the appearance in its place of various *reinos de taifas* (kingdoms of factions, rival principalities at war with each other), the *Reconquista* gained impetus. Toledo was captured by Alphonse VI on May 6, 1085, and Spain was gradually won by advancing Christian armies. This "lengthy and unsteady" process[8] took more than four centuries and was dotted with disastrous defeats, such as the battle at Zallaqa on October 23, 1086, when the army under the command of Alphonse VI was routed by the Almoravids and three thousand of his men killed. The king managed to escape with a few hundred knights.[9] The *Reconquista* was complicated by divisions within the Christian camp and frequent alliances that its leaders concluded with the Muslims against their coreligionists. For example, the hero of the struggle against the Spanish Moors, Rodrigo Díaz de Bivar, known as El Cid Campeador (the Challenger), when he fell into disgrace with Alphonse VI and was banished from his kingdom in 1081, offered his services to the *rey de taifa* of Saragossa. El Cid's siege of Valencia was a revenge for his Saracen friend al-Qadir. He was likely motivated not so much by the high principles of the war against the infidels as by a desire to acquire his own principality.[10]

In the battles of the *Reconquista* was born that spirit that in a few years became the driving force behind European conquests in Asia Minor, known to us as the Crusades. The capture of the fortress of Barbastro, not far from Saragossa, in 1064 by an expeditionary force that included a large number of French knights, was sanctioned by Pope Alexander II. The papal bull "became the model for the subsequent pontifical documents which came to constitute the canon law of the crusades: the bull granted as an indulgence remission of sins to anyone participating in the enterprise."[11] So when news reached Europe of the Seljuks' occupation of the Holy Places in Asia Minor, at the Church Council at Clermont, France, in 1095, Pope Urban II appealed to Christians to liberate Jerusalem from the "Hagarens." This call was met with enthusiasm by European knights who were resolute in their desire to wrest the Holy Sepulchre from the Muslims. But one cannot explain the Crusades only by religious fervor. More earthly motives lay behind this march to save the Holy Places.

The Crusades were a complex phenomenon, clouded in numerous myths and legends that have distorted their real nature. The very word "Crusades" is misleading; it was used only much later. Contemporaries talked instead of *iter* (military expedition) or *peregrinatio* (pilgrimage).[12] Likewise, it is erroneous to present the Crusades as wars of religion and as a clash between Christendom and Islam, because neither the conversion of the infidel nor his suppression was proclaimed as the ultimate goal of the expeditions. They were "holy wars" only in the sense that they were sanctified by the popes and reflected the growing role and prestige of the papacy in the eleventh century, and its claim on the leadership of all of Europe.[13] Along with religious enthusiasm, the participants of the Crusades, like their counterparts in the *jihad*, were characterized by greed, ambition, and a lack of scruples in dealing with local populations of any faith. These shortcomings led ultimately to the inglorious end of the Crusades, when their leaders failed to reconcile their contradictions in the face of the Muslim counteroffensive.

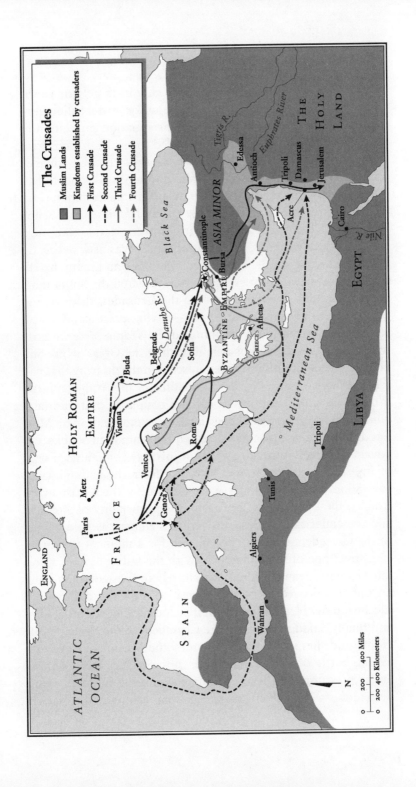

The Crusaders' initial success was due in large part to the weakness and division of Islam in the wake of the Seljuk conquests. We have already seen a similar situation in relation to the Byzantine Empire. The Seljuks failed to establish a coherent state in conquered territories, which soon became divided among rival military leaders (amirs and atabegs) who fought one another and were unable to unite against the common rival. According to the *Cambridge History of Islam*, "Rival Seljuk armies, and Turcoman and Arab tribes, were scattered through the country, dominating a population which was itself deeply divided, including large Christian communities and many heretical Muslims who, at times, seem to have hated the Sunni more than the infidel. Far from resisting the Crusades, they were at first ready to cooperate with them—having presumably calculated that a precariously maintained Crusading state in Syria would be a less dangerous neighbor than the Great Seljuk Sultanate."[14] The situation was reminiscent of the disarray that had reigned three centuries earlier at the time of the Arab conquests in Europe—and would be repeated a couple of centuries later when the Ottomans began their invasion. Because of these Muslim divisions, the Crusaders defeated the Anatolian Seljuks and advanced rapidly through Syria. On July 15, 1099, after a siege of five weeks, they captured Jerusalem from the Fatimid garrison. Soon four Latin states were created by the Christian intruders: the kingdom of Jerusalem, the principality of Antioch, and the counties of Edessa and Tripoli. Damascus paid tribute to the Crusaders while Aleppo agreed for a moment to place a cross over one of the minarets.[15] With the fall of Tyre in 1124, the Mediterranean coastline was entirely in Crusader hands.

But this proved to be the apogee of the Crusades. Soon a succession of able Muslim leaders, including Zangi, Nur al-Din, and finally Saladin, deprived the Crusaders of their gains in the Holy Land. Jerusalem was retaken by the Muslims in 1187 after the battle of Hattin. The Latin possessions rapidly shrank under pressure from Islam during the ensuing hundred years, despite the resistance efforts of Christian armies and new Crusades proclaimed by the popes. In May 1291 the Mamluk sultan al-Malik al-Ashraf Halil captured the last capital of the kingdom of Jerusalem, Acre. The remaining Frankish possessions were surrendered or captured with little resistance. The Crusader rule in the Levant was at an end.

That the Crusades should not be regarded as a great conflict between Christianity and Islam is demonstrated by the Muslim attitude toward the Crusaders. They saw in the Christians a foreign force that intruded on their internecine struggle and only complicated it. They always referred to these intruders by an ethnic name, the Franks (*Franj* in colloquial Arabic, a word used to designate Westerners and the French in particular[16]). The alliances that the Crusaders formed with various Muslim leaders and factions[17] during this period only strengthened such an impression. Besides, the territory affected by the Crusades included none of the large Muslim population centers, and their expeditions meant little to the eastern Fertile Crescent and, further east, Persia.[18] In Bernard Lewis's opinion, instead of a "great debate" between the worlds of Christianity and Islam, the Crusades were rather a monologue "from which the Muslim interlocutor was absent and of which he seems to have been unaware."[19]

Even for Europe, the Crusades cannot be regarded as evidence of the perennial conflict between Christianity and Islam. Although religious motives seem to have been stronger among the wearers of the cross, their aims were limited to the liberation of the holy places from the infidels and never involved the elimination of Islam. Furthermore the popes evidently regarded the Crusades as a powerful weapon in the struggle to unify the Catholic and Orthodox churches and to combat the many heresies that were spreading throughout Europe at the time. The capture of Constantinople during the Fourth Crusade, and crusades against the Albigean heresy and for the conversion of the Baltic peoples to Christianity, clearly demonstrate the protean character of the Crusades. And this distraction and scattering of European forces proved to be fateful, as it became one of the causes for the loss of the Crusaders' gains in Palestine and the discrediting of the movement.[20] When the popes tried to revive the crusading spirit in the face of the Ottoman invasion of Europe, they could not overcome these earlier doubts.

Throughout the period of the Ottoman threat to the continent, never was Christendom able to unite its forces for a prolonged stand. That Europe might be unified on the basis of Christian ideology and a holy war against the Ottomans was either a myth or an effort to exploit public opinion in Europe in order to legitimize the policies of the individual states.[21] Every European state participated in the struggle against the Turks— but only for its own interests, and more often than not for considerations of sheer *realpolitik*.

In the fifteenth and sixteenth centuries European powers were preoccupied with the struggle for supremacy on the continent. The Habsburgs' ambitions to play a leading role in politics and to dictate their will to neighbors met resistance from France, England, and the Low Countries, as well as from the Protestant princes in Germany. These ambitions had been strongly enhanced by fortunate marriages and unexpected deaths, with the result that by the early sixteenth century enormous powers had been concentrated in the hands of the Habsburg scion, Charles V. Heir to the original Habsburg duchies in the eastern Alpine region and to much of the Netherlands, Charles also became king of Spain, with its dependencies the Balearic Islands, Sardinia, Sicily, and Naples. He also held wide and rich possessions in the New World. His election as emperor of the Holy Roman Empire made him head of the jumble of states that stretched from the Baltic and North Sea coasts to the Gulf of Genoa and the head of the Adriatic.

Such a concentration of power in the hands of one sovereign naturally led to growing concern among other European rulers. France was especially worried since it found itself an encircled power, and the French king Francis I undertook efforts to counter Charles's ambitions with his own conquests in Italy and the Low Countries. In this competition the Most Christian King of France was not averse to grasp "the Turkish sword to throw it into the scales of the European balance."[22] In February 1525 Francis, who waged war against Charles's forces for the mastery of north Italy, was defeated and captured and sent as a prisoner to Spain. Out of this disaster came the Franco-Turkish alliance. Francis decided to create a second front against the Habsburgs, addressing his appeal for help to Sultan Suleiman the Magnificent.[23] For the rest of his life Francis played a double game, pretending to be an eager defender of Christendom yet secretly allied to Suleiman—whom he did not hesitate to betray in pursuing his own interests. Francis allowed the Turkish fleet to use Toulon as its headquarters. He also nurtured plans to employ it in a direct attack on Naples or other Spanish lands in Italy, or to capture a port there that was to serve as the Turkish base in Suleiman's attack against Rome once the Turkish war with Persia had ended.[24]

France continued to employ the Ottoman threat in achieving its objectives in Europe well after the death of Francis I. And France was not the only country eager to resort to the help of the "enemy of Christendom." Venice, whose trade interests often clashed with the goals of the struggle against the Turks, frequently sacrificed this struggle in favor of economic preferences with the Ottoman Empire. More than that, Venice was able to enlarge its possessions in the Aegean, using the fear of Turkish attack as an inducement for local rulers to seek Venetian protection, then making temporary agreements with the sultan. In this way Venice acquired Durazzo and Scutari in Albania; Lepanto, Patras, Argos, and Nauplia in Morea; Athens; as well as more lands around Negroponte and more islands in the Aegean.[25] Little wonder that Venice was vociferously accused of seeking an understanding with the Turks against its Italian rivals. The Serenissima, being the most vulnerable to Turkish aggression, appealed for crusades when at war and yet was ready to come to terms with the infidel whenever it suited its interests.[26]

The only power that seems to have been consistently opposed to the Ottoman advance, and mounted an effort to build a united front against Turkish threat, was the papacy. The new equilibrium in Europe formed after the end of the Hundred Years War, and the healing of the schism inside the Catholic church, making the pope the only Christian leader possessed of real authority and prestige, placed the Roman pontiff at the center of crusading schemes being planned in Europe after the fall of Constantinople. But the crusading spirit, though widespread among the people as well as the ruling classes, could not overcome the growing division of Europe into nation-states more preoccupied with their own safety and rivalries than with the vague idea of war against the Christian enemy, especially if that enemy was many miles away from their borders. All the pope's attempts to rally princes for the struggle against the Turks met only duplicity and reticence. Nor were they eager to unite with their rivals who might reap profits at their expense. As the danger subsided, enthusiasm for a new crusade began to cool.

In 1453, when the fall of Constantinople signaled the imminent threat of the Turks' advance into Europe, Pope Nicholas V's call to arms was well received by the princes. It seemed that the idea of a united front was close to being realized. But two assemblies of the Holy Roman Empire, at Ratisbon and Frankfurt in 1454, which were to work out concrete plans of action, including expenses, failed to produce results: even the emperor did not show his face, leaving his chancellor, Enea Silvio Piccolomini, to conduct the meeting. A third assembly, held in February the following year, broke up when news of the death of the pope reached the delegates. In his testament, Nicholas V denounced the collaboration between the princes and the Christian states as halfhearted.[27] Piccolomini, who became pope under the name of Pius II, was likewise disappointed with the indifference and obstructionism of the European monarchs, to such an extent that he published a highly controversial *Letter to Muhammad*, in which he declared that the sultan was greater than the Christian monarchs and could therefore succeed to the emperors of Rome. If the sultan were to renounce Islam and accept baptism, the pope would place the crown of the world on his head. Although this letter was evidently written as a polemical pamphlet and was never sent to the sultan, Muhammad II might have read it, as various printed editions were circulated after 1469.[28]

In their efforts to build an alliance against the Ottomans, the popes did not hesitate to seek the help of other Muslim powers, if only they were rivals of the Ottoman Empire and responsive to the overtures of the Holy See. In this endeavor the papacy used a vast network of missionaries who traveled as far as Central Asia and China, pursuing the conversion to Christianity of peoples who were either pagan or hesitant in their faith. Even before the Ottoman invasion, Rome had attempted to contain the threat of Islam by rallying the support of the Mongols, and it had responded favorably to the proposal of the Il-Khans of Persia to conclude an alliance against Mamluk Egypt.[29] Persia was again atop the list of possible allies after the accession to power there of the Safavids, who were implacable enemies of the Ottoman Empire and who forced the sultans to divert their attention from their schemes of conquest on the European continent. Thus throughout his reign Selim I's war with Persia kept him away from Europe; the war between Suleiman the Magnificent and Tahmasp I repeatedly distracted Suleiman from staging an offensive in Europe.

Pope Julius II, weary of his unfruitful efforts to revive the zeal of the Crusades among the indifferent monarchs of Europe, in addressing the king of Bohemia, Ladislas II, pointed out the value of action while the Turks were involved in a serious war with the Persians. He suggested that the king send a religious and educated man to the shah in the hope of effecting an alliance.[30] Yet it was the shah who first tried to establish contact with Europe in order to lay the foundation of an alliance against his Ottoman enemy. After having vainly tried to arouse Venice's interest in the prospect of a collaboration with Persia, Shah Ismail wrote to the Emperor Charles V with a similar proposal. Despite difficulties of distance and primitive communications, ties between Persia and Europe were finally established, and by the middle of the sixteenth century the idea of a Christian-Persian alliance was evidently a commonplace among the European monarchs. Its advantages had been demonstrated during the Turco-Persian War of 1578–1590, during which the shah received artillery and experienced gunners from the Spanish king Philip II. As a result of the Turks' defeat in 1585 at Persian hands, Venice was freed that year from the fear of Ottoman attack, while in North Africa the sultan was obliged to postpone his aggressive designs, and on the Hungarian frontier he was forced to maintain peace.[31]

These efforts of the papacy were significantly undermined by the beginnings of the Reformation. In Martin Luther and other leaders of the movement to reform the Catholic church the sultan quite unexpectedly found allies who prevented the full mobilization of the Habsburg Empire against the Ottoman advance. Of course there was no deliberate cooperation, though some extremists among the Reformers might have nurtured plans of addressing the sultan for help in their struggle against the papacy. The damage was more indirect. Luther and his supporters undermined papal prestige at a time when the papacy was the only force that could unite an otherwise divided Europe.

For the Reformers, the popes were no less an evil than the Turks. In the Reformers' polemic they referred to two Antichrists who clashed for supremacy in Europe, the papacy and the Ottomans, both unbelievers and tyrants linked together as soul and body. The Antichrist of the West, the pope, was the spirit, or the soul, while the Antichrist of the East, the Turk, was the body, or the flesh.[32] In this light it becomes apparent that the Reformers denied the pope's role as a leader in the struggle against the Ottomans. Luther's objection seems to have been less to fighting the Turks than to fighting under papal leadership. In the material realm, this denial of the pope's leading role was the reflection of reluctance by much of Europe to contribute funds for the crusade. Instead of spending money for the organization of crusades, the Reformers claimed, the popes wasted them for other purposes. Ulrich von Hutten initiated the charge that these funds could have been far better used by the emperor.[33] But when the question of raising imperial armies to fight the Turks actually arose, there was no conspicuously greater public eagerness to provide funds and soldiers.[34]

STRUGGLE ON THE SEA: PIRACY

Similar disunion and mutual suspicion characterized Europe's response to Ottoman dominance on the seas. For many countries the Turkish invasion of the continent was a faraway prospect, thus they paid only slight attention to the wars in Hungary, Austria, Poland, or Transylvania.[35] But growing Ottoman seapower presented a more immediate danger. France, Italy, and Spain could not feel secure while Turkish ships cruised the Mediterranean.

The conquest of Constantinople provided the Ottomans with a base for their naval operations. In 1454, just a year after the fall of the Byzantine Empire, two Turkish squadrons put to sea but confined their activities to "showing the flag" and plundering where possible. The transformation of the Porte into a great seapower continued with occupation of Syria in 1516 and Egypt in 1517. By the end of the sixteenth century the eastern Mediterranean had become an "Ottoman sea," with most of the islands and the archipelago in Ottoman hands. Negroponte was captured in 1479; Rhodes fell in 1522; Chios was occupied in 1566; Cyprus was annexed, after two sieges, in 1570–1572. After twenty years of war, the Turks conquered Crete in 1669.[36]

That the Porte would not be satisfied with the eastern Mediterranean became clear in 1480 when a Turkish force landed and seized Otranto on the Italian peninsula, and from that base overran the countryside and struck at Brindisi, Tarentum, and Lecce. Fear among the Italian states was extreme. The pope thought of fleeing to Avignon. The danger united the Italian princes, who stopped their fighting with one another. Yet it was not their efforts but the death of the sultan in 1481 that prompted the conquerors to evacuate Otranto and leave Italy.[37]

Turkish plans to spread their influence to the western Mediterranean were partly realized after Khair ad-Din (known in the West as Barbarossa), a dreaded pirate who already controlled the coast of Morocco, recognized himself as the sultan's vassal and occupied Algiers in his name. Nevertheless the western Mediterranean remained an area where the rules of the game were dictated by the Habsburgs' Spain.[38] The Ottomans and the Spanish fought the major sea battles of the sixteenth and early seventeenth centuries.

European efforts to contain the spread of Turkish influence at sea were no more consistent and coordinated than on the land. Each country pursued its own selfish objectives, which often undermined the declared struggle against the infidels. France was alarmed by the Habsburgs' growing influence in Europe and regarded with apprehension Charles V's conquests in North Africa. To block its rival, the French king was prepared to enter into agreement with any adversary of the emperor, be it the Netherlands or the Ottomans. The Italian states, particularly Venice and Genoa, did not wish to sacrifice their trade priorities for the lofty principles of a struggle against the Muslims. Whenever a peace with the Turks could guarantee them a continuation of their commerce, they were ready to abandon any anti-Turkish alliance and sign a truce with the hereditary enemy. Besides, Venice and Genoa also feared the Habsburgs' aggressive policy in Europe. Thus no alliance of European powers against the Porte during the most acute period of struggle in the Mediterranean could survive its victories or defeats.

The first League of the Christian Countries of Europe (1538–1540) was concluded between Charles V and Venice with the fate of the Mediterranean at stake. A fleet under the command of Barbarossa, with the secret support of France, threatened the Habsburg possessions in Italy as well as Venice's empire. Yet neither participant of the League trusted the other, and the alliance fell apart soon after an embarrassment at Prevesa, on September 27, 1538, when the Spanish fleet abandoned the field to the galleys and foists of Barbarossa without putting up a fight. Two years later Venice left the League and, with the aid of French diplomacy, bought peace with the Ottomans.

The situation soon became acute for the Christian powers. "Without the Venetian fleet," Braudel notes, "it was impossible for the western alliance to offer any resistance to the Turkish armada, soon to be reinforced by French galleys which took to plundering the Catalan coasts and the waters round the Balearics. The collective security of Mediterranean Christendom was gravely threatened; the Turks would now not merely attack, but go beyond Malta and the Sicilian channel. Christian sea-power was reduced to a defensive, ineffectual but nevertheless costly strategy."[39] In 1543 Barbarossa ravaged the Sicilian and Neapolitan coasts and captured Reggio. The Ottoman and French fleets then combined in an attack upon Nice, which belonged to Charles's ally, the Duke of Savoy. In August 1551 the Turkish fleet captured Tripoli, which the Spaniards had seized in 1510 and then handed over to the Knights of St. John. With this operation the Ottomans secured a valuable military position.

The Turks seemed to be on the offensive throughout the Mediterranean. An attempt by Spanish King Philip II, Charles V's son, to reverse the situation by sending expeditions to the African coast led nowhere. The capture of Djerba in April 1560, as revenge for the loss of Tripoli, resulted only in a swift counterattack by the Turkish fleet, which reached the island in twenty days and routed the Christian armada; thirty galleys and thirty-two boats were lost. The Djerba disaster marked the low point of Western power in the Mediterranean and the apogee of the Ottoman fleet.[40] After that, Turkish dominance began to decline, yet the Turks continued to menace the European powers, as the siege of Malta in May–September 1565 demonstrated.

The island of Malta belonged to the Knights of St. John, who had moved there after the capture of Rhodes by the Turks in 1522. The loss of Malta, because of its important strategic position south of Sicily, would undoubtedly have been a disaster for Christendom. The defense of the island by the knights, with the help of the Spanish fleet, therefore took on profound importance. Whether the siege of Malta should be regarded as a clear collision between Islam and Christendom,[41] however, remains a question of perspective. In any case, the heroism of the knights received its full due while no one mentioned the contribution of the Spanish fleet, which delivered a landing party to the island and thus forced the Turks to abandon hopes for victory and to retreat from Malta. The cautious and indecisive Admiral Don Garcia wished to avoid excessive risk. But soon the Spanish fleet received an opportunity to be fully exonerated, on October 7, 1571, when the forces of the two opposing camps met in battle in the Gulf of Lepanto.

Despite the retreat from Malta, the Turkish peril was not about to vanish overnight. The sultan stepped up his ship-building to prepare for new conquests in Malta, Sicily, and Apulia. When this news reached Europe, it stirred great anxiety on the continent and posed once more the need to unite forces against the Ottoman threat. Toward this objective Pope Pius V, an energetic leader committed to a new crusade, devoted all his energy. What the pope dreamt of was a formally constituted league that would include all the leading European powers with himself at the head. This dream was finally realized in the Holy League, formed to wage a united struggle against the Turks, formally signed on May 20, 1571. But it included only Spain, Venice, and the pope. An attempt to draw France into the alliance failed because of its implacable hostility toward the House of Habsburg. As a contemporary observer noted: "Here in France, everyone is doing his utmost to prevent the league from taking shape and to encourage an entente between Venice and the sultan."[42] Evidently, hatred of its Christian rival was stronger in France than an aversion toward collaboration with the infidel.

The Holy League's fleet consisted of 316 ships under the command of Don John of Austria. Other Italian cities—Genoa, Florence, Turin, Parma, Lucca, and Ferrara—as well as the Knights of St. John contributed their ships and manpower to the forces of the League.[43] After having received information that the Turkish fleet had just returned to Lepanto, off the Greek coast, for the winter, Don John made a decision to fight. The council of war supported it, despite the objections of the cautious and pusillanimous. News of the fall of Famagusta, the last stronghold in Cyprus, to the Turks only increased the resolution of the men in the Christian fleet.

The battle of October 7, 1571, resulted in a resounding victory for the League's forces. Of 230 Turkish warships, only 30 escaped; the others were sunk or captured and divided among the victors. The Turks lost more than 30,000 dead and wounded and 3,000 prisoners; 15,000 galley slaves were freed. The Christians lost 10 ships, 8,000 men killed, and 21,000 wounded. The victory undoubtedly spelled the end of Ottoman supremacy in the Mediterranean. But, no less important, it ended a period of profound depression, of a "genuine inferiority complex" in Christendom.[44] If one considers this victory in terms of the confrontation between Europe and Islam, however, its results are not so simple. Lepanto did not deal a mortal blow to Ottoman might. In the years that followed, the Turks consolidated their conquest of Cyprus and continued their expansion into North Africa, eliminating the remaining Habsburg fortresses there. In 1669 the Porte captured Crete while nurturing plans for the siege of Vienna.

On the other hand, the Christian world remained as divided as it had been before the battle of Lepanto. Not every Christian rejoiced in news of the victory. One notable exception was Charles IX of France, who drew up a memoir for the sultan's guidance in the difficult circumstances the Porte found itself after the battle. Charles's main idea was that Selim should aim at separating his enemies and defeating them one by one, lest he find himself with a land attack by a united Christendom. To this end, Charles advised the sultan to make overtures either to Venice, where peace was much desired, or to Spain.[45] The Holy League itself did not endure more than two years. In May 1572 Pius V, the principal inspirer of the League, died, and his death was sufficient to throw into question the entire future of the alliance. The next year Venice, disappointed with the meager results of its participation in the League, suspicious over Spanish intentions, and itself exhausted, abandoned the League, having signed a harsh and dishonorable peace with the Porte.

Furthermore, Lepanto proved to be the end of the age of crusades. Never again would Christendom unite its forces to launch an offensive against the followers of its rival religion. Never again would thousands of people be ready to leave their homes for the sake of lofty religious ideals and travel to faraway lands to war against infidels. This lot was left to a few fanatics firmly resolved to revive the lost spirit of the past. Now people were preoccupied with more earthly needs. And the Catholic church reflected this change. At the end of the sixteenth century the popes thought primarily about the struggle against the Reformation rather than defense against the Turks. In 1581 the Spanish church protested not against the abandonment of the Turkish wars but against paying taxes to no purpose.[46]

The story of the struggle for supremacy in the Mediterranean would be incomplete without an analysis of piracy, which played an increasingly important role in the confrontation between Europe and Islam. The name of Khair ad-Din Barbarossa has been noted in referring to sea battles between the Turks and the Europeans. To it should be added Uluj Ali Reis, Turghud Ali (known in the West as Dragut), and many other corsairs and pirates whose ships plied the seas of the Mediterranean, sowing terror among ships of war and peaceful populations alike.

Piracy is as old as the history of navigation. As long as ships loaded with goods, weapons, and people sailed the seas, there were always those who sought profit by capturing and plundering them. The Mediterranean, always an area of intensive traffic, had been an attractive locale for the robbery of ships from time immemorial. Phoenicians who showed themselves to be skillful and audacious sailors were also fearless and cunning robbers. They were not averse to brigandage and rarely demonstrated charity toward their victims. The legendary Greek Argonauts who set to sea to obtain the Golden Fleece were also pirates who ravaged the coast in search of treasure and a better life. These objectives were uppermost in mind for most pirates then and later; their nationality, faith, or allegiance never played a significant role.

When a monk who happened to meet one of the Barbary corsairs asked him why he was a pirate, the latter responded: "I live according to the tradition of the sea."[47] This tradition, rooted in the ancient past, continued unchanged through many generations. Its practitioners took advantage of geography—the many inlets, small islands, and river estuaries that offered good shelter for pirate ships. The appearance of Islam on Mediterranean shores did not significantly alter pirates' activities in the area. For Muslim pirates, religion only concealed the same desire for wealth and a better life that were always powerful stimuli for sea robbers.

Initially the Arabs, children of the desert, feared the sea and avoided distant travels by water. When the Caliph Omar was first asked to approve a sea crossing and attack on the islands of Greece, he forbade the expedition as he feared the dangers of the deep. "The safety of my people is dearer to me than all the treasures of Greece."[48] A principal obstacle for the Arab landing in Spain on the eve of its conquest was the need to cross the strait that separated the European continent from Africa (later called Gibraltar, after the name of the leader of the first expedition on Spanish land, Tariq ibn Ziyad).[49] As time passed, however, the Arabs learned the science of navigation, not least with the help of the Chinese and Indians, with whom they were in constant exchange and from whom they borrowed compass and astrolabe. They became good sailors, and some of them turned to piracy, which proved to be a profitable enterprise.

Among the first Muslim pirates in the Mediterranean were probably those rebels who were expelled from Cordoba by the Arab ruler and who decided to practice piracy in the central and eastern parts of the inland sea. The first object of their attack was not a Christian country but Muslim Egypt, where they established a sort of maritime republic based in Alexandria. It required strong measures by the legitimate ruler of this province of the Abbasid caliphate to expel them from the country. After being chased from Egypt, these adventurers from Spain decided to attack Crete, which belonged to the Byzantine Empire. Under the command of their leader, Abu Hafs Umar al-Balluti, they landed on the island and occupied it. They successfully repelled a sequence of Byzantine attacks and ruled on Crete until 961, transforming it into a piratical nest and terrorizing this region of the Mediterranean with their raids against naval traffic as well as against the Aegean islands.[50]

In the western Mediterranean the subjects of the emir of Cordoba not only led pirate raids against ships and neighboring shores, they also penetrated deep into the continent, as far as the Western Alps, attacking parties of travelers and pilgrims as they crossed the mountains. In 842 they reached the outskirts of Arles, plundered it, and retreated without loss. In 869 they captured the bishop of Arles, Roland, who had taken command of the local defenses and attacked the pirates' landing party. The courageous prelate died aboard a pirate ship at the moment he was about to be ransomed. Yet the Saracens, who did not wish to be deprived of the money, dressed his body in his priestly clothes, placed it on a chair, and handed it over to his redeemers, pretending that the bishop was still alive.[51] In the last decade of the ninth century these pirates established their base on the coast of Provence at the place known as Fraxinetum (now La Garde-Freinet), not far from Saint-Tropez. From there they terrorized the county of Fréjus and infiltrated the surroundings of Marseilles. They destroyed the famous monastery of Saint-Victor and pillaged the Valentinois and Viennois provinces. An expedition sent against them in 931 was unsuccessful. Only in 972 or 973 was this nest of piracy eliminated.

Although one may be tempted to see in these raids of the Muslim pirates a continuation of the *jihad* against Christians, the facts do not support this argument. As the example of the bishop of Arles clearly indicates, the principal object of pirates' activities was loot. They attacked Christian monasteries not out of hatred toward these centers of Christianity but with the aim of capturing the enormous treasure that the monasteries already possessed. The Saracen attack on the abbey of Saint-Gall in 939 was dictated primarily by this motive.[52] The scarcity of extant sources limits information about the composition of the pirates who acted in Provence and who were usually called the Saracens, but there is reason to suspect that the most audacious among them were neither Arabs nor Berbers but the indigenous inhabitants of the Iberian peninsula, whether converts or Christians, and that the language widespread among them was the Roman dialect.[53] This does not excuse the brutality of pirate attacks on peaceful populations, but it argues that purely mundane motives, rather than religion, played a dominant role in the activities of pirates from al-Andalus.

The pirate situation changed somewhat during the period of acute confrontation between Europe and the Ottoman Empire. While the caliphs of Cordoba consistently denied their responsibility for the actions of pirates against Christian countries, the Ottomans were eager to rely on piracy in their plans for conquest on the European continent. Thus piracy in the sixteenth and seventeenth centuries increasingly assumed a role as auxiliary to Turkish regular forces, and its leaders were elevated to the ranks of the commanders of the naval forces of the Sublime Porte. In that period Muslim pirates in the Mediterranean were transformed into corsairs who, after acknowledging the suzerainty of the sultan, received permission from him to commit aggressive acts against enemy vessels.[54]

The raids of Muslim pirates who had settled on the North African coast harassed primarily Spanish ships, and in the early sixteenth century Spain undertook efforts to extinguish this piratical nest. But its efforts proved unsuccessful. Piracy spread in the western Mediterranean, soon becoming a powerful factor in the confrontation between Europe and the Ottomans. After the title of supreme commander of the Turkish naval forces was conferred on Khair ad-Din Barbarossa by Suleiman the Magnificent, the fleet of Barbary corsairs[55] took an active part on the Turkish side in sea battles between the adversaries, while organizing independent expeditions to ravage the seacoasts of European countries. With the help of the corsairs, the Ottomans spread their dominance, albeit precarious, over African coastal regions to the west of Egypt and threatened their principal adversary, Spain, from the immediate vicinity. When war on the seas ended after 1574 and the center of gravity moved to land war on the European continent, the corsairs continued their raids. Piracy became a "secondary form of war," in the words of Fernand Braudel. "Already a force to be reckoned with between 1550 and 1574, it expanded to fill any gaps left by the slackening of official war. From 1574–1580, it increased its activities even further, soon coming to dominate the now less spectacular history of the Mediterranean. The new capitals of warfare were not Constantinople, Madrid, and Messina, but Algiers, Malta, Leghorn, and Pisa. Upstarts had replaced the tired giants, and international conflicts degenerated into a free-for-all."[56]

From then on the activities of the Barbary corsairs were not limited to the Mediterranean. In 1627 they ravaged the shores of Iceland; they inflicted damage on trade routes in the North and Baltic Seas, capturing ships and kidnapping their crews. Between 1613 and 1621 Hamburg lost 56 ships to the corsairs, and in January 1662 alone the Hanseatic cities were deprived of 8 commercial vessels. To defend its trade fleet from these attacks, beginning at the close of the seventeenth century Hamburg accompanied it with heavily armed battleships with soldiers aboard. Despite these precautions, between 1719 and 1747 the corsairs captured 50 of Hamburg's ships and took 682 seamen into captivity.[57]

If during the active phase of the sea war in the Mediterranean the Barbary pirates might be seen as participating in the *jihad* against the infidels, these expeditions to the north were clearly dictated solely by a craving for booty and slaves. The very existence of the Barbary states in North Africa depended on successful thievery at sea. When corsairs came home empty-handed, there would be famine in Algiers.[58] In these circumstances nationalities or faiths had no importance whatsoever. Among the captains of corsair ships (*re'is*) were representatives of many nationalities, most of them from European countries, who had denounced their original faith and converted to Islam. The attraction of a freer life and the opportunity to rid themselves of oppression and poverty in their native lands brought many aboard ship on the Barbary Coast, in pursuit of a better fate. Entire shiploads of such individuals sometimes came to North Africa together to seek their fortunes. Thus most of the famous corsairs were of European origin. Aruj and his brother Khair ad-Din Barbarossa were Greeks from Mytilene; Dragut, another famous corsair who served at the siege of Malta, was also Greek born in Asia Minor; Muhammad from Chios (1633–1649), who received the title of pasha from the Ottomans and who became the dey of Tripoli, was from Genoa. Such examples are numerous.

Muslim privateers were not the only ones whose ships plied the Mediterranean in the years of confrontation between Europe and the Ottoman Empire. Malta and Livorno were bases of Christian pirates, while the Uskoks of Segna and Fiume continuously robbed Turks and Christians alike. Ragusa took up arms against the Uskoks one day, and Venice blockaded their two ports and carried out reprisals against the captains of the pirate ships. In the mid-sixteenth century the boldest Western corsairs were the Knights of Malta. Their audaciousness and abilities were equal to those of the Barbary pirates. In 1561 alone the Knights captured three hundred slaves and several rich cargoes at the mouth of the Nile.[59] Even merchants were not averse to plundering a weaker vessel that they encountered on the way to their destination.

While the Barbary corsairs dominated the western Mediterranean, the Christians acted mostly in the Levant, with its trade routes that linked various parts of the Ottoman Empire with Constantinople. Christian pirates inflicted serious damage on the Ottomans' commerce and by their brash actions even impeded the development of political relations between European powers and the Porte. France particularly frowned at the activities of the Knights of Malta, because the Franco-Turkish alliance was frequently strained by the close link between the knights and French nobility, such as the House of Lorraine, whose scions had led the Maltese knights in the sixteenth century. The actions of the Order in 1614 provoked a diplomatic crisis and the raid of Malta by the Turkish fleet in the course of its punitive expedition to the Barbary Coast. In 1643 a Maltese squadron captured a vessel carrying an Ottoman court official, Kizlar Aga, and a valuable cargo. The prisoners included a young woman who was suspected of being an Ottoman princeling, an impression later confirmed by the sultan's wrath upon hearing news of the capture. This seizure may have influenced the Turkish decision to invade Crete, in whose harbors the Maltese had been received on their return voyage.[60] In the pirate wars that raged in the Mediterranean, the Barbary corsairs, albeit the protagonists, were not the only actors.

What's more, in the war of all against all, it was often hard to distinguish between acts of piracy and a legitimate defense against aggressors or intruders. The post of the captain of the gulf in Venice may serve to illustrate this situation. His duties varied widely, ranging from surveillance of the Adriatic Sea to the escorting of merchant galleys in threatening situations. He often had to decide independently what actions to take. Since Venice regarded any armed vessel appearing in the Adriatic without its consent as piratical and as a legitimate object of seizure, the actions of the captain of the gulf sometimes were regarded as arbitrary. This was especially so because Venice's claims to superiority over the Adriatic, which the republic considered its "gulf" (hence the title of the captain), were continually contested by other sea powers.[61]

SLAVERY: MUSLIM AND CHRISTIAN

The most despised feature of the Barbary corsair war was the capture of individuals who then were sold as slaves and subjected to merciless exploitation in North Africa. Like the Crimean Tatar raids into the territory of Muscovy, corsair expeditions deprived European countries of human resources and forced them to divert from other spheres of their economies the money necessary for ransoming the captives. The damaging effects of this sordid business were acutely felt in France, England, Italy, and Holland. And the human spoils of privateering were enormous. For example, between November 1593 and August 1594 the Tunisian corsairs brought in some 28 prizes with 1,722 captives; between 1628 and 1634 the Algerians managed to capture 80 merchant vessels from the French alone, taking 986 captives in the process; the rovers of Tripoli, though running one of the smaller slaving fleets, between 1677 and 1685 nonetheless brought in 75 Christian ships with 1,085 captives.[62] Corsair expeditions on land specifically aimed at the capture of slaves proved even more productive: in 1544 the Algerians took 7,000 captives in the Bay of Naples; 6,000 were snapped up when they sacked Vieste in Calabria in 1554; 4,000 men, women, and children were seized in Granada in 1566.[63] Yet the most damaging were smaller expeditions led by, say, a score of pirates in a felucca against a handful of poor fishermen caught too far out at sea, or a couple of village women seized while working in the fields. These petty piracies cost Christendom more in material and human losses than all the spectacular expeditions together.[64] As a result, between 1530 and 1780—that is, at the peak of corsair activity—about a million or as many as 1.25 million European Christians were enslaved by the Muslims of the Barbary Coast.[65]

The European slaves were used in various economic pursuits in the Barbary principalities. Most of them were intended for work as galley slaves or for heavy construction; some were sent out to labor on small farm plots; still others, mostly women, became maids or servants in the houses of their proprietors. The life of most slaves was difficult, and they often died from abuse, disease, overwork, lack of food, or despair. But some, especially among the private slaves, became managers of their masters' property and members of the family.[66] Others, after their conversion to Islam, were promoted to high administrative posts or became commanders of their own ships. Still, the plight of the majority was miserable, and they dreamt of being ransomed by their relatives at home. Ransoming the slaves became the duty not only of private citizens but also of states and various religious orders. In Denmark, for instance, on the king's order, special *Slavebøger* (slave books) were issued that permitted the relatives of captured sailors to gather money at church doors. Often special funds were established and taxes levied to cover ransom payments for Christian slaves.[67] But many of them could not wait for ransom: the death rate among slaves was usually very high.

However unfortunate was the lot of those who were captured and enslaved by the Barbary corsairs, it is important to note that slavery was also widespread on the European side of the Mediterranean. Christian pirates, while seizing material goods on the vessels of their victims, did not ignore human prey. In many cases this business was legitimated by the authorities. It is well known that the Sicilians practiced piracy widely. In 1415 it was decided that a fifth of the slaves captured by Sicilian pirates would go to the admiral of Sicily after deducting expenses for arms and equipment. A ship that set to sea specifically to hunt for slaves had to pay the admiral two florins for each person sold. Slaves could not be exported from the kingdom without a special license from the admiral.[68]

The Genoese were the most notorious players in the slavery business. They sold slaves to the Mamluks of Egypt and to their Italian neighbors, using any opportunity to capture them on the shores of the Black Sea or in *Reconquista* Spain. Immediately upon the reconquest of Valencia, slaves from that Moorish kingdom appeared for sale in the market at Genoa. The same happened after the fall of Murcia and Minorca. But while the slaves from Spain were mostly Muslims, among those who were sold in Caffa were Christians from Russia, Georgia, and Byzantium's provinces. Slaves of Russian origin are mentioned in notarial documents throughout Italy.[69]

The popes deplored the enslavement of Christians, even of those whose rites Rome considered schismatic or heretical,[70] but the Vatican was generally not above using slaves as rowers on papal galleys and did not wish to liberate them after conversion to Christianity. Pius V, the instigator of the Holy League before the battle of Lepanto, in 1571 possessed four hundred slaves, primarily Turks, whom he used on his galleys. In the seventeenth century the popes frequently acquired their slaves from the Knights of Malta; they were chained to one another during rest time and at night. Even at the close of the eighteenth century the popes used slaves in their galleys, though this practice had already disappeared everywhere due to the introduction of sailing vessels in the fleets of the great powers.[71]

Slavery was observed in Europe as late as the early nineteenth century. In 1812 it was still possible to meet a slave in Palermo and other towns of Sicily.[72] Although among Christian states slavery was not as massive as on the Barbary Coast, and died out in most countries sooner, one must not forget the peculiar character of the principalities created in North Africa by pirates and corsairs. While in Europe slavery was an auxiliary branch of the economy and never occupied a dominant position, mostly satisfying housekeeping needs, the prosperity of the Barbary states depended directly on slave labor, because their sole economic activity was privateering and related activity. When piracy was suppressed by the European powers in the early nineteenth century, slavery disappeared.

FOUR

Religion's Role in the Confrontation

Having considered the development of armed conflict between Europe and Islam in its most acute phase for Europeans, one may ask how crucial religious factors were in this confrontation. Did they play a dominant role? Is there something inherent in both Islam and Christianity that made this confrontation inevitable? Or can other motives explain the intensity of the conflict and its manifestations?

What one first notices about the history of the relationship between Christians and Muslims is the exceptional cruelty that accompanied their wars. Some modern Western authors have counted the number of people beheaded or crucified by "savage Islamic warriors" during their conquests in the lands of Christendom. In comparison with these atrocities, the Crusaders or Conquistadores do not look so bloodthirsty. They even demonstrated clemency toward their adversaries, as prescribed by the injunctions of the Gospels. Yet such a view is misleading in several respects. First, we tend to judge the behavior of people who lived five or ten centuries ago from the standpoint of today's morality. In the course of history, man's attitude toward his own actions has changed, as has his system of moral values. Today we have different views about the treatment of people, even if they are our enemies. And these views are common for most of mankind, regardless of religion and rituals.

Second, how can we measure which side was more cruel in wartime? Should we attribute savagery to Islam or to the atrocities of war, an unfortunate feature of any armed conflict? In describing battles between Christian and Muslim forces, historians often refer to bloody acts committed by the latter. Here, for example, is a passage from a description of the aftermath of the battle of Nicopolis in 1396: "Aghast at the numbers of his own dead, greater than the Christians, he [Bajazet] ordered all his prisoners—perhaps three thousand in all—to be decapitated on the spot. They were paraded before him in the morning, naked and tied together in bunches of three or four. The mass beheading ceremony started early in the morning and went on without a break until the late afternoon. The battlefield became a lake of blood."[1] In the picture thus presented, the leaders of the armies of Islam—emirs, sultans, and shahs—are depicted as monsters, with bloody hands and all possible vices.

Let us turn to another episode of medieval history which is no less famous than the battle of Nicopolis: "Regular forces of the Crusaders began to flow into the city; they slaughtered inhabitants on the streets and encircled the church. Among the sound of bells and the groans of the dying, priests sang the funeral Mass; the church doors fell as the brigands rushed into the church. Their comrades, meanwhile, spread through the city, thinking only of plunder. They murdered everyone they found, including monks and priests; the Crusaders were searching for heretics. Neither women nor babies were spared."[2]

This is not an account of battle between Christians and Muslims. It is about the slaughter of the French town of Bézier, and a slaughter of Christians by other Christians who considered the former heretics. It is one of the episodes of the Crusade against the Albigensians, who were condemned in 1215 at the fourth Lateran Ecumenical Council.[3] Simon de Monfort, after the capture of one of the towns during this Crusade, ordered that more than one hundred people be blinded and have their noses cut off.[4] Surely de Monfort could compete with the cruelest of the Ottoman sultans.

Examples of Christian cruelty may be found in considerable number in the history of confrontation between Christendom and Islam. In the encounter at Pontuvium, in Galicia in 768, the army of the Asturians under Fruela I massacred many thousands of Muslims. The proper son of the emir of Cordoba, Umar, was captured in the course of the battle and then beheaded, following the order of the Austurian king.[5] In another battle, the siege of Evora, again in Galicia, in 913, King Ordoño II ordered the governor of the caliphate of Cordoba and seven hundred soldiers of the town garrison massacred. After plundering the city, the attackers led four thousand women and children into captivity.[6]

In those times Christians and Muslims alike demonstrated behavior that seems abominable to modern man. But to what extent may such behavior be attributed to the respective religions? True, the spirit of *jihad* was strong among the Turkish tribes that in the eleventh century flooded into the Byzantine Empire. They founded the so-called ghazi states in the areas that bordered on Christian-populated regions, constantly harassing and plundering them. The ghazis were "warriors of faith," and the idea of enlarging the home of Islam was the raison d'être of their activities. The state that was created about 1300 by Othman, the founder of the Ottoman Empire and a leader of the ghazis, was typical in this respect. His ghazis, upon crossing to Europe, soon conquered most of the Balkans and posed a serious threat to Christendom.[7]

In the course of their invasion of Anatolia, Turkish tribes pillaged towns and villages, destroyed churches or converted them to mosques, and killed or enslaved the Christian population. Nur al-Din of Aleppo, the son of Zangi, a famous hero of resistance against the Crusaders, took Nisibis, a Byzantine town in Anatolia, in 1171, and ordered all new churches as well as those built in the reign of his father to be demolished. The treasure of the Nestorian church of Mar Jacob and its library of one thousand volumes were pillaged and destroyed.[8] During the Ottoman invasion of Thrace under "Ghazi Suleiman," son of Orkhan, after 1351, the Turks followed the same policy of the forcible imposition of Islam. One Turkish author wrote, describing this onslaught: "Where there were bells, Suleiman broke them up and cast them unto fires. Where there were churches he destroyed them or converted them into mosques. Thus, in place of bells there were now muezzins. Wherever Christian infidels were still found, vassalage was imposed upon their rulers. At least in public they could no longer say 'kyrie eleison' but rather 'There is no God but Allah'; and where once their prayers had been addressed to Christ, they were now to 'Mohammed, the prophet of Allah.'"[9]

Yet there is ample evidence that most of the Turkish Seljuk tribes that invaded Anatolia were not the staunch Muslims they sometimes presented themselves to be. Having adopted Islam not long before their conquests, the tribesmen, subjects of the Seljuk and Ottoman sultans, retained much of their shamanistic inheritance at the level of folk religion.[10] Their religious chiefs were direct descendants of the older tribal shamans in Central Asia and represented a fusion of the tribal shaman and the itinerant Muslim dervish. Not surprisingly, Sufism, a form of mass religion that combined Islamic norms and injunctions with the personal experience of serving divinity and mysticism, spread broadly among these tribes.[11]

The religious heterodoxy of the Turkish tribes corresponded to their militancy. According to Speros Vryonis, "If the folk character of Turkmen religion found its Muslim equivalent in the heterodox wandering Sufis, Turkmen martial order was well suited to the Ghazi life and the tradition of the holy war against the Christians. By association with the religious war on the boundaries against the Greeks and Armenians, the warlike practices and proclivities for plunder of the Turkmens were not only satisfactorily accommodated but even religiously justified."[12] This combination of their pre-Islamic customs and particular Islamic forms produced the cruel and savage behavior of the ghazis during the Seljuk and Ottoman conquests. The banditry of these tribes was recognized even by Muslim authorities. The great Seljuk sultans of Persia made strenuous efforts to shunt them into Anatolia in order to spare their own domains from their ravages. The tribesmen were also a constant source of difficulty for the Ottoman sultans. The Kĩsĩlbash tribes of Anatolia openly supported the Safavids and forced the sultans to adopt a policy of partial extermination.[13]

Nevertheless this savagery aimed at Christians was typical mostly during battle. In peacetime the tolerance of Islam usually prevailed. Christians and Jews who submitted to Muslim rule quietly and peacefully became *dhimmi* (*zimmi* in the Ottoman Empire), that is, members of a community whose non-Muslim subjects had agreed to recognize the primacy of Islam and the supremacy of the Muslims. They symbolized their submission by paying a poll tax and accepting certain limitations in their social status, such as the prohibition to bear arms, to ride a horse, to wear certain clothes and certain colors, to build houses higher than those built by the Muslims. In return they were allowed to practice their religion and to enjoy a large degree of autonomy under their own religious leaders. They lived chiefly by their own and not by Muslim law, though they were forbidden any public or loud expression of their religious beliefs. Among other things, this meant that Christians were generally prohibited from displaying the crucifix outside their churches and from tolling their church bells. Nor were they allowed to raise their voices in prayer or to hold processions or other religious ceremonies outdoors.

Despite some discrimination against the Christians who lived under Muslim rule, their life was generally not intolerable. They enjoyed certain freedoms that seem unthinkable in light of the ferocity of war that was waged between Christendom and Islam. Even savage Seljuk tribes, as soon as they settled on conquered lands, often turned to a policy of protecting the local population, which in many cases formed a majority. In 1197 the sultan Kaykhusraw settled five thousand Christians in Philomelium. The sultan lavished great care upon these Christian colonists, giving them land and seed to plant and bestowing upon them a five-year tax immunity with the provision that afterward they should pay the customary taxes they had paid in Byzantine territory.[14] The Ottomans likewise sought to avoid the immediate breakdown of the social system that existed on the conquered lands in Europe. They tolerated the existence of Christian feudatories, both secular and ecclesiastic, which were recorded in the official Turkish land registry. Christian *vakifs* and *timars*, that is, landholdings belonging respectively to God and to the sultan (the latter granted as fiefs to those who served the empire), existed side by side with comparable Muslim holdings. The notion widespread in Europe at that time—that Christians lost all their land when the Ottomans arrived—was erroneous.[15]

As a result of Ottoman conquest, Christian peasants were freed from the oppression and arbitrariness of their local lords. No serfdom existed in the Ottoman Empire. Every person was the direct subject of the sultan and had to pay taxes that were uniformly applied as long as the Ottoman system functioned properly. This may explain why so many inhabitants of the Balkans helped the Ottomans during their conquests and why living under direct Ottoman rule was initially preferable to living under a local lord. The Turks pursued a similar policy with respect to the cities. The conquerors not only confirmed the privileges of artisans and traders in each city that fell into their hands, they also worked to build flourishing centers of manufacture and trade. They maintained the roads that linked one with another, and made the *zimmis* who repaired roads exempt from various taxes. The merchant marines too received special privileges.[16]

Although non-Muslims in the Ottoman Empire lived under their own laws, they might nonetheless appeal to the Ottoman law courts based on Sharia, the sacred law of Islam, in certain internal matters involving relations between the Christian and

Muslim communities. For example, in Cyprus, after its conquest by the empire in 1571, Ottoman *kadis* (judges) were ordered to apply the same standard of justice for both *zimmi* and
Muslim. *Zimmis* were entitled to the same protection of life and
property as Muslims, and the court was to strive diligently to secure that equality. As a consequence *zimmis* used the Sharia
courts with considerable frequency. In the Cyprus city of
Nicosia, of the overall number of cases under consideration by
the courts in various years, more than one-third involved at
least one *zimmi*. Fifteen percent involved only *zimmis*. Another
19 percent of all cases were intercommunal, indicating significant economic and social interaction.[17]

The Ottoman Turks demonstrated flexibility in their religious
policies as well. Most people in the conquered lands in the first
years of Ottoman expansion were Orthodox Christians. Not
surprisingly, the largest of the *millets* (groups of non-Muslim
people considered as legal-administrative units by the Ottomans)
was the Orthodox. Mehmed II, who captured Constantinople,
while creating a Christian *millet* limited to the adherents of the
Eastern Rite, pursued several goals. He considered himself the legitimate successor of the Byzantine emperor and wished to retain
his position and prerogatives in dealing with the Orthodox
church. Furthermore he hoped to rebuild his new capital, Istanbul, and make it a great trading and manufacturing center. For
this he needed loyal Christians, and he trusted only the Orthodox.[18] Finally, he wished to guarantee the submission of the
Christian population in the newly conquered countries of the
Balkan peninsula. By entrusting responsibility for the conduct of
the flock to the church hierarchy, the sultans smoothed the
process of consolidation of their European conquests.

The power conferred by the Ottomans to the Orthodox
church made it a state within a state. The Turks were generally
indifferent to both its teachings and internal affairs. Orthodox
clergy took advantage of this attitude not only to protect their
flock but to spread the word of God. Frequently they did not
limit themselves to religious ministrations but seized every op-

portunity to condemn the Turks for their tyranny. This covert opposition may have helped create an image in the West that the subject peoples of Greece and the Balkans were heavily oppressed by the Ottomans and were waiting for any pretext to rise against their oppressors.[19] This image rekindled the spirit of the Crusades and led to tragic failures and disappointments, when European forces not only failed to gain the support of the local population but sometimes were met with hatred. Yet the Orthodox church never announced a policy of official opposition to the Turks. Leaders of the clergy knew full well how harsh the conqueror could be and were therefore loath to provoke him, especially since the Turks allowed the church to exist in relative freedom and did not meddle in its internal affairs.[20]

Ottoman authorities displayed their leniency not only toward Orthodox Christians but also toward Catholics, though the latter were not as numerous in the empire and did not constitute a separate *millet*.[21] Most noticeable among the representatives of the Catholic church were monks of the Franciscan mission in Jerusalem. They had attracted attention with their public religious ceremonies, which were a source of constant discord between them and the vigilant upholders of Muslim law. Particularly troublesome was the annual ceremony on Palm Sunday, in which the Franciscans recalled Christ's entry into Jerusalem. They reconstructed this event and staged the glorious evangelical scene in a solemn procession that descended the Mount of Olives, crossed the Valley of Jehoshaphat, ascended toward the Temple Mount, went round its walls, and walked into Jerusalem through the Gate of Zion—all before the eyes of the Muslim inhabitants of the Holy City. The event was a great violation of the limitations imposed by Muslim law on the religious practices of non-Muslims in the domains of Islam, and recurrent complaints were lodged before the *kadi* of Jerusalem by the Franciscans' Muslim neighbors.[22]

The Ottoman authorities faced a dilemma in considering these accusations and claims. On the one hand, they had to follow strictly the Sharia as it related to the behavior of the infidels.

On the other hand, the empire was committed to permit its European guest—in this case the Franciscan monks—to practice their religion unimpeded and to protect them from being harassed. The Ottomans tried to get around the impasse with an array of contradictory imperial edicts that sustained the protests of the wounded Muslims and acknowledged that some acts had violated Muslim law outright. As a result, everything was left the way it was.[23] All these events took place in the mid-seventeenth century, that is, when the confrontation between Europe and the Ottomans had not yet entered its most acute phase, and when the sultans still nurtured plans for a general offensive in Europe and the capture of Vienna.

It may seem that Jerusalem was a special case, and that the Ottoman tolerance toward the Franciscans can be explained by the obligations of the Turks to a city considered holy by three different religions. While the Ottoman authorities were shutting their eyes to the religious processions of Christian monks in Jerusalem, other information reached Europe about the exigencies of the Turkish rule in the conquered lands: forcible conversions to Islam, the horrible practice of a child tribute imposed on Christians in the Ottoman domains, the destruction of churches or their transformation into mosques. This information was undoubtedly distorted and the Ottoman atrocities somewhat exaggerated. Although such exigencies did indeed occur in some regions in time of war, they were not a permanent practice of any Muslim state, including that of the Ottomans.

The problem of conversion is much more complicated than it sometimes appears to the uninformed observer. Arab rulers of the conquered empire initially were not preoccupied with a desire to convert all people to their faith, allowing the inhabitants of the countries they occupied to keep their religion. Considering Islam a privilege that distinguished the ruling Arabs from ordinary mankind, they regarded it as their duty to strengthen Islam among their kinsmen and paid most attention to their own religious education, rather than to the spread of Islam among the vanquished peoples. Large numbers of non-Muslims nevertheless embraced the faith of their conquerors. This gave rise to the problem of diminishing taxes, because the converts, having become Muslims, were generally exempt from paying a poll tax (*jizya*), which was considered a payment by non-Muslims to the Muslim community in return for protection. Responding to this problem, Arab rulers took different measures that had the same basic aim: to make new converts pay taxes. These measures seemed to the converts, whose motive of conversion, among others, was to evade heavier taxation, a trickery. It prepared the ground for various sorts of opposition.[24]

The situation changed during the invasion of the Turkish tribes of Asia Minor and their conquest of Anatolia. We have already noted the high religious zeal of the Turcoman *ghazis*, who often presented the peoples of invaded territories with a choice between conversion and death or enslavement. The most spectacular example of this was an attempt to convert to Islam Theodore Gabras, the virtual ruler of Trebizond, who in about 1098 was captured by the Turk Amir Ali. The captor tried to force the conversion of Gabras, who was first laid out on the snow, face down, and beaten on the back. Failing to convince him of the righteousness of their religion by this method, Gabras's captors then proceeded to dismember him alive, severing his tongue, plucking out his eyes, and then removing the scalp, limbs and other parts. His remains were burned, and the Amir Ali had a golden drinking cup fashioned from his skull.[25]

Notwithstanding this and similar stories of Christian martyrs that were included in Byzantine chronicles of the period, it would be an exaggeration to regard all conversions that took place during the turbulent period as forced. The very fact that the Turkish conquest of Asia Minor was a long process that lasted four centuries implies that Islamization was gradual. After the establishment of Anatolian Turkish principalities, other motives for conversion were uppermost in people's minds, rather than fear of being slaughtered or tortured. In addition to economic and social attractions—an opportunity to escape onerous taxes, the possibility of gaining an administrative position, or removal of the discriminatory restrictions imposed on Christians—other factors played a prominent role. One of the most important was the close relation of Islam and Christianity at the level of folk religion.

As already noted, Sufism spread among the Turkish tribes that could be considered newcomers to Islam by the time of their irruption in Anatolia. The main feature of Sufism is its stress on "inwardness over outwardness, contemplation over action, spiritual development over legalism, and cultivation of the soul over social interaction."[26] For the Sufis, externals were secondary. For many of them, even the difference between Islam and other monotheistic religions, such as Christianity, was not important. What mattered was the inner longing for the heart of God. This piety could accommodate all sorts of people's beliefs and hopes, even without their intimate acquaintance with Koranic prescriptions and rules. At the same time such piety could bridge the gap between Muslim and infidel.[27] Indeed, what is the difference between the heart of the faithful and the *kafir* (unbeliever) if both find their consolation in God?

Sufi orders had long been instrumental in the missionary expansion of Islam. Less concerned with the formalities of Muslim law, Sufi teachers more easily adapted to local customs and practices. On the other hand, local populations, lacking religious training and often estranged from the "established" churches with their close cooperation with oppressive lay authorities, found in Sufism a ready alternative for their aspirations. Many of the Sufis constantly moved from one place to another, disseminating the word of Allah. They represented a combination of holy man, miracle worker, medicine man, and teacher, and were often regarded as living saints. After their death their shrines often attracted devotees of any spiritual allegiance. Not surprisingly, this flexibility and adaptability to local conditions, combined with religious zeal and a desire to convert infidels, contributed significantly to the spread of Islam in the lands conquered by Muslims in Byzantine Anatolia or in the Balkans. When conversion became increasingly attractive to people who lived in the lands occupied by the Ottomans, inner resistance to such a change of allegiance was seriously weakened by the preaching of Sufi teachers. Christians whose faith was superficial and filled with superstition might adopt a similar but more secure folk version of Islam. What emerged was a curious blend of Islam and Christianity, with icons, baptism to prevent illness, and many other decidedly non-Muslim features.[28]

Although voluntary conversion was most common in the countries conquered by Muslims, forcible methods were sometimes applied. Occasionally there were large-scale persecutions of entire cities or regions, where non-Muslims faced the choice of conversion or exile. These persecutions were largely linked to external events, such as failures in the wars with Christian powers, European invasions of Muslim territories, or the need to support the demands of Muslim envoys in negotiations with the adversary. In many cases they were organized by official authorities, but popular Muslim feeling might supplement official persecution with rioting. Sometimes, however, street riots directed against non-Muslims had to be suppressed by the authorities. Sometimes, after the crisis ended, those who had been subjected to forced conversion were allowed to return to their former status.[29] Or those who had been forced to convert maintained a pretense of Muslim belief while secretly practicing Christian rites, sometimes for the rest of their lives. The descendants of such "Crypto-Christians" often found it impossible to resist the pressure of their surroundings, and their fidelity to the ancestral religion slowly eroded. Thus "Crypto-Christianity" constituted a transitory phase in the process of real conversion to Islam.[30]

Sometimes the Muslims demanded conversion of those people whom they regarded as useful and whom they wished to retain in their service. While in the Barbary states there was generally no requirement for conversion, local authorities did attempt to convert Christians who were skilled craftsmen—artillerymen, shipbuilders, experienced sailors—or whom they wished to undertake important missions to European countries.[31]

The most detested form of forcible conversion was of course the tribute of children (*devşirme*). It was instituted by the Ottomans, according to some evidence, as early as 1395.[32] At certain times traveling commissioners selected Christian boys from about eight to fifteen years of age for the sultan's service. After a period of general instruction in Turkish speech and customs, and physical training, the boys were sent into the army or the government. The reasons for this child tribute are unclear. Some assert that the system was adopted to fill the ranks of the Janissaries, the elite corps of Turkish troops. Others regard it as a means by which the sultan could replace nobles of Turkish origin who held administrative posts and who might challenge his power. Soon after the introduction of the child tribute, the replacement of freeborn Turks in the administration was completed. From then on, for two hundred years, most of the state's officials were of Balkan-Slav-Christian origin.

By some estimates the number of young Christian children "officially" removed from their homes by the tribute was approximately 200,000 during the roughly 200 years while it was practiced.[33] In this connection the question arises, What was the attitude toward the *devşirme* of the people of the Christian lands conquered by the Ottomans? Did they really abhor this institution as it was frequently presented in Europe, or did they profit from friends and relatives in high places in the Ottoman administration? Although some Christians may have benefited from well-placed relatives,[34] obviously for most people the child tribute constituted an abhorrent manifestation of Turkish rule. Not surprisingly, the Turks used its renunciation as a strong bargaining chip in the surrender terms they offered to citizens of some besieged cities.[35]

To sum up, in its policy toward Christendom the Muslim world demonstrated not only hatred and an insatiable appetite for conquest. Examples of peaceful interaction with non-Muslims, within the domains of Islam or outside it, show that the religious factor often gave way to other motives, momentary or permanent, which were devoid of spiritual connotation but dictated by demands of government, *realpolitik*, or mere opportunism. In this sense Islamic leaders sometimes displayed more flexibility, tolerance, and openness than their Christian counterparts.

THE CHRISTIAN ATTITUDE TOWARD MUSLIMS

At a time when Christian communities were widely scattered in the domains of Islam, when Christian pilgrims traveled to the Holy Land and European merchants established their colonies under the protection of Muslim rulers in Istanbul, Egypt, Morocco, and Tunis, Christendom developed a barely tolerable attitude toward the Muslims who lived in its territory. Torn by contradictory tendencies that characterize the Middle Ages as a childlike period in the history of civilization, with its combination of humility and violence,[36] Europeans paid scant attention to the canon law that recognized Jews and Muslims as *neighbors* in the evangelical sense. This law left to the adherents of Islam very limited rights, comparable to those of tributary Christians in Muslim countries. They might hold no position of public authority, must wear distinctive clothing, and could not employ Christians in Muslim households on any pretext. Papal decrees forbade the call to prayer and pilgrimages within the territory of Christian princes.[37] Yet even this restricted freedom was soon abolished in favor of a policy of forcible conversion or expulsion, as happened in Sicily and Spain.

In Sicily, where a Muslim community was established in 902 as a result of the Aghlabid conquests directed from North Africa, an initial policy of toleration after the reconquest of the island by Christians under Count Roger I de Hauteville (1031–1101) and his successor Roger II (1111–1154) soon came to an end when the latter, in the last years of his reign, launched a policy of religious persecution. Forcible conversion of the Muslim population, or its extermination in the course of various uprisings and riots, was accompanied by a steady immigration of Christians from the mainland. As a result, the ethnic and demographic map of Sicily was changed irreversibly at the expense of the Muslims. Frederick II, king of Sicily and Holy Roman Emperor, albeit well known for his sympathies for Islamic culture and his friendly relations with the sultan of Egypt (from whom he received the Holy City in 1229, which gave him the right to crown himself king of Jerusalem), continued the policy aimed at ending all vestiges of the Muslim presence in Sicily. By the mid-thirteenth century, Islam and the Islamic presence in Sicily had disappeared.[38]

In Spain, with the completion of the *Reconquista* in 1492, the previous policy of toleration, which had left Iberian Muslims or *mudéjares* in peace to ply their trades as carpenters, masons, gardeners, or tailors, was reverted. Muslim subjects now faced a choice of baptism, exile, or death. In 1502, after a rebellion in the region of Alpujarras, all the Spanish *mudéjares* chose to be converted en masse. Yet the Christians never trusted these Moriscos, as the converted Spanish Muslims were called from then on.

As Spain's power was threatened by rebellion in the Netherlands and defeats at the hands of the Ottomans in North Africa, the continued existence of a potentially disloyal minority in Spain became a more acute problem. Philip II decided to revive old decrees aimed at Moriscos. He ordered the use of Castilian in place of Arabic, the wearing of Castilian rather than Moorish clothing, and the cessation of other Morisco customs. The provocative character of these decrees led to another revolt of the Moriscos in Alpujarras in 1568. Unlike earlier uprisings, this rebellion demanded a resort to naval and military units from Italy to contain it. Philip II and his Spanish officials raised the issue of Moriscos as a fifth column that aided both the Ottoman advance in North Africa and the Protestant cause in Europe, thus making the suppression of the rebellion an issue of the larger struggle against the menace to Christendom.

In fact there is some evidence that Ottoman politics made the existence of the Morisco community a danger to Spain.[39] But other factors—internal economic difficulties, heightened religious feelings associated with the Counter-Reformation, the failure of the *mudéjares* to join the Christian world and resulting religious tensions between Old Christians and Moriscos—contributed to the Morisco problem. In 1570 the rebellion was contained. Thereafter Philip II directed the dispersal of the Moriscos throughout Spain. The final solution occurred in 1609 when the Moriscos were expelled from the country.

After this expulsion there remained not a single Muslim community in western Europe save for those territories conquered by the Turks. And this has continued to be so until relatively recent times. European hostility toward Muslims has sometimes strained common sense. When in Venice, which traded actively with the Levant, a proposal was put forward in the late sixteenth century to establish a hostelry for traveling Turkish merchants, it provoked long and bitter arguments before the city finally allowed Turkish merchants to settle at the Hostelry of the Angel, which served as the Fondaco dei Turchi. If Venice, which lived by its trade with Islam, was so reluctant to admit the Muslim presence, one can imagine how intolerant others were.[40]

The use of force against Islam was but one aspect of Christendom's struggle with a serious rival that threatened to undermine its position in the world. Although victory was seen as essential for the glory of the Christian church, force alone was considered insufficient for many reasons, not least because of the lack of resources for war on such a grand scale. Hence special importance was attached to the refutation of the rival religion, the demonstration of its false character that deluded the people and led them away from the path of God. It was necessary, in other words, to respond to Islam's charges that Christianity was an abrogated religion, superseded by God's final word as expressed in the Koran. Proofs to the contrary were to be the task of scholars, not warriors. But to realize this task successfully it was necessary for Christian learned men to familiarize themselves with the foundations of Islam and its basic tenets. Therefore medieval European scholars sought to learn more about Islamic doctrine in order to refute it effectively.

Principal attention was paid to the sacred book of the Muslims, the Koran. At the initiative of the Abbot of Cluny, Peter the Venerable, a team was formed which, with advice from Muslims and Jews, in July 1143 completed the first translation of the Koran into Latin. It bears the name of Robert of Ketton in Rutland.[41] This translation remained in use for four centuries. Other scholars studied various Muslim texts and busied themselves with a genealogy of Muhammad, his life and deeds, as well as with writing pamphlets criticizing and sometimes ridiculing the main tenets of the Muslim faith, such as its notions of revelation, paradise, *jihad*, and morality.

Christian scholars challenged the Islamic Revelation. They tried to show that the Koran was incongruous with the other revelations with which it associated itself. Its style was supposedly too human and too poorly written to be of God. Stressing Muhammad's illiteracy and his dependence on supposed collaborators, Christian polemic was designed to discredit the Prophet. It was presumed that if he could be shown not to be a prophet, the whole fabric of Islam would come undone. When Christian writers turned to the life of the Prophet, they revealed shocking facts; they demonstrated that Muhammad could not be a prophet because he was a robber, a murderer, a traitor, and an adulterer. They described scabrous episodes of the Prophet's life, based in Islamic scholarly treatment of his marriages and his relations with his wives, and concluded that no true prophet could conduct his personal life as Muhammad did his.[42]

Summarizing accounts of Muhammad's life, which varied from the accurate to the ridiculous, Christian scholars outlined three points that were thought to undermine Muhammad's claim to the Prophethood: the violence and force with which he imposed his religion; his salacious appeals to his followers; and his evident humanity, which, in the Christian view, was incompatible with his pretended closeness to God. On these grounds European writers made of Muhammad a great blasphemer whose religion justified sin and weakness.[43]

Learned men of Christendom also scrutinized the Muslim attitude toward women and the pleasures of life, the conception of the Islamic Paradise, and the role of violence and war. According to the renowned theologian St. Thomas Aquinas, sexuality and violence were characteristic of Islam.[44] Muslim ideas of Paradise only confirmed this. It opened its doors to those who had died in the struggle against the infidels with sword in hand, and it was filled with various delights for the flesh rather than for the spirit. This Paradise was in sharp contrast to the idea of a purely spiritual apprehension of God, the Beatific Vision of Christian tradition.

Based on their analysis of Muslim doctrines, the Christians came to regard Islam as the culmination of all the world's heresies. They found in it features in common with Nestorians, Manicheans, Arians, and many other deviations from the "true faith." And as in the case of these heresies, Christian theologians were prepared to fight Islam by exposing its falsity. But was the object of their polemic the Muslim faith, or did they fear that their Christian coreligionists might be attracted by the material wealth promised by Islam in this and the next world? According to the historian Norman Daniel, the highest probability is that "the public intended by the polemists was Christian. . . . Nearly all the arguments . . . were well calculated to be effective with such an audience, and only with such. They were admirably formulated to uphold faith."[45] Daniel notes that in practice Christian missionaries devoted their attention chiefly to Christians, Latin and oriental, living under Islamic rule, rather than to the Muslims themselves. If they addressed a Muslim audience, it was with the purpose of seeking martyrdom.

Nevertheless the idea of converting the Muslims appeared to be a constant preoccupation of Christian church authorities for most of the period of confrontation. This idea was stimulated mostly by the Crusades and the success of the *Reconquista* in Spain. It gained strength by the middle of the twelfth century with the translation of the Koran. Peter the Venerable had himself urged winning over the Saracens "not as our people [so] often do, by weapons, not by force but by reason, not by hate but by love."[46] Thus for Church authorities, conversion became a supplement to, or sometimes even a substitute for, efforts to

advance Christianity by military means. Pope Innocent III, in-
clining to a popular belief that the world might end around
1284, envisioned a final crusade in East and West to prepare the
mass conversion of both Jews and Muslims.[47]

The most propitious ground for conversion was Spain and
its principalities of North Africa. After the last Almohad fled
from Morocco to the Aragon's court with a group of relatives
and retainers, to become pensioners of the crown of Aragon at
Calatayud and Valencia, some of these relatives became Christians. Five years after the last Valencian revolt, the sultan of
Bougie, Ibn al-Wazir, offered to become a Christian as well as
the king's vassal. Abu Zayd, the ruler of Valencia and eastern
Spain, who descended from the great Almohad founder, had two
sons baptized at Murcia in 1241, with St. Ferdinand of Castile
and Prince Alfonso present as godfathers.[48] The famous school
of Arabic studies founded by San Ramon de Peñaforte, who regarded such schools as useful instruments to train specialists in
controversy, especially with Muslim academics, claimed ten
thousand conversions, primarily among the educated.[49]

Although Europeans succeeded in their missions to Spain
and to faraway countries, such as India and China (where John
of Montecorvino established his diocese at Peking), and to the
Mongols, efforts at conversion met little response in the core
lands of Islam. Conversions might really be expected only where
Christian arms were successful. Otherwise Muslims remained
unmoved by the preaching of monks from mendicant orders,
which constituted the mobile and main missionary force of
Christendom. That is why the mendicants often resorted to fa-
natic confrontation, venturing to breach and act openly at times
in order to precipitate a dramatic response. There are numerous
examples of attempts by Christian missionaries to break into
mosques or to abuse Muhammad and Islam openly in the streets
of Muslim cities. For some of them, like Friar Livin, who was
martyred in Cairo in 1345, provoking violence against themselves became a goal in itself.[50] Even St. Francis of Assisi followed this tactic that required a prior commitment to death,

while St. Thomas Aquinas, in response to a request to prepare a handbook for polemical efforts at conversion, wrote his famous *Summa contra gentiles*.[51]

With the rise of the Ottoman threat to Christian Europe in the fifteenth century, the policy of conversion was revived. But this time, due to the expanding intellectual horizons of Europeans, the peaceful conversion of the Turks occupied the attention of theologians and statesmen. The most dedicated and unswerving advocate of the new policy was the Spaniard Juan de Segovia. He treated the doctrine of Islam in the Renaissance spirit and insisted on approaching Muslims on the basis of beliefs that they and Christians held in common. In place of the crusade or the usual preaching mission, Segovia recommended reconciliation. In a situation of peace, a mutual understanding would develop between the adherents of the two religions while fanaticism and prejudice diminished.[52] Although such views by no means met with general understanding, and there remained many who favored crusades against the Muslims and who censured cooperation with the enemy, Segovia found support from such renowned theologians and thinkers as Nicholas of Cusa, who admitted in his work *De pace fidei* that even non-Christian religions worshiped, however imperfectly, the true God and possessed some knowledge of Him.[53]

As time passed, the dream of converting the Muslims became less and less a reality. It died with the radical change in relations between Christendom and Islam, when Europe, quickly developing new technologies and expanding into the New and Old Worlds, passed from a defensive policy toward its "hereditary enemy" to a counteroffensive that opened a new chapter in Christian-Islamic relations.

FIVE

Europe Ascendant

On Sunday, September 12, 1683, joint Habsburg and Polish forces under the command of the Polish king Jan Sobieski won perhaps the most decisive victory in Europe's long war against the advancing Ottoman Empire. They routed the army of Kara Mustafa, which for two months had besieged Vienna in its second attempt to subdue the capital of the Ottomans' staunchest enemy in Europe and thus inflict a most humiliating defeat upon the Habsburgs and the whole of Christendom. Mustafa had persuaded Sultan Mehmed IV of the need for war against the Habsburg monarchy rather than a consistent policy of opposition. He was able to prevail over that faction of the Ottoman court that had strong reservations about the planned campaign.[1]

In Europe, where the spirit of the Crusades had not yet died, the siege of Vienna was regarded as the continuation of the Ottoman Empire's ambitious plans to expand its sway over the Christian world. Thus several hundred noblemen from various countries had joined the imperial and Polish army as volunteers. Among them was the future king of England, George I, and the nineteen-year-old Eugene of Savoy, who was to become, in later years, one of the most famous leaders in the wars against the Ottomans.

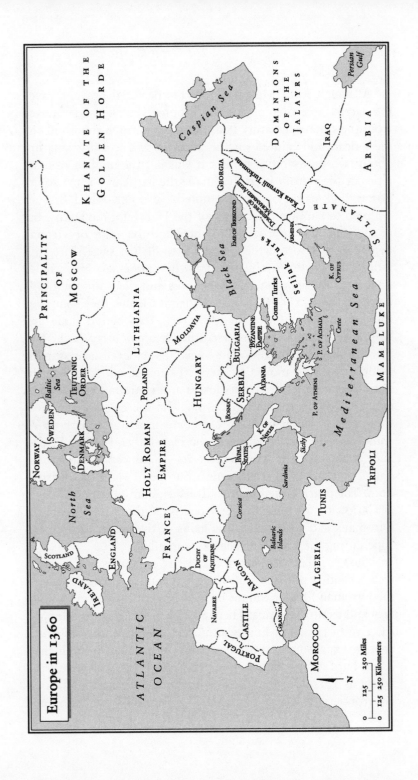

Europe in 1360

Although Kara Mustafa, with his personal bravery, saved the sacred green banner of the Prophet that he had received from the sultan, his army fled, leaving about ten thousand soldiers dead and injured on the battlefield. The Christians lost about two thousand men.[2] But it was not the number of casualties or the victory itself that made the battle at Vienna so important. In 1529, as already noted, Suleiman I had first attempted to capture the capital of the Habsburg monarchy, but at that time the approaching winter and the valor of Vienna's defenders had forced the Ottomans to lift the siege. After this failure the Porte's conquests in Europe nonetheless continued unabated. But in 1683 the Habsburgs and their allies not only defeated the army of the Grand Vizier at Vienna, they continued their offensive in Ottoman territories. They seized Buda and Belgrade, and in 1687 dispersed the Ottoman army in the battle at Mohacs in Hungary. The Venetians achieved success in the Peloponnese and moved to the Greek mainland. Although the Porte was able to recover its losses and confound expectations of its early expulsion from Europe, the successes of the Holy League—formed against the Ottomans in the aftermath of Vienna, with the participation of the Habsburgs, Poland, Venice, and, a bit later, the Muscovite tsars—significantly altered the balance of power in southeastern Europe in favor of Christendom. The peace signed by the adversaries on January 26, 1699, at Carlowitz, affirmed this new reality. Within fifteen years the Ottomans had surrendered the gains of their expansion in Europe during the preceding century and a half.

The Christian victories of the last two decades of the seventeenth century and the shift of fortunes in the struggle against the Ottoman Empire cannot be measured only in terms of military and territorial gains. They must be placed in a broader perspective of trends in European development, precursors of the coming expansion of Europe and its future world dominance. After hard times dating from the mid-fourteenth century—when, as a result of the "closing of Europe's internal and external frontiers,"[3] society had entered a period of stagnation and even decline; when the Black Death had arrived from central Asia and wiped out one-third of the population in a number of regions and brought progress in every field to a standstill; when Europe's capitalistic innovations had proved inadequate and its economy unable to survive the Hundred Years War and the advancing Ottomans on its borders—the sixteenth century marked the beginning of "an unstoppable process of economic development and technological innovation" which made Europe the world's commercial and military leader.[4]

Paul Kennedy sees the principal cause of Europe's rise as the absence of a "centralized authority, which insisted upon a uniformity of belief and practice, not only in official state religion but also in such areas as commercial activities and weapons development."[5] Instead, competing economic and military centers of power stimulated commerce and led to the rise of a market economy which linked all parts of the continent. In knowledge, a parallel upward spiral rooted in the Renaissance resulted in important innovations in industry, navigation, the exploration of mineral resources that helped initiate the Industrial Revolution, oceanic discoveries, and improved education. Economic changes were accompanied by the transformation of the social order: the disappearance of old classes and privileges and the development of new political and public institutions. New nation-states replaced outdated kingdoms, duchies, and counties with their dependence on the wills and whims of local rulers more concerned with retaining their power and riches than with the welfare of their subjects.

The effect of these transformations was felt especially in the military sector, where new techniques of warfare gave rise to the "gunpowder empires"[6] that were soon to compete with one another for world supremacy. In this struggle Europe occupied a leading position, with its sense of innovation, enterprise, and spontaneity, resulting in a more effective use of resources. In Europe one found the impetus for constant improvements in the size, shape, and design of new arms. The "gunpowder revolution" influenced not only land armies but warfare at sea. The steady improvement of ships' armaments led to the building of the full-rigged ship, which "married technology of both the northern seas and the Mediterranean in one vessel."[7] Known as carracks, these ships armed with modern weapons guaranteed European control of oceanic trade routes and intimidated those societies that were vulnerable to seapower. At the same time improvements in compasses and charts made possible transoceanic voyages, which further expanded European horizons. By 1431 the Portuguese had reached the Azores and pushed considerably south of the Congo along the west African coast. In 1492 Christopher Columbus, attempting to explore routes to India, discovered the New World. Six years later Vasco da Gama was able to sail round the south coast of Africa, thus launching the Portuguese into the trade of all the southern seas.

The benefits of these first European discoveries helped to accelerate an already existing dynamic. Gold, silver, precious metals, and spices added to European prosperity and stimulated the development of a market economy. But sugar, indigo, tobacco, rice, furs, timber, and exotic plants like potatoes and maize also enhanced the wealth of the continent and its place in the world. All this overseas trade, in turn, served as a powerful incentive for the European shipbuilding industry, which stimulated many crafts directly or indirectly related to it. As a consequence, in the sixteenth and seventeenth centuries Europe laid the basis for further worldwide expansion and the domination of overseas areas. By the eighteenth century this expansion had moved beyond the Western hemisphere—where all previously unknown lands had been divided among Spain, Portugal, England, and the Netherlands—to the mostly maritime zones of the southern seas, where the Portuguese established their fortified trading posts at Hormuz (at the mouth of the Persian Gulf), Goa (on the west coast of the Deccan in India), and Malacca (at the straits leading into the South China Sea), as well as at Macao in China. Having struck root in the New World, Europe, in a permanent search for new markets for its industrial goods and new sources of raw materials, turned toward the territories long known as the Orient, where the Ottoman Empire loomed as a bulwark against outside penetration and as a watchman controlling the sea and land routes that linked them with the rest of the world. When Christian Europe had been a relatively backward civilization, struggling for its very survival under the pressure of the expanding Muslim world, setting foot on Ottoman lands seemed out of the question. Not only were the Europeans weak and without means of transportation, they had nothing to offer in exchange for oriental wonders. With the age of discoveries and modernization, everything changed. Not only did European merchants have vessels strong enough to reach South and Southeast Asia, escaping the Ottomans, they were also able to challenge Muslim supremacy in trade with those territories, offering cheaper commodities of better quality. Besides, the Ottoman Empire itself became less impenetrable as it entered a period of gradual decline, manifested in the defeat at Vienna and the ensuing war with the Holy League.

For centuries the Muslim world had displayed its superiority in political, military, and intellectual activities. With a religion considered to be God's final revelation, proud of their conquests and achievements, the Muslims could afford to be insulated. They despised other peoples who had not yet become adherents of the true religion but who eventually were destined to be included in the House of Islam, whether by force or voluntarily. Yet Islam's "iron curtain" isolated Muslims from the outside world and proved to be fateful. When history took a new turn, Islamic civilization's response to new challenges was insufficient and ineffective.

A civilization is not a physical organism that passes through stages of birth, growth, aging, and death. This comparison, albeit attractive, obscures many factors that play a role in the historical process. The decay of Islam was not unavoidable, nor can it be attributed to inherent defects of religious obscurantism or political weakness. It is reasonable to conclude that if the processes of modernization had not occurred in Europe when they did, they could have occurred at another time in the realm of Islam.[8] But events in Christian Europe exerted a strong influence on Islam, compounding its internal weaknesses and in many ways accentuating them. In other words, the period of relative decay that the Muslim world entered in the seventeenth and the early eighteenth centuries, and that might have been temporary or even transitory on the way to a new expansion, was significantly transformed by a rapidly developing and expanding Europe.

How Islamic civilization responded to these external forces depended largely on the mind-set, traditions, experience, and patterns of behavior that prevailed among its peoples. Viewing the world beyond Islam as inferior and not worthy of consideration; demeaning everything about infidel countries, whether language, history, or education; avoiding contacts with "unbelievers" except through intermediaries—Christians, Jews, *zimmi* subjects of Muslim rulers, or renegades[9]—the Muslims deprived themselves not only of the knowledge and experience of other peoples but, more important, of an understanding of developments in other lands. When it was crucial for a society "to take up the new patterns more or less *pari passu* with their development in the most advanced Occidental countries,"[10] Islam's general attitude toward the outside world retarded the process and led to further backwardness.

THE OTTOMAN EMPIRE IN A TIME OF CHANGE

The example of the Ottoman Empire well illustrates Islam's predicament. The Ottomans occupied a unique position in the Muslim world, located in the very heartland of Islam and in control of those territories that were the birthplace of Islamic civilization or experienced its earliest influence. In this sense, as Bernard Lewis has pointed out, the empire of the Ottomans "was not a single country but a whole world."[11] And for more than four centuries the Ottoman Empire had been Europe's principal adversary in the confrontation between Christianity and Islam. It was still a threat at the close of the seventeenth century, despite failures of the period after 1683. But by then Ottoman power had already showed clear signs of weakness and internal disorder. Principal among the causes of this decline were those related to the empire's purpose as the *ghazi* state that stood on the front lines of the struggle of Islam against the world of infidels.

The need to wage constant war against other powers led to a strategic overextension of Ottoman forces. The empire was forced to deploy large armies in central Europe, to build an expensive navy operating in the Mediterranean, and to send troops to North Africa, the Aegean, Cyprus, and the Red Sea, to say nothing of spasmodic wars in the East and with Safavi Persia, and support and encouragement for its client state in the Crimea. Yet this military strain was not solely responsible for the Ottoman decline. The principal problem was rather the excessive centralization of the system as a whole, its despotic and orthodox character. In the words of Paul Kennedy, an "idiot sultan could paralyze the Ottoman Empire in the way that a pope or Holy Roman emperor could never do for all Europe."[12] The consequence of the system's complete dependence on the ruler was its inevitable decay and decomposition as soon as the sultans became unwilling or unable to direct it.

Hence after 1566 the reign of thirteen incompetent sultans in succession created a power vacuum at the top and led to nepotism, inefficiency, dishonesty, and anarchy in all parts of the empire. As time passed these tendencies became even more persistent. With the weakening of central control and the advent of misrule in various provinces of the empire, separatist movements developed that were used by autonomous figures (generally called *ayans*) for the consolidation of their own power. These individuals, relying on their wealth and their religious and social prestige, came to be looked upon as arbiters and leaders by the local population, which suffered from the arbitrary rule of Ottoman officials and their inability to guarantee law and order. In fact, representatives of the central power themselves increasingly came to *ayans* to secure local compliance with their orders and desires. Gradually the positions of the *ayans* became hereditary and almost completely independent of the central government.[13]

Another symptom of the weakening central power, increasingly visible by the eighteenth century, was the appearance of bandit armies composed of peasants and townsfolk driven from their homes by oppression and insecurity, soldiers fleeing from the tyranny and incompetence of their officers, and tribesmen and mountain dwellers who were always somewhat independent of the Ottomans because of their inaccessible dwelling places or the thin control extended over newly conquered lands. These bandit armies devastated the provinces of the empire, from the mountains of Bosnia to the valleys of the Tigris and the Nile, terrorized the population, and generally added to disorder and internal upheaval. They came to control entire districts and even provinces, and their chiefs (*derebeys*, or lords of the valley) almost entirely ignored central authority.[14]

The Porte could maintain friendly ties with the *ayans* and *derebeys* only in order to retain the tribute and military assistance they provided. The sultan elevated them to official rank, often as governor of the district they dominated. But imperial control was extremely precarious and in most cases ephemeral.

Ottoman political instability was matched in the economic sphere as Western trade supplanted the commerce of traditional relations. The general transformation of the European economy made its goods increasingly competitive with those produced in Ottoman lands. The great inflation of the sixteenth and seventeenth centuries caused by the inflow of American gold and silver also disrupted the empire's economy; the purchasing power of these precious metals was greater in Islam than in the West. Grain and textiles had been the two most important Ottoman exports to Europe, the latter at one time having consisted largely of manufactured goods. This trade was gradually reduced, and only cotton cloth remained a while longer as an important export from the Middle East to Europe. Now the situation was reversed: Europe sent manufactured textiles, including Indian cloth, to the Middle East and imported raw materials such as cotton, mohair, and especially silk. The Ottomans thus experienced a chronic lack of precious metals, insufficient even to meet the needs of coinage.[15]

The situation in agriculture, as in industry, was characterized by technological and economic stagnation. The European industrial and agricultural revolutions found no parallel in the Ottoman economy; instead the Ottomans showed little progress in agriculture, industry, and transport. This backwardness directly affected Ottoman military effectiveness and consequently its power and resources in relation to those of its rivals. The Porte depended more and more heavily on new military technology developed in Europe. But even some isolated efforts to find remedies for the army's ills met with opposition from the older corps, such as the Janissaries.

Previously the most efficient unit in the Ottoman army had been formed using children of tribute, wholeheartedly devoted to the sultan. In the eighteenth century the Janissary corps became a loose, badly disciplined, and unruly band that resisted attempts at reform. In 1790 it was estimated that of the twelve thousand names on the Janissary rolls, only two thousand could or would serve when needed. Others were women, children, artisans, and merchants, untrained in the military arts and retaining their membership only for their pay.[16] After the disappearance of the child-tribute recruiting system sometime in the sixteenth century, the Porte reinforced the corps with men sent by provincial notables and vassals, and with rabble dragged from the streets of major cities. The result was a body of untrained and undisciplined soldiers, more prone to plundering and looting than to withstanding the well-armed and well-trained troops of the enemy. The general shortage of officers trained in the military arts, most of whom held their positions only for the salaries they earned, completes the picture of an army in which disorder, desertion, and revolt were normal conditions. As the historian Marshall Hodgson has observed, the army tended "to take on a civilian character, probably inherent in the bureaucratic structure of absolutism. In the course of the seventeenth century and above all in the early eighteenth century (when the process culminated), this gradually resulted in a serious weakening of the central armed forces. The weakening of the armed forces, in turn, undermined the absolutism itself, which had depended on its monolithic army for its strength and for its prestige."[17]

Not surprisingly, in the course of the eighteenth century the Ottoman army suffered increasingly painful defeats at the hands of its Austrian and Russian enemies, who could scarcely be considered industrially and technologically advanced. After the peace of Carlowitz in 1699, the Porte retained most of its possessions in Europe, leaving to the Habsburgs only Hungary (without the Banat of Temesvár), Transylvania, and part of Slavonia, and successfully resisting Russian claims for territories north of the Black Sea (Kerch and small fortresses on the Dnepr River).[18] In the hundred years that followed, the Ottomans lost to Russia considerable territories on the northern shores of the Black Sea and in the Caucasus (including Kerch, Azov, Kinburn, and Kabarda), the Crimean khanate (annexed to the Russian Empire in August 1783), some fortresses in the area of the Bug and the Dniester (according to the peace treaties of Küçük Kaynarca and of Jassy), and later all of Bessarabia. Russia thus gained access to the Black Sea, which had hitherto been entirely under Turkish Muslim control. The Ottoman positions in Moldavia and Walachia, though these two principalities remained under the suzerainty of the sultan, also became more precarious. To Austria, during these hundred years, the Porte had to cede only the Banat of Temesvár, but its losses could have been greater. The new Austrian emperor Leopold II, after the death of his brother and predecessor Joseph II, had no desire to pursue an active policy against the Ottoman Empire; and Prussia and Britain feared the strengthening of Russia and Austria at the expense of the Porte, and so intrigued against them.[19] But more important than these territorial losses was the transformation of the Ottoman Empire: no longer a threat to Europe, it became a pawn in the great-power games of the continent.

EUROPEAN PENETRATION AND DOMINANCE

By about 1800 European world hegemony was firmly established. In the course of the nineteenth century a number of the countries which were to be called great powers steadily expanded their possessions on all the continents, including Africa, Australia, and Asia. They converted their small enclaves in the tropics into extensive domains. While in 1800 Europeans occupied or controlled 35 percent of the land surface of the world, by 1878 this figure had risen to 67 percent, and by 1914 to more than 84 percent.[20] Even more important than these territorial acquisitions was the preponderance of the European powers in technology, productivity, commerce, and intellectual activity. As Marshall Hodgson has said, it was "not merely, or perhaps even primarily, that the Europeans and their overseas settlers found themselves in a position to defeat militarily any powers they came in contact with. Their merchants were able to out-produce, out-travel, and out-sell anyone, their physicians were able to heal better than others, their scientists were able to put all others to shame."[21] The European powers did not need troops to establish their supremacy, save in a few cases. More important was the inclusion of their overseas territories into a worldwide economic and political system. On the one hand, this made indigenous nations dependent on the proper functioning of the world market, according to the rules of the game as determined in Europe; on the other hand, it guaranteed the interests of merchants, missionaries, and even tourists from Europe, who even in African jungles were protected by an international law invented and adapted to the needs of European hegemony.

The Muslim world was most seriously affected by this hegemony, whether from the viewpoint of its territorial losses and political subjugation or the "impact of Western man." The nineteenth century was a time of constant European advance into Islamic possessions. The first attack was directed against principalities on the Barbary Coast, the main source of piracy that posed a continuing threat to European trade routes that ran through the Mediterranean. The landing of French troops in

Algiers in July 1830 began the occupation of the Barbary state by France. French protectorates were established over Tunisia and Morocco in 1881 and 1912 respectively, while Tripolitania became a colony of Italy and in 1934 was united with another province, Cyrenaica, under the name of Libya. The piracy that had terrorized Europe for more than three hundred years came to an end.[22] In 1882 the British occupied Egypt and established their protectorate over the country. Using it as a springboard for penetration deeper into the African continent, British armies conquered the Sudan in 1899. By the end of the century Great Britain, along with France, Germany, Italy, and Portugal, also acquired territories in the Indian Ocean coastal areas of Africa.

On the opposite fringes of Islamic civilization, another European power, Russia, quickly expanded its possessions at the expense of Muslim states. By 1828 the Russian tsars had established their rule over most of the territory that now forms three Trans-Caucasian states—Georgia, Armenia, and Azerbaijan—which had previously belonged to the Ottoman or Persian empires or had been contested by them. By mid-century the Russians were generally able to crush popular resistance in the Caucasus, in the long war against Adyges, Kabarda, Chechens, Ingush, and Dagestanis. They now turned to Turkestan, inhabited by nomad tribes and a sedentary population, a region of fertile oases controlled by the emirate of Bukhara and the khanates of Kokand in the Fergana Valley and of Khiva in Khorezm to the south of the Aral Sea. The Russian conquest of the area began in 1855 when a column under the command of General Mikhail Chernyaev moved into Turkestan, seizing Tashkent in May 1865 and Samarkand in May 1868. After the defeat of his forces at the battle of Zerabulak, the emir of Bukhara was obliged to sign a treaty by which his state was placed under Russian protection. Khiva's turn came in 1873, and Kokand was invaded in 1875 and the khanate—Russia's most dangerous enemy in Central Asia—abolished. The conquest was rounded off between 1873 and 1881 by the occupation of the Turkmen country. On the territory of Central Asia was constituted the Turkestan "governorate-general" along with two protectorates.[23]

The only opposition to this Russian drive to the east came from Britain, which frowned at the prospect of a consolidation of the tsars' influence in this region and a potential threat to British India. Throughout the nineteenth century the Russian and English frontiers in Central Asia slowly but steadily grew nearer. In 1895 the Pamir boundary commission agreed to award Pamir to Russia and a northwestern extension of Kashmir to England, with a strip between them left to Afghanistan. Then, after a long negotiation between the two countries, an Anglo-Russian convention was signed in August 1907 dividing Persia into spheres of influence while the tsar recognized British interests in Afghanistan and refused to interfere in the latter's affairs except through London.[24] When in 1911 Russia introduced its troops into the northern provinces of Iran, London in turn consolidated its presence in the south, so that Iran was effectively divided between the two powers until the end of World War I.[25]

THE OTTOMANS ENCOUNTER EUROPEAN EXPANSION

The position of the Ottoman Empire was now rather precarious. Its process of decay only intensified in the course of the nineteenth century, when Istanbul was unable to organize sufficient resistance to the annexationist appetites of the European countries. They acquired parts of the Ottoman possessions in North Africa, Arabia, and the Caucasus, though by this time they had long been under only the nominal power of the sultan. At the same time the Ottoman government failed to halt the internal disintegration of the empire furthered by national liberation movements in the Balkans and the growing independence of local notables.

By the nineteenth century, to the power of *ayans* and *derebeys* was added the rise of a national consciousness among Ottoman subjects in the countries of the Balkan peninsula. This consciousness was aided by the very character of Ottoman rule, which never aimed to suppress or even mitigate the ethnic, cultural, and religious differences of the conquered population. Before the nineteenth century the empire made no effort to provide a legal, political, or cultural basis for a common Ottoman citizenship embracing the diverse elements of the state. The *millet* system and the flexible forms of incorporating European lands into the empire, albeit initially fruitful, eventually led to national and local particularism, which was only reinforced with the passage of time. As Charles and Barbara Jelavich write, "In some localities Muslim, Serbian, Bulgarian, and Greek villages existed side by side for centuries with no cultural or personal intermixing. In the towns different peoples lived in their own quarters. When in the nineteenth century the Ottoman government tried to introduce the principles of the modern European state system, the attempt foundered because the empire had been organized on quite a different basis during the previous four centuries."[26]

With nation-states rising in Western Europe and ideas of the Enlightenment penetrating the educated masses of those European countries under Ottoman rule, with a market economy influencing local populations, and the impact of the French Revolution reaching even the faraway corners of the Balkan peninsula, Ottoman possessions in Europe entered a period of "concentrated national revolution."[27] The European great powers saw an opportunity to benefit from the liberation struggles of the "oppressed" Christian subjects of the Turks.

The first country to win independence was Greece. As a result of an agreement signed in London in February 1830, an independent kingdom was established in that country under the guarantee of France, Britain, and Russia. This independence was limited—only about 800,000 Greeks became free while three-quarters of the Greek people remained under Ottoman rule;[28] but this "victory" was followed by others. Between 1804 and 1878 three other independent states, Serbia, Montenegro, and Romania, were established. An autonomous Bulgaria came into being. Later threatened by territorial claims of other national groups, Albania proclaimed its independence in November 1912.[29] Thus within a century the Porte had lost all its Balkan provinces. The Treaty of Bucharest, concluded on August 10, 1913, after the Balkan wars of 1912 and 1913, marked the

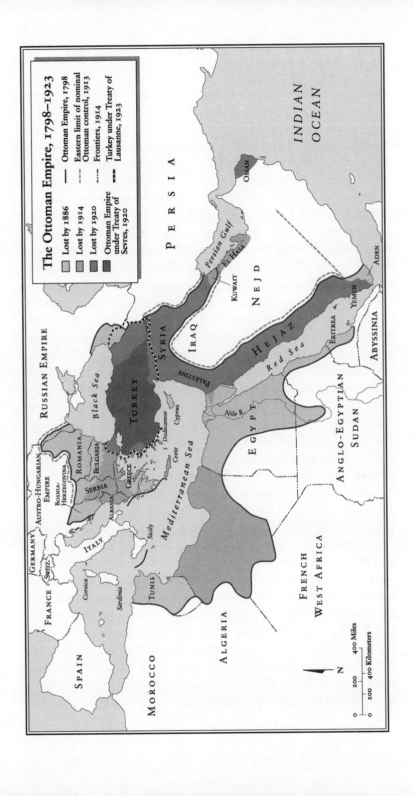

The Ottoman Empire, 1798–1923

	Lost by 1886	——	Ottoman Empire, 1798
	Lost by 1914	– – –	Eastern limit of nominal Ottoman control, 1913
	Lost by 1920	–·–·–	Frontiers, 1914
	Ottoman Empire under Treaty of Sèvres, 1920	▪▪▪▪▪	Turkey under Treaty of Lausanne, 1923

INDIAN OCEAN

PERSIA

OMAN

Persian Gulf

NEJD

KUWAIT

ADEN

RUSSIAN EMPIRE

IRAQ

EL HASA

SYRIA

Black Sea

HEJAZ

YEMEN

TURKEY

PALESTINE

Red Sea

ERITREA

ABYSSINIA

Dodecanese

Cyprus

Nile R.

EGYPT

ANGLO-EGYPTIAN SUDAN

Crete

ROMANIA

BULGARIA

GREECE

Mediterranean Sea

SERBIA

ALBANIA

AUSTRO-HUNGARIAN EMPIRE

BOSNIA-HERZEGOVINA

GERMANY

SWITZ.

ITALY

Sicily

Sardinia

Corsica

TUNIS

FRANCE

SPAIN

MOROCCO

ALGERIA

FRENCH WEST AFRICA

N

400 Miles

400 Kilometers

0   200

0   200

expulsion of the Ottoman Empire from Europe with the exception of the city of Constantinople and a small section of Thrace.

While in Europe the Ottoman possessions were threatened by Balkan national movements supported by European powers, in the Arab lands of the empire the challenge came essentially from coreligionists. The spread of a rigorous fundamentalist movement under the leadership of Muhammad ibn Abd al-Wahhab (1703–1792), allied with one of the local chieftains, Muhammad ibn Saud of Dariyah, undermined Ottoman rule in the heartland of the Muslim world and challenged the authority and prestige of the sultan. This alliance of fundamentalists called for a return to the original religion of the Prophet, and for moral and spiritual regeneration and the abandonment of idolatrous practices. It supported the extension of the holy war to include all Muslims, and it produced a militant Islamic state that expanded rapidly on the Arabian peninsula. In 1803 the Saudi-Wahhabi forces raided the Shii holy cities in southern Iraq and captured Mecca. Although defeated in 1818 and suppressed, the first Saudi state laid the foundations for the twentieth-century emergence of a successor fundamentalist state that would enjoy the support and encouragement of the British.[30]

A strong separatist movement in the nineteenth century also developed in Egypt. Its leader, Mohammed Ali (1769–1848), born in Macedonia of a Turkish-Albanian family, traveled to Egypt in 1798 at the head of an Albanian force to fight Napoleon. Although his troops were defeated, Ali remained in Egypt and later rose in the military and administrative service. In 1806 he was named governor of Egypt. The next year he was able to resist a British attempt to intervene, and by 1811 he had broken the power of the Mamluk troops and slaughtered their chiefs. Ali's troops were commissioned by Istanbul to suppress the Wahhabis in the Hijaz, where he established Egyptian rule under Ottoman suzerainty. In 1825 the Porte again relied on the help of the ambitious ruler to suppress a rebellion that had broken out in Greece, promising Ali in return the island of Crete for himself and the governorship for his son Ibrahim. But the Ottoman government's failure to fulfill these promises led to Ali's attack on Syria in 1832, which caused a major European crisis. Like other local notables, Mohammed Ali typified the effort to break up the Ottoman Empire through the formation of separate states under Muslim military leaders.[31]

Under these conditions of internecine struggle, the Ottoman Empire became an easy prey for European powers. They completed the expulsion of the Turks from Europe and recovered Christian lands that had fallen to the infidels several centuries earlier. But the Crusades were long ended. New considerations were already uppermost in the minds of European leaders, for whom the Ottoman menace had given way to the vicissitudes of the "Eastern Question."

THE "EASTERN QUESTION"

Just as disunity among the Christian powers had smoothed the advance of the Turks on the continent, rivalries among England, France, Germany, and the Austrian and Russian empires became a new "ally" of the Ottomans in decline. Although Turkey was not regarded as a serious religious adversary (growing European secularism had deprived the Turkish threat of its former religious overtones) and gradually ceased to be even a serious military threat, it remained an important element in the European balance of power. But now this was due to its weakness rather than its strength.[32] European powers, now competing for supremacy on the continent, sought to prevent the use of Ottoman territories by their rivals as "weights" in the equilibrium of forces. The historian Ivan Parvev has observed, "Any moment after 1699, when two states engage in a direct (or theoretical) territorial dispute over the Ottoman succession, fearing that the other may become [stronger], could mark the birth of the Eastern Question."[33] The Ottoman Empire had thus been drawn into the Concert of Europe, at first merely as an instrument that every musician tried to play according to his own score. Only later, first at the convention of the Black Sea Straits in 1841 and especially after the Crimean War of 1853–1856, was the empire accepted as a member of the community of nations.[34]

The greatest antagonists in the struggle for the heritage of the "sick man of Europe" (an expression of Tsar Nicholas I's) proved to be Russia and Britain. To each the Ottoman lands occupying strategically important positions between East and West represented an attractive object, if not for conquest at least for furthering their influence.

For Britain, the Porte's territories were the key to the imperial system that included India as the most valuable possession of the British crown. What is more, by the 1850s the Ottoman Empire formed the third largest market for British manufactures.[35] Not surprisingly, London dreaded the thought that Russia might endanger the British position by subordinating Ottoman lands, either through direct conquest, domination of the government in Constantinople, or the establishment of satellite Balkan states. Britain therefore usually preferred to keep the Ottoman Empire intact, preventing other states, especially Russia, from taking advantage of the Porte's weakness.[36]

Russia's policy toward the Ottomans was more complicated. Undoubtedly the tsars were not averse to enhancing their country's prestige and territory at the expense of the Turks. But their primary concerns were defensive in nature. Throughout the nineteenth century the Black Sea area was Russia's most vulnerable region. Its acquisitions in Tauria and Crimea, as well as in the Caucasus, could not be considered secure as long as any rival power in Europe, or the Ottomans themselves, might send their naval forces into the Black Sea and threaten Russian positions on its shores. Too, there existed serious obstacles to the development of Russian trade in the Mediterranean because of Istanbul's restrictions on free navigation in the Black Sea. Thus in negotiations with the Porte, in addition to territorial and security issues, Russian envoys consistently called for freedom of commerce.[37] Of special importance for Russia was control of the Bosporus, which would guarantee not only the security but the commercial interests of the Russian Empire.

Like Britain, Russia in the nineteenth century was initially interested in preserving the territorial integrity of the Ottoman Empire, fearing its dissolution might impair the European balance of power.[38] Russian statesmen recognized that no single government would decide the fate of the region; they understood full well that any attempt by Russia to increase its influence there would meet strong reaction from other European powers, especially Austria and Britain, and that the benefits of having a weak neighbor in a vulnerable region far outweighed the advantages of acquiring new lands and client states there. A memorandum to this effect had been prepared by the Russian foreign minister Count Nesselrode in the immediate aftermath of the Russo-Turkish War of 1828–1829, and received the full approval of Nicholas I. It suggested that the preservation of the Ottoman Empire was more advantageous than harmful to Russian interests, that it would be vain to think that Russia would benefit in the event of Turkey's disintegration. "Russia needs not new acquisitions," the memorandum stated, "nor the expansion of its territories, but their security and the spreading of its influence among the neighboring peoples. This could be best obtained by prolonging the existence of the Ottoman Empire on certain conditions."[39] Furthermore, according to Nesselrode, the expulsion of the Turks into Asia Minor, with its homogenous Muslim population, might well lead to the renewal of their state—which would be dangerous for Russian interests in the Caucasus and in the Trans-Caucasian region.[40]

While declaring its defense of the territorial integrity of the Ottoman Empire, Russia did not wish to abandon its efforts to enhance its influence among the neighboring countries of the Balkan peninsula. The government objective was to sponsor the establishment of autonomous and independent national regimes in the region, then either cooperate with them or attempt to dominate them. This aspect of tsarist policy was justified by Russia's claim to be the sole protector of those Orthodox Christians who lived under Ottoman rule. It was a claim based on the myth of Moscow as the Third Rome, that is, successor to the

Byzantine Empire as the bastion of the Orthodox church, after Constantinople, the Second Rome, in 1453 had fallen to the infidels, the Ottoman Turks. The idea had been born at the time when the fledgling Russian state had freed itself of the "Tatar yoke" and entered the international arena as a powerful factor in European life.[41] It was quite a popular notion among the Russian people, and in the nineteenth and early twentieth centuries it became a weapon in the movement of the Russian intelligentsia known as Slavophilism during the reign of Nicholas I, Panslavism during that of Alexander II, and, finally, Neoslavism before 1914. Because of the influence of the myth among the educated classes of Russian society, it played a role in the tsars' foreign policy. But it must not be exaggerated because, however important, religion was not the sole factor in determining the course of Russia's Balkan policy.

The names of these Russian popular movements might indicate another powerful component: nationalism, which emphasized the Slavic heritage of the Russian people and their links to other Slavic peoples in the Balkans—Serbs, Bulgars, and Montenegrins. Successive tsars combined these popular sentiments with geopolitical considerations and their concerns for the empire's security and prestige in their policy toward the region. The personalities of Russian rulers—their perception of honor and duty—sometimes also played a decisive role in the formulation of policy on the Eastern Question.[42] This was certainly the case with Nicholas I, whose sense of his prestige aggravated his relations with other European leaders and precipitated the Crimean War. Thus Russian claims to spiritual and cultural interests carried strong political connotations, and tsarist policy toward the Eastern Question was, in general, contradictory and confused.

The confusion only increased after Nicholas I, impressed by the growing disintegration of the Ottoman Empire under the impact of national liberation movements in the Balkans and separatist tendencies elsewhere, concluded that it might be impossible to maintain the unity of the Ottoman lands. His proposals for the division of the Ottoman possessions were met with suspicion and apprehension in London and Vienna, Russia's principal rivals in its policy toward the Porte. And his tough stance on the issue of protection of the Orthodox church in Jerusalem (which was determined by his understanding of Russian obligations and privileges under previous treaties with Istanbul) transformed the Eastern Question into one of Russia's relations with the rest of Europe.[43] The consequence was a coalition of Britain and France, formed with the Ottoman Empire, which took arms against Russia in the conflict known as the Crimean War.

For the second time in modern history, Christian powers entered into an alliance with a Muslim state against another Christian power in order to impose their will on it. There is no better example of a repudiation of the principles of holy war in favor of geopolitical considerations. Nor can the proponents of the "clash of civilizations" find in the Crimean War a validation of their theory (which places Russia in a civilization different from that of western Europe), for the first European alliance with the Ottomans had been formed in 1798 against revolutionary France.

The European powers followed the strategy of preserving the Ottoman Empire as a bulwark against Russian expansionism until the early twentieth century. By the eve of World War I, however, the balance of forces in Europe had gradually shifted, and rapidly growing German imperialism now presented an immediate threat to European concert. Turkey's alignment with Kaiser Wilhelm II during the "Great War" sealed the Ottomans' fate.[44] Since Russia was allied with Britain and France, the need for the "Ottoman factor" evaporated. The three powers concluded the Sykes-Picot agreement in 1916 to partition the Ottoman territories according to their own interests. Later, after the Bolshevik Revolution of 1917, Russia abandoned the agreement and even concluded a military arrangement with the Turkish leader, Mustafa Kemal, as soon as the war ended; but French and British troops occupied the Turkish capital while the territories of the empire were being divided among the French,

British, Greeks, Armenians, Kurds, Italians, and revolting Arabs. Only because of Kemal's valiant resistance to the aggression of the European powers, primarily Greece, which occupied even ethnically Turkish territories in Anatolia, was Turkey able to recover some of the lands it lost after the Treaty of Sèvres (1920). According to another treaty, of Lausanne, signed in July 1923, the Turks retained possession of all of Anatolia, eastern Thrace, the Bosporus, and the islands of Tenedos and Imbros. Nevertheless the Ottoman Empire ceased to exist. On November 1, 1922, the Turkish assembly declared the abolition of the sultanate. On October 29, 1923, the Turkish republic was proclaimed with Mustafa Kemal, known in history as Atatürk (the Father of Turks), as its president. With these events the Ottoman epoch came to the end while European expansion in the Muslim world reached its apogee.

THE EUROPEAN IMPACT ON ISLAMIC CIVILIZATION

By the 1920s most of Islam's territories found themselves under various forms of European control. This subordination was not always direct, as in the formal annexation of territories and the imposition of colonial rule. Rather, in most cases it assumed more subtle forms—economic, military, and cultural. Egypt, for example, though occupied by British troops in 1882, remained nominally under the rule of the Khediv. But in reality Great Britain established a protectorate over the country, and the British consul general in Cairo was empowered to intervene whenever he saw fit. Algiers became a colony of France with all the characteristics of this position, while in 1912 Morocco became a French protectorate. Notwithstanding these forms of dependence, the more important changes came with the political, economic, and cultural structures that the European powers brought with their rule. As Paul Kennedy has noted, the impact of European man "manifested itself not only in variety of economic relationships—ranging from the 'informal influence' of coastal traders, shippers, and consuls to the more direct controls of planters, railway builders, and mining companies—but also in the penetrations of explorers, adventurers, and missionaries, in the introduction of western diseases, and in the proselytization of western faiths."[45]

European domination led to a deep transformation of Muslim societies under the influence of new methods of economic practice, management, and administration. Reforms in law, police, and the courts; the abolition of old taxes; the introduction of machines and the building of contemporary infrastructure in industry and agriculture—all these innovations were beneficial. But many others had a negative aspect. For instance, in Egypt the elimination of customary law was in some cases calamitous for the poor who must have primarily profited from this, and the new courts made little sense to them and were often regarded as a new form of injustice.[46] In Algeria, French colonial authorities attempted to introduce European-style education that was free, secular, and obligatory. They believed they were "developing" the people, spreading literacy and modern knowledge among the younger generations. But in their desire to replace a religious education with a secular one, they did not recognize that Muslims regarded a secular school—one that excluded any relationship to God—as even more redoubtable than a Christian education, for they considered atheism, the rejection of Divinity, a greater sin than apostasy.[47]

In other words, European reforms, despite their generally beneficial effect in many spheres of activity, ran counter to the traditional Islamic way of life and undermined the very foundations of Islam as an all-embracing principle of people's existence. What the Europeans failed to see, Marshall Hodgson writes, was that "an alien community was being introduced into the society, an alien community which, as part of the Modern Western society, was possessed of both economic and political power to mould the life of the land without regard to the wishes or interests of the established population."[48] The "civilizational mission of the white man" turned out to be a considerable shock, which produced resistance among the indigenous peoples.

Even in their efforts at modernization, European "missionaries" pursued objectives that were far from purely altruistic. Instead they reflected the interests of the dominating powers as well as the need to establish an order best suited to these interests. The redistribution of lands in favor of foreigners, the latter's privileged positions in business and government, the adjustment of economies to the requirements of European production and trade, often in complete disregard of local needs, only perpetuated or widened the development gap.

Europeans generally made no sustained effort to eradicate Islam or convert Muslims to Christianity. On the contrary, in most cases—for example, the French in Algeria—the new rulers declared themselves protectors of the Muslim religion and its establishments. Nonetheless many of the reform measures undertaken by European authorities—the nationalization of religious property, the secularization of justice, new education and tax systems, the requirement of prior permission for travel to Mecca, the public sale of food and drink that were prohibited by the Koranic law—were contrary to the spirit of Islam. In the twentieth century the expansion of Western mass culture, with its movies, popular music, fashions, and lifestyles, further endangered Islam's position in Muslim countries. Thus Europe's offensive against Islam generally assumed indirect forms rather than the use of force.

MUSLIMS IN RUSSIA: A CASE OF SURVIVAL

Russia represents a different case in the European dominance of Islam, because the conversionary zeal of the tsarist government and the Orthodox church did not abate even by the late nineteenth century. Attempts to convert the Tatars by force began immediately after the conquest of the khanate of Kazan in 1552 and continued until the start of the seventeenth century. During this period an important community of converted Tatars, the Kryashens, was formed. After a period of relative tolerance during the seventeenth century, a new wave of religious suppression

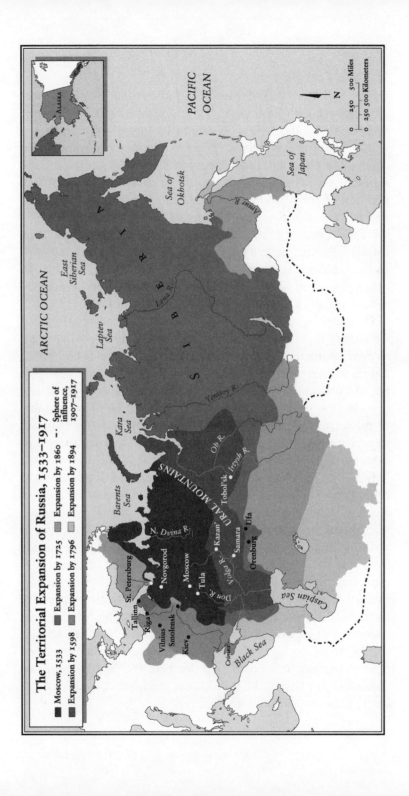

The Territorial Expansion of Russia, 1533–1917

- ■ Moscow, 1533
- ■ Expansion by 1598
- ■ Expansion by 1725
- ■ Expansion by 1796
- ■ Expansion by 1860
- ■ Expansion by 1894
- -·- Sphere of influence, 1907–1917

ARCTIC OCEAN

PACIFIC OCEAN

ALASKA

N

0   250   500 Miles
0   250   500 Kilometers

Barents Sea

Kara Sea

Laptev Sea

East Siberian Sea

Sea of Okhotsk

Sea of Japan

Caspian Sea

Black Sea

S I B E R I A

URAL MOUNTAINS

Lena R.

Yenisey R.

Ob R.

Irtysh R.

Tobol'sk

Amur R.

N. Dvina R.

Volga R.

Don R.

St. Petersburg

Novgorod

Moscow

Tula

Tallinn

Riga

Vilnius

Smolensk

Kiev

Crimea

Kazan'

Samara

Ufa

Orenburg

was inaugurated by Peter the Great and continued by his daughter Elizabeth with fresh vigor. During Elizabeth's reign, mosques were burned and converts liberated from taxes and military service.[49] The *waqf* properties (Muslim religious endowments for educational and charitable purposes) were secularized and seized by the state. Catherine the Great ended this wave of suppression of her Muslim subjects by banning forced conversions and economic and other pressures aimed at the conversion of the Tatars. In 1773 she issued a ukase that declared a toleration for all religions; in 1789 the muftiat as the Muslim's supreme spiritual body was established in Orenburg. Six years earlier the office of a mufti had been created in the Crimea in the immediate aftermath of its annexation by the Russian Empire.[50]

Pressure against Islam was renewed under Nicholas I and Alexander II, but this time missionizing became mostly defensive in character. Its main purpose was to prevent baptized Tatars from returning to Islam rather than to convert new people to Christianity. Still, attempts to spread Christianity among the Muslims were never abandoned. In 1830, with the opening of the Kazan mission, the Kazan Spiritual Academy was meant to prepare missionaries for work in the East. In 1854 three missionary departments were added to the academy—for the Tatars, the Mongols, and the Cheremiss-Chuvash populations, respectively.[51] This seems to have been important in light of Russian expansion into Turkestan in the second half of the nineteenth century. Contrary to expectations, however, the tsarist government's policy in the region was to isolate it from outside influence and maintain it in a state of medieval stagnation, thus removing any possibility of national resistance. It was no surprise, therefore, that Russian administrators sought to preserve an archaic form of Islam in religion and education. Clerics were retained and supported by Russian authorities. Koranic schools of the most conservative type were favored and protected against modern influences. The learned and Sharia-conscious *ulema* did not regard the Russians as infidels but counseled political accommodation with them.[52]

Tsarist conversionary efforts were concentrated instead in the Volga region, where the most influential Muslim community, the Tatars, lived. Their special position was due to a number of factors. They represented one of the empire's largest ethnic and religious minorities and were situated in the very heartland of the Russian-dominated state. From early times the Volga Tatars had played a leading economic and spiritual role among the Muslims of Eurasia and had acted as intermediaries in relations between Russia and various Islamic peoples. These conditions led to the early rise of a Tatar national self-consciousness and a special attitude toward the Islamic response to the advent of modernization and national revolutions.

Principal efforts aimed at suppressing the leadership positions of the Volga Tatar community were undertaken by the Russian Orthodox church, whose general stance toward Russia's Muslims was extremely negative. The church encouraged the government to convert the Tatars forcibly or deport them to central areas of Russia that were populated predominantly by Orthodox Christians. Although sharing these goals with the church, a group of the most influential Orthodox missionaries among Russia's Muslims—including such figures as M. A. Miropiev, N. I. Baratinskii, P. D. Shestakov, and N. I. Il'minskii—emphasized more flexible tactics. Nikolai Il'minskii, for example, believed that the best way to convert Tatars and other Muslims was through their native teachers and native language. He regarded the Christian mission as a long process of cultural rapprochement with Muslims and other groups, which eventually would lead to their Christianization.[53] Since these intellectuals had powerful connections in the Russian political establishment, most of their views were translated into practical government action.

Yet Russian policy toward Muslims was not limited to efforts aimed at their conversion. Russia's unique position among the European nations, until roughly the mid-twentieth century, was due to the fact that it contained within its borders a sizable Islamic community, thus dictating the need for a clear-cut policy. But apart from recurrent attempts to convert Muslims to

Christianity, no such policy existed before the Bolshevik Revolution. The tsarist course of action in dealing with Muslims was simply part of a general nationalities policy, whose guiding principles were Russification and the suppression of national self-consciousness or any feeble efforts at local autonomy. The granting of privileges to noble and propertied classes, regardless of their religion, helped the ruling circles subjugate the majority of the Muslim population.[54]

After 1917 the situation in Russia changed. Now the government pursued a radical policy of extreme secularization, and Islam became an object of repression on equal terms with other religious denominations.[55] At the same time the Bolsheviks closed mosques and *medreses*, prohibited the public display of religious feelings, arrested imams and *ulema* for their allegedly anti-Soviet activities, and intensified propaganda against Islam, they likewise undertook repressive measures against the Russian Orthodox clergy, transformed churches into clubs and libraries, and sent church bells to be melted. Undoubtedly the impact of this anti-religious policy was stronger in the case of Islam, due to its penetrating nature in all aspects of Muslim society. But it would be erroneous to present the Bolshevik regime as especially hostile to Islam.

Nonetheless the Muslim community in the Soviet Union suffered severely under the Bolsheviks' anti-religious policy. In the 1970s, the decade that marked the height of Soviet rule in Russia as well as the beginning of its end, about 50 million persons in the USSR belonged to nationalities that before 1917 had acknowledged their adherence to Islam. Although only a small fraction of this population openly observed religious rites and obligations, opportunities were not great for those who did. According to some estimates, there remained only 40 to 50 mosques of the 24,321 that had existed in the Russian Empire. Only one *medrese*, Mir-i-Arab, in Bukhara, was legally permitted to offer religious training, while before 1917 there had been 185 medreses in Bukhara alone.[56] Of the five "pillars of the faith" incumbent on all believers, only *shahada*, the belief in one

God and in Muhammad His Prophet, had eluded control of the authorities, since it was a matter of the heart. Public observances were either forbidden, restricted, or placed under strict state control (like the *hajj*, the pilgrimage to Mecca).[57]

Although prohibited by the Soviet authorities, Islam nonetheless remained for most Muslims part of their national past, their family traditions, and their way of life. It remained an object of respect and sometimes curiosity, just as Christianity was for Russians who, despite obstacles, sought to attend some church ceremonies, such as Easter, even though they did not belong to the church. Similarly, great Muslim festivals attracted especially young people who wished to share the legacy of their fathers. The absence of an established Islamic hierarchy prompted the spread of "unofficial" mullahs, often elected by the people. They eluded the control of state officials and were often barely tolerated by Islamic authorities who enjoyed the protection of the Soviet government.

These authorities formed four departments to provide for Muslims in the Soviet Union. The Department of Religious Affairs for the European region and Siberia had its center in Ufa; for Central Asia and Kazakhstan in Tashkent; for the trans-Caucasus in Baku; and for the northern Caucasus in Buynak.[58] These offices were supervised by the government's Council for the Affairs of Religious Cults, established in 1944. Contemporary Russia has inherited this structure from the Soviets, though now the profession of faith is not formally limited. The survival of spiritual departments guarantees the state's important role in religious affairs.

ISLAM'S RESPONSE

As Islam lost its position in the world and gradually retreated under the pressure of an expanding Europe, Muslims sought explanations. Why was it that a once flourishing and powerful civilization, which had demonstrated its superiority for centuries and had radiated the light of its cultural and spiritual achievements to the remotest corners of the world, now had succumbed before the advance of a previously weak and barbarous Europe—which moreover adhered to a religion superseded by the teachings of the Prophet Muhammad? The psychological shock of Islam's fallen prominence was reflected in a saying current in the eighteenth century: "This world is the paradise of the unbelievers and the hell of the believers."[59]

An immediate answer to the imposition of Europe's hegemony was resistance. The Ottoman Empire still occupied a dominant position in the lands that bridged the two continents of Europe and Asia. After the Ottoman withdrawal from Vienna, it was still able to resist the encroachments of Austria and Russia upon its possessions. Occasional Turkish successes in eighteenth-century wars against the two powers may have inspired hope that recent disappointments in the struggle against the aggressive Europeans were only temporary, soon to be overcome by a new display of vitality and endurance in the Muslim world. Some countries and regions experienced armed resistance to European expansion in the name of the Islamic faith and the preservation of Islamic values against secularism and alien laws and customs. For fifteen years Abd al-Qadir in Algeria resisted the installation of the French in North Africa (1832–1847). The rebellion of the "Sepoys," Muslim and Hindu troops maintained by the British, in northern India in 1857–1858 sought to reestablish the rule of the Timurid emperor at Delhi and of his former Muslim and Maratha vassals.

In this respect the war of Shamil in the Caucasus against Russian troops, part of the Caucasian War, as an example of Muslim resistance to Russian rule[60] stands by itself. Islam played a secondary role in this war, serving as a justification for the struggle against the expansion of Russian power, which hampered the development of early feudalism among the local tribes. Islam spread among most of these tribes relatively late, in the seventeenth and eighteenth centuries, where paganism had occupied an important place in the system of beliefs among the local peoples. For example, among the Chechens Islam had taken root only in the late eighteenth century and was not widely recognized until the Caucasian War.[61] One could hardly say that the native Caucasian population fought for the values of Islam, because these values had only recently been acquired and were only superficially understood. Nor had the splendor of Islamic civilization reached these wild and remote territories, perhaps with the exception of Dagestan. Imam Shamil himself, rethinking the experience of his struggle during his exile in Kaluga, emphasized that the principal cause of the Caucasian war was robbery,[62] that is, the raiding tactics of the local tribes which brought riches and prestige to their chieftains and the necessary means of survival to ordinary kinsmen. The war in the Caucasus should therefore be regarded rather as native resistance to a colonial intruder, not as part of the Islamic struggle against European expansionism.

As we have seen, Muslim armed resistance to the advance of modern Europe proved to be unsuccessful. In the course of the eighteenth century the Ottoman Empire suffered further defeats in Europe while European penetration into the lands of Islam intensified. Having lost to the Christians on the battlefield, the Turks, not surprisingly, saw the problem of their weakness and decline in purely military terms. They believed that the remedy lay in adopting the victor's weapons, techniques, and methods of training. Efforts were made to introduce European cannons, rifles, and other weapons along with new military organization, discipline, and tactics. These new approaches were advanced by foreign renegades who entered the Ottoman service. One of them was the French Marquis (in some sources Count) Alexander de Bonneval, who had been a personal friend of Eugene of Savoy's and also had a reputation as a highly talented officer. When his relations with the prince deteriorated, fearing for his life, Bonneval sought shelter in the Ottoman Empire. There he adopted the Muslim religion and entered military service. He became known as Humbarajıbashı Ahmed Pasha and was charged with the task of reforming the bombardier corps. Later he established the first engineering school in the empire to introduce some of the basic elements of the new science and technology of the West.[63] Soon one of the school's instructors, Mehmed Said, wrote a geometry book. Other books appeared on medicine, military sciences, and European affairs.

These innovations followed the so-called Tulip Age, 1717–1730, and were led by Sultan Ahmed III and Grand Vizier Ibrahim Pasha. The latter envisaged, as a partial solution to the decline of the Ottoman army, inviting Christian Europeans to train certain corps of the Ottoman forces that were notably weak. Although nothing came of these plans, limited reform efforts continued and were crowned by a major attempt during the reign of Sultan Selim III (1789–1807). The sultan, who came to the throne in the midst of the war with Austria and Russia, used the respite of peace to inaugurate a far-reaching military and political reform of the empire. Like his predecessors, he paid chief attention to the military and spent most of his energy creating an entirely new army, the *Nizam-i Jedid* (New Order), and an independent treasury organized specifically to support it, the Treasury of the New Revenue (*Irad-i Jedid Hazinesi*). Selim sought to produce modern weapons like those sent to him from Europe, invited European experts and engineers to help open factories, and expanded old technical schools while establishing new ones. He made strenuous efforts to revive Ottoman shipbuilding and to provide the empire's fleet with modern ships capable of competing with European vessels.[64]

However successful these reforms, they could not breach the technological gap that now existed between European nations and the Ottoman Empire. Since modernization in Europe was itself the product of social, economic, and political revolutions that had been going on over a long period of time, it could be successfully applied only in the context of similar changes in Ottoman society. Buying, imitating, or adopting foreign technology could not solve the problem of inferiority. Yet the Ottoman ruling classes were not about to consider radical changes in the society as a whole and its way of life. They were ready to adopt elements of European technology but not European civilization, being ill prepared to accept a civilization so different from their own. As a result, the reforms of Selim III were abortive. He himself was deposed by Janissaries and *ulema* who were concerned that these reforms would disrupt the old order.

Nevertheless Selim III's reign was not entirely without progress. The establishment of first Ottoman permanent embassies abroad; the arrival of large numbers of European diplomats, soldiers, and merchants in the principal cities of the empire; the dispatch of numerous Ottomans to reside in the capitals of Europe—these increased contacts between Ottomans and Europeans led to a growing recognition of the need for substantial changes in the Islamic state and society. The solution appeared to be modernization through Europeanization, that is, through the reshaping of government, education, and the armed forces on the European model, even if this meant rejecting some of the basic prescriptions of Islam, as had happened during the *Tanzimat* reforms in 1839–1876, when all subjects of the sultan, of whatever creed, were proclaimed equal, and the doctrine of the equality of Christians and Muslims was made the central principle of the Ottoman revival.[65]

Some leaders went even further, seeing the abolition of Islamic society and the adoption of European practices over a wide range of public and social life as the only way to bring their countries into the community of "civilized nations." The most radical of such reformation was the Kemalist revolution of the 1920s in Turkey, the first Islamic nation to adopt Western practices in all spheres of activity. Turkey's immediate proximity to Europe, its history of military incursions and the occupation of extensive territories on the continent, and its numerous contacts with pilgrims, travelers, and merchants from European countries made the Turks more accustomed to foreign culture and more responsive to the challenges of alien societies. This does not mean that Mustafa Kemal's reforms were easily accepted by all strata of the population. But resistance was not so formidable as to impede their realization. Gradually Islam was disestablished in the country and made a private matter. All the clerical orders were abolished and their property seized; *medrese* colleges were closed, and the state ceased to support the training of *ulema* scholars; the government-controlled system of *waqf* endowments became a secular matter. Sharia was replaced by European law codes, in particular the Swiss personal law. In order to make the reforms complete and irreversible, and to eliminate even the slightest possibility of a regression, in 1928 it was decreed that Latin letters be used for writing Turkish; printing in the old Arabic letters was forbidden. This act was designed to ensure that the younger generation would be cut off from the Ottoman literary heritage and thus from old ideas.[66]

The Turkish example was followed by other Muslim countries, but with different priorities and degrees of success. Iran, Iraq, Syria, and Egypt underwent similar transformations, adopting much of the experience and practices of European countries. Yet these reforms were not simply an attempt by farsighted and progressive political leaders to meet the challenge of the modern world. They reflected the profound changes that had occurred in Islamic civilization under the impact of European expansion. They reflected too the rise of nationalism.

The formation of national self-consciousness began in the Muslim world before World War I, notably in the Young Turks revolution of 1908 and the development of Pan-Arabism in the Arab provinces of the Ottoman Empire. The war provided a powerful impetus to nationalism, and the emergence of new states from the wreckage of the empire—under the control and with the encouragement of the British and French—created an organizational basis for the compartmentalization of the Muslim *ummah*. While the Islamic component was important in mobilizing popular support for independence, nationalist leaders initiated reform programs that left just a little space for Islam. As John Voll has observed, "There was less conscious effort to integrate the Islamic heritage with modern ideas and techniques, and more attention paid to creating modernized nation-states."[67] Although most nationalist spokesmen still recognized Islam as a part of their identity, they took a more secularist attitude toward its role in their society. They were determined that Islam should serve the nation rather than the nation serve Islam.[68]

This trend developed between the world wars, and the success of reforms in Turkey provided an attractive example for other nationalist leaders who sought to modernize their societies and achieve genuine independence and equality with the industrially developed countries of Europe. When European dominance waned after the world depression of the 1930s and World War II, nationalist leaders recognized that the introduction of European institutions and methods did not necessarily save their countries from dependence on the West. It did not eliminate poverty, inequality, and privation at home while the fruits of modernization were falling largely into the hands of a corrupted elite and the masses still lacked the means of subsistence. This recognition gave rise to a new ideology that combined radical secularism—inspired by the Soviet example of successful modernization—and liberal nationalism in the form of political, economic, and juridical institutions patterned after the West. Unlike the nationalism of the interwar period, the new movement that emerged in the first decade after World War II placed greater emphasis on Islam. It was used to support and justify the objectives of the reforming leaders: "Islam as a revolutionary faith could be cited as a support for contemporary revolutionary ideology, and Islam as part of a great heritage could provide support for national unity," Voll writes.[69] The new ideology was frequently called "socialism," often with a qualifying adjective, as in "Arab socialism."

The most telling example of Arab socialism was Nasserism, a movement named after its leader, Gamal Abdel Nasser (1918–1970) in Egypt. Its watchwords were Arab liberation and unity, and a radical socialist transformation of society. In Nasserism, Islam provided the starting point for an independent socialist ideology, but the program rejected those institutions and intellectual habits of Islam that were associated with traditional society. Nasser came to power in 1952 after a coup that drove the royal house out of Egypt. He became a popular leader not only in Egypt but in other countries that waged a struggle against imperialism and colonialism. By the mid-1960s Arab socialism had spread widely in the Arab East: Arab socialist regimes held sway in Syria, Iraq, and Yemen, and there were active movements of that nature in Lebanon, Jordan, and Saudi Arabia. Among other leaders who espoused similar ideas of the new radicalism were Ahmad Ben Bella in Algeria, Sékou Touré in Guinea, and Sukarno in Indonesia.

This merger of socialism and nationalism occurred not only in the Arab East. Even before the Bolshevik Revolution, Muslim nationalists and socialist leaders in Russia had not hesitated to cooperate in the struggle against the tsarist regime. In 1911 some of the nationalist leaders and socialist intellectuals had established the Musavat (equality) party in Baku. Socialist in origin, the party became the mouthpiece of Azeri nationalism.[70] "Muslim Communists" such as Mulla-Nur Vahitov and Said Sultan Galiev combined adherence to Communist dogmas with strong leanings toward the national liberation of Muslim regions from foreign tutelage, Western or Russian. These movements were suppressed by the Bolsheviks, who regarded them as a threat to the territorial integrity of the Soviet Union and as contrary to the basic tenets of Marxism-Leninism.

Modernization in the form of European and Western secularism represented only one of Islam's responses to European expansion and domination. Other responses continued to see Islam as the only remedy for the decay of the Muslim world and its submission to foreign dominance. Yet among these adherents of Islam there was a principal distinction. Some tried to redefine the Muslim religion in order to meet the new challenge: to adapt it to new ideas and trends; to find in it the inner strength and resources to withstand the pressures of secularism, liberalism, nationalism, and other modern theories; and, finally, to demonstrate that Islam was able to provide answers to most of the questions posed by changing realities. Others, however, insisted on a return to the pure, authentic Islam of the Prophet and his

Companions, and a rejection and elimination of the accretions and innovations that had supposedly corrupted the faith and weakened Islamic society.

A leading figure among the reformers was Jamal al-Din al-Afghani (1839–1897). An advocate of all kinds of reform—political, religious, and social—at the same time he preached that enduring strength would be found only in Islam. Afghani insisted on the necessity of Islamic revival and asserted the full compatibility of Islam with reason and modern science. His followers were Muhammad Abduh (1849–1905) and Muhammad Rashid Rida (1865–1935). Abduh's goal became the reformulation of Islamic thought and the revitalization of Islamic society through the integration of modern ideas and techniques with those of Islam. Rida criticized the stagnant conservatism of traditionalist *ulema*, on the one hand, and the excessive secularism of Muslim nationalist reformers, on the other.[71] In Russia the advocates of adapting Islam to the requirements of modernity were Ismail Bey Gasprinskii (Gaspraly) (1851–1914) and the so-called *Jadids*, the proponents of Tatar educational reform who developed the idea of Muslim unity as a minority within the Russian state.[72]

Opposition to nationalist reformers and to those who would combine traditional Islam with various conceptions of modernity originated in the Wahhabis movement in Arabia in the late eighteenth and early nineteenth centuries. Its emphasis on the strict observance of the basic tenets of Islam, as they were expressed in the Koran and the *Sunnah* (the corpus of traditions, describing the actions and utterances of the Prophet) as the two fundamental and binding sources for Islamic faith and law, made this movement the "prototype of rigorous fundamentalism in the modern Islamic experience."[73] Wahhabism was revived in the twentieth century as a result of the consolidation of the Saudi state, which adopted its ideology. It came to exert considerable influence on various movements in the Muslim world after World War II and especially after the end of the cold war. One can find another example of this trend in the views and activities of the Muslim Brotherhood in Egypt. Established by Hasan al-Banna (1906–1949), it too insisted that the weakness of Islamic society could be cured only by returning to the sources of its strength, the Koran and the *Sunnah*. Although they viewed themselves as pupils of Afghani, Abduh, and Rashid Rida, the Wahhabis and the Muslim Brotherhood were unwilling to engage in intellectual speculation and were thus fundamentalists in style.[74]

The line that separated the followers of these two ideological positions in the Islamic community was always vague and volatile. It is worth noting that even those Muslims who emphasized the values of Islam and a return to its fundamentals did not totally reject the achievements and experience of European civilization. They preferred to adapt the Muslim world to new realities and to borrow all that was valuable in modernization without sacrificing their identity, of which religion constituted an integral part.

SIX

Cooperation, Coexistence, and Influence

If war embodied the confrontation between Europe and Islam, trade and commercial interaction demonstrated their ability to cooperate. Even when Christendom and the Muslim world were at ideological loggerheads, trade continued to flourish and benefit both sides, and to serve as a common point of interest.

Europe and Islam established commercial relations soon after the establishment of the Islamic faith. Contrary to Henri Pirenne's assertion,[1] authorities have shown that Arab conquests did not interrupt trade in the Mediterranean, that even during battle it provided a bridge between Europe and Islam.[2] It was conducted in Italian cities—Naples, Amalfi, Sorrento, Gaeta, and Venice—and prospered despite the pope and the emperor's efforts to suppress it.[3] Provençal Jews managed vigorous trade at the ports of Provence.[4] And on the eastern outskirts of the European continent, commercial routes to the Muslim world ran through the lands of Kievan Russia, which maintained fruitful relations with the Volga Bulgars who served as middlemen in trade with Muslim merchants from Samarkand, Bukhara, and Persia.[5]

Evidently both sides wished to maintain trade ties. Although in the early Middle Ages Europe's economic development and culture were inferior to Islam's, nevertheless its exports were not confined to "Slavonic slaves, Frankish weapons, and English wool."[6] In addition to armor and slaves, Venice exported timber for shipbuilding; Provençal Jews loaded ships in France with brocade, beaver and marten skins, and other furs that were highly valued in Muslim countries; and North Gaul, Scandinavian countries, and Russia sold Arab merchants furs (sable, ermine, marten, fox, and beaver), honey, wax, birch bark, hazelnuts, fish glue, leather, amber, cattle, and many other goods that were in high demand in Eastern bazaars. The prosperity generated by this commerce is evidenced by the contents—including enormous coin hoards—of tombs excavated in Scandinavia.[7] For their part, European merchants imported spices, pearl and stone-encrusted jewels, tapestries, silk vestments, dyes, incense, perfumes, and papyrus. From sea and river ports, these commodities were dispersed throughout the continent.

The church generally denounced trade with the infidels, and clerics were especially disdainful of selling European slaves to Muslims. While the church reconciled itself to the enslavement of pagan Slavs inhabiting eastern and southern Europe, it could not tolerate the selling of Christians. Slave trading (as well as any trade relations) was banned by Popes Zachary and Hadrian I, though this did not bring the lucrative business to a halt.[8] Other popes attempted but also failed. For instance, Leo V (813–820) proscribed trade between Venice and Alexandria, and Doge issued an edict in conjunction with this prohibition. Yet apparently this had little effect, for Venetian merchants continued trading with Muslim Egypt.[9] Despite these and similar measures undertaken by the church against European trade with Islam, clerics themselves eagerly consumed its fruits, both in a literal and figurative sense. In 1062, anticipating the visit of an emperor, the powerful abbot of Montecassino went to Amalfi, an Italian city famed for its trade with Asia and particularly with North Africa, to buy silk garments suitable as a gift for such an exalted guest. Ecclesiastic and lay lords from all of Western Christendom could acquire these same items on their occasional visits to Rome, and their numbers brought Amalfi's merchants an important market.[10]

Trade largely determined how European countries reacted to Arab military incursions. In the ninth century the Maritime republics of southern Italy cooperated with Muslim invaders of the Apennine peninsula, and with the Aghlabids who conquered Sicily in 902. Arab raiders used the harbors of Naples, Amalfi, and Gaeta to refit their ships and unload their spoils. Even when, in August 846, Arabs attacked Ostia and plundered Rome's surroundings—including the famous basilicas of St. Peter and St. Paul—Naples and Amalfi did not intervene on behalf of the endangered papacy. Indeed, despite considerable pressure these republics refused to take active roles in the anti-Arab league. It was not until 849, when Arabs aimed to attack Rome, that Naples and Amalfi armed and deployed their ships. The pope found their swift action highly unusual, particularly in light of their earlier reluctance, and suspected the leaders of illicit intentions. Assisted by a storm, the Italian fleets were victorious over the Arabs and saved Rome.[11] The rulers of Naples and the merchants of Amalfi demonstrated that, except under the most extreme circumstances, they were prepared to compromise their solidarity with fellow Christians in order to profit from friendly ports in Sicily and North Africa.

Early relations between Europe and Islam not only involved trade but also colonization. Amalfi established colonies in Egypt, Palestine, and Syria, and its merchants obtained permission from the ruler of Egypt to build a church, a monastery, a hospital, and two hostels for Christian pilgrims. These establishments, most of which withstood even the Norman conquest, preceded the arrival of European merchants in the wake of the Crusades.[12]

Nor did the Crusades interrupt commercial relations between Europe and Islam. On the contrary, states formed by the Crusades established relations with Europe that were preserved by their Muslim successors.[13] Protected by the Crusaders, European merchants feverishly developed a system of colonies in the Levant ports. These were formed by European chiefs and governed by European laws. Muslims who later reconquered these ports did not end Europe's colonizing activities. Rather, they encouraged merchants to continue. Patterns established in the eleventh and twelfth centuries therefore survived not only the downfall of kingdoms created by the Crusades but also the Mamluk occupation and the Ottomans' later conquest of the Levant.

Merchants from Venice were among the most enterprising of those who settled in the Levant after this territory was invaded by those who wore the cross. They were also some of the most privileged, for Serenissima had won for the Crusaders undisputed control of the sea and helped them gain Tyre and Ascalon. These ports of the kingdom of Jerusalem became not only secure means of receiving reinforcements from the West but also centers of exchange between Europe and Asia.

This exchange grew increasingly important. Europeans found in the Levant a vast marketplace to sell their goods in exchange for what they lacked. Syria and Palestine provided Europe with lemons, oranges, almonds, figs, cotton, silks, and sugar. Egypt, in addition to spices, was for Europeans the chief source of alum, sugar, and wheat. The Levant market was also a center for trade in wood, metals, and slaves. Venetians settled in Acre and close to Tyre; they built a church, a consulate, a warehouse, and other buildings for their everyday needs, and they owned palaces, private homes, and country estates around Acre and Tyre.[14] Assisted by their navy, which now dominated the eastern Mediterranean (and would continue to do so until the eighteenth century), Venetians generally occupied influential positions in trade in the Levant.

Europe's flourishing trade with this area was not terminated when Crusaders were evicted from the regions they had conquered. The Mediterranean seaports on the coast of Asia that fell into Muslim hands continued to provide an important commercial link between Europe and Islam. Bills issued by the pope after

Acre was conquered by the Mamluks in 1291, which prohibited trade with Muslims, did not deter European merchants; indeed, trade between the two worlds was livelier than ever. Arabs traded wool, linen, and silk. With the decline of agriculture in the early fourteenth century, Levantine countries increasingly demanded foodstuffs. Copper and tin had good markets in both Syria and Egypt. The Levant also kept soap in high demand.[15]

Although spices, aromatics, and dyes continued to form the bulk of the Levant's exports, Near Eastern countries also produced sugar and precious textiles eagerly bought by European traders. But none of this compared to Europe's interest in the growing cotton trade of Syria and Egypt. Cotton grown in those countries was mainly exported to Europe and processed through its growing fustian industry.[16] Soon Europe became the principal source of cloth for countries in the Middle East, particularly since the Levantine industry had begun to wither. Almost every European country exported cloth, but by the seventeenth century England was predominant.

Muslims in the Levant demanded metals, especially copper, which came from central Germany and Slovakia, and agricultural products, chiefly olive oil, honey, and fruits. But European trade with the Islamic world aroused controversy as a result of shipments to the Muslims of materials that could be used in war: weapons, but also timber, iron, and other metals used to manufacture arms. Papal prohibitions mainly concerned such commodities. Yet European merchants, interested in laying claim to trade's substantial profits, generally ignored papal law and continued selling war materials to Muslims. Italian traders supplied Egyptian rulers throughout the Crusades.[17] Later, when Turkey menaced Europe, England was accused of providing the Ottoman Turks with tin for their guns. An English ship, bound for the Ottoman Empire, was seized with a cargo of woolens, kerseys, gunpowder, guns and gun barrels, and sword blades, as well as gold and coins.[18] Neither decrees of excommunication nor sanctions brought to a halt this highly profitable trade.

Generally Europe's commerce with the Muslim world promised substantial revenues and attracted merchants who hoped
quickly to return their money spent for the delivery of goods to
and from the Orient. For example, while the cost (including
freight) of importing cloth from the Levant ranged from 10 to
20 percent of the anticipated profit, cloth in southern Europe
cost 20 to 40 percent more than in the Levant. This means that
merchants' net profit on cloth reached and sometimes surpassed
15 to 30 percent. Similarly, since pepper and ginger cost 50 percent more in Venice than in the Levant, net profits could exceed
25 percent.[19] With this kind of financial incentive, it is not sur-
prising that trade continued to flourish. Late in the fourteenth
century Venetians annually invested 400,000 to 500,000 ducats
in Levantine trade; the Genoese invested 200,000 to 300,000;
and the Catalans 200,000 to 250,000. Add the investments of
minor trading nations—southern Italy, Ancona, Ragusa, and
Provence-Languedoc—and it would be safe to say that 1 million
ducats were spent annually on the Levantine trade.[20] By the end
of the fifteenth century this amount had increased to 1.1 million
ducats—entirely the result of investments by Venetians in dominant positions in the eastern Mediterranean. This increase
amounted to almost two and a half times what they had invested in a similar period a hundred years before; Genoese and
Catalan investments, by comparison, were considerably less.
France and Naples began playing an increasingly important role
in Levant trade and augmented their investments substantially.[21]

European merchants traded not only with the Levant. They
penetrated deep into the Muslim world and established relations with Persia as well. Mongol's Il-Khans were particularly
interested in trade with Europe, as they hoped it would lead to
a political alliance against their rivals in the Middle East. Merchants were interested in raw silk from Caspian borderlands
for Italy's developing silk industry.[22] Of European nations,
Genoa most actively pursued contact with the Il-Khans, establishing colonies in Caffa, Crimea, and Tana at the mouth of the
Don River, which served as bases for commerce with Mongol's

khanates east of the Black Sea. From 1280 the Genoese accelerated their expansion in this direction and, after 1313, when violent rivalries between Mongol rulers subsided, the Genoese carried on a lively trade with Tebriz—where they would soon build a consulate—and even undertook expeditions to India and China.[23]

As the Genoese were highly favored by the Il-Khans' court, their relations were not confined to trade. With their Venetian counterparts, they managed political relations between the Mongols and Western Europe. And soon Italian merchants who traded with the Il-Khans joined in.[24] Thus politics and trade were closely intertwined in Persia.

This was not always the case, especially when commercial interests clashed with the political and religious objectives of Christian rulers. Trade with Muslims, prohibited by the pope in order to inflict damage upon the infidel countries, was a rich source of income for the Holy See. Merchants who defied these prohibitions preferred to pay the penalty than lose profits. Eager to capitalize on their disobedience, popes issued absolutions that authorized the sale of goods, including war materials, to the infidels, and these could be obtained by paying a considerable sum of money. Absolutions were issued to entire merchant communities or to individual traders and were valid for one commercial transaction or for a certain period of time. The popes sacrificed the principles of the holy war out of economic need. Embargoes imposed by the papacy on trade with the Muslim world were never enforced to the fullest.[25]

The zeal of certain secular rulers to recapture the Holy Land also damaged trade in the Mediterranean. King Peter I of Cyprus was eager to renew the Crusades and was obsessed with the idea of winning back his ancestral kingdom of Jerusalem. He tried to persuade other European rulers of the need for a campaign, even enlisting the support of the pope, who remained uncertain whether the immediate goal was the Mamluk sultanate—whose possessions included former Crusader states in Palestine—or the regions in the Aegean and Balkans that were ruled by the Turks.

In 1364 Peter sailed to France and England to publicize and gather support for another Crusade.[26]

Peter's chief aim was the conquest of Alexandria, an important seaport for trade with Egypt. His Christian fleet arrived at Alexandria on October 9, 1365, surprised and scattered the local garrison, and sacked the city. The Crusaders seized everything of value, including the property of Western merchants who had large colonies in Alexandria. Venetians, Genoese, and other merchants who traded with Egypt were incensed by the disruption to their business. They not only lost merchandise in the pillage; Westerners in Egypt when Alexandria was attacked were held captive by the sultan as a reprisal against Christians. The Mamluks, worried about further attacks by the Crusaders, pressed trading cities to work for peace. Venetians, with their predominant positions in trade with Egypt, had every reason to pressure Peter into negotiations. But the king of Cyprus prepared a new invasion of the sultanate. It was only after this invasion failed—partly because of a Venetian embargo on the export of arms and horses to Cyprus, and partly because of a storm that dispersed Peter's fleet—that, on the pope's advice, Peter put an end to hostilities and in 1367 entered into negotiations with the sultan.

Peter's Crusade had not only evangelical but also worldly objectives related to Cyprus's role in European trade with the Levant. A draft of the treaty from 1367 makes it clear that he wanted the sultan to favor Cypriot merchants with preferred commercial facilities, tariff reductions, legal franchises, and guarantees for trading in his lands. Peter threatened and used aggression to derive commercial advantages for his subjects at the cost of the sultan and European competitors.[27] Evidently greed was more important than the goals of a holy war, even for a "romantically minded knight" like Peter I.[28]

From the late Middle Ages to the eighteenth century, piracy also threatened trade between Europe and Islam. We have already seen how widespread piracy was in that period when all Mediterranean nations scudded across the high seas in search of plunder.[29] Pirates voyaged during war and peace, commissioned by their native governments or at their own whim, and made navigation treacherous for all nations. The Aegean became particularly dangerous for ships loaded with valuables. Christian and Muslim merchants suffered alike the raids of pirates whose only religion was easy money.

The most violent and acquisitive pirates were the Catalans. In 1312 they extended their activities to the eastern Mediterranean when the Catalan Company acknowledged a nominal suzerainty of the house of Barcelona, thus becoming a base for merchants from the mother country in this region. The Catalan Company, a mercenary organization formed in 1303, was involved in regional wars and enlarged its territorial possessions in the general turmoil and confusion. Catalans seized control over the duchy of Athens in 1311, a state established by Latin crusaders after they captured Constantinople in 1204 and partitioned Byzantium. By trading with the Levant and establishing consulates in Constantinople, Alexandria, and Acre, Catalan merchants put an end to the Italian monopoly on long-distance commerce in those waters. Relying on territorial acquisitions of the Catalan Company, Catalan pirates also hoped to compete with the Venetians and Genoese in the Aegean trade, but the resources of Barcelona's merchants could not compete with such powerful rivals.[30] Nevertheless they challenged the Venetians at the heart of the Levantine trade.

Like their compatriots in the Catalan Company, Catalan merchants were known to be violent and unscrupulous. In 1408 they boarded one of their own ships, which had been chartered to transport merchandise, and sold the Muslims aboard into slavery. In 1422 they attacked Alexandria at night and set fire to a Muslim merchant ship with a rich cargo. Although Muslim merchant ships and Mamluk's coasts were the Catalans' preferred targets, they were not averse to Christian ships. After the Catalans attacked Alexandria in 1422, they sailed to Syria and, in the port of Beirut, attacked a ship with an envoy of the sultan and a Genoese merchant on board.[31]

Such maltreatment of Muslims enraged the sultan, and he often inflicted his reprisals not only upon the guilty Catalans but also upon Christians residing in Mamluk dominions. After the Catalans attacked Beirut, the sultan threatened to expel all European merchants. He closed the church of the Holy Sepulchre in Jerusalem and a church in Bethlehem; had Franciscans in Jerusalem arrested and deported to Cairo; and enforced an embargo on Catalan merchandise, upbraiding Europeans who traded with them.[32]

Piracy nevertheless continued. In the sixteenth century, as England became a strong naval power, English pirates displaced the Catalans and became the principal threat to Mediterranean commerce. English piracy rapidly developed after the Spanish armada was defeated. English privateers targeted mainly French vessels, because England was competing with France for trade with the Ottomans. Yet English pirates attacked ships of almost any stripe that traded in the Mediterranean, including those of the Ottoman Empire. They took advantage of the superiority of their vessels, which were stronger and better armed than those of other nations. The legendary exploits of England's pirates increased the British flag's prestige in the Levant as well as the influence of Queen Elizabeth's representative in the Porte.[33]

Aside from piracy, other obstacles sometimes hindered Europe's trade with Islam. Muslim rulers, though generally interested in trading with Christians and in protecting European merchants residing in their domains, sometimes imposed excessive duties on foreign traders. In 1426 the Mamluk sultan Barsbay monopolized the spice trade, established compulsory prices, and compelled Europeans to sell him their merchandise at a fifth of its commercial value.[34] In response Venice's senate minimized trade with the Levant and issued permits. Genoese and Catalan merchants likewise reduced trade with the Mamluk domains. Stubborn opposition by foreign merchants undermined Barsbay's monopoly and his policy of compulsory prices.

European trade with the Ottoman Empire depended little on the whims of a particular ruler and was regularized under the so-called Capitulation, which the sultan granted to European nations. This term originates from the Latin *capitula*, an itemized document, and designated privileges granted to Christian states, "allowing their citizens to reside and trade in the Muslim dominions without becoming liable to the fiscal and other disabilities imposed by those Muslim rulers on their own non-Muslim subjects."[35] The first Capitulation, granted to France in 1536, was a turning point in the history of the Franco-Turkish alliance.[36] It covered the entire Ottoman Empire and accordingly increased French influence in the Levant. The document entitled the king of France to exercise jurisdiction over Christian traders in the Levant, which meant that they had to do business under the French flag and the exclusive surveillance of French ambassadors and consuls, and that the latter had to represent them.[37] This jurisdiction enhanced French prestige and confirmed the country's dominance in eastern Mediterranean trade; it also generated substantial profits, for French representatives in the Ottoman domains could collect consular fees on all imported goods. The sultan's Capitulation with France became official law in the treaty of 1581.

Yet France could not long maintain its monopoly on trade with the Ottomans. When the English entered the Levant toward the end of the sixteenth century, they were determined to free themselves from French jurisdiction and to supplant France as the Ottoman Empire's favorite power. With its vigorous economy and superior navy, England presented a significant threat to French positions in the Levant. Furthermore France had been weakened by civil and religious strife and by continual conflicts with England, Italy, and Spain. Consequently France's political influence and share in the Levantine trade were wavering.

England exploited these circumstances and used its able diplomats in Constantinople—William Harborne, Edward Barton, Henry Lello, Sir Thomas Glover, and Sir Paul Pindar—to strengthen its position in the Porte and advance its ambitions against other European merchant competitors, primarily French and Dutch. In 1593 the English ambassador, Barton, obtained a treaty of capitulation from the sultan similar to what he had granted the French. On July 6, 1612, the sultan also granted a treaty of capitulation to the Dutch, conceding to them the privilege of free trade in his domains under their own flag. These new powers enjoying privileged relations with the Ottoman Empire increased competition among Europeans; they put aside their religious differences and fought instead over profits from trading with the Muslim world.

DIPLOMATIC CONTACTS: MISSIONS AND EMBASSIES

Commerce did not provide the only occasion for contact between Europe and Islam. No matter how acute their military opposition, wars came and went. In periods of peace, diplomatic missions traveled between Christian and Muslim rulers primarily to establish a common ground for political relations and alliances. In 840, when the Byzantine emperor Theophile was planning an offensive against the caliph of Baghdad, he sent an embassy to the court of the emir of Andalusia, Abd al-Rahman II.[38] Theophile also entered into negotiations with the Frankish king, Louis the Pious, and with Venice. Nor was he averse to establishing allies in the Muslim world. He knew that the Umayyads who ruled Cordoba were adversaries of the Abbasides in Baghdad, and he sent his mission to Spain to form an alliance.

Although little is known about this mission, the Arab chronicler Ibn Haiyan logged the Byzantine emperor's proposition to the emir of Andalusia as well as the emir's response. The emperor sent Kartiyus, a Greek who knew Arabic, to settle a treaty of friendship and to offer the emir's assistance in restoring the Umayyads to the throne of their ancestors in Baghdad's caliphate. For his part, the emperor asked that Crete, which the emir's former subjects had occupied, be returned to him. Abd al-Rahman honored the Byzantine emissary, for the arrival of an envoy from Constantinople augmented his prestige among Muslim rulers. He immediately sent two envoys back to Byzantium

with a politely worded response that rejected the emperor's offer of friendship and cooperation against the Abbasides and
their allies, the Aghlabides of Ifrikiya. In the words of É. Lévi-
Provençal, the Spanish emir's message was "a masterpiece of
Cordobian diplomacy even at its infancy: many good words, a
protective and hardly polite tone, and no engagements for the
present or for the future."[39] His envoys were nevertheless well
received in Constantinople, and one of them—Yahya ibn al-
Hakam al-Bakri of Jaen, known as al-Ghazal (the gazelle) for
his beauty[40]—roused the interest of Theophile, the empress
Theodore, and the crown prince Michael (the future Michael
III) with his intellectual charm.

A better-documented exchange of missions between Christian and Muslim monarchs in 797 is provided by historians. In
that year the great Frankish ruler and founder of a European
empire, Charlemagne, sent a diplomatic mission to the caliph of
Baghdad. Its purpose is unclear, and some scholars even doubt
that it took place.[41] Yet Christian chroniclers wrote at length
about the exchange between the Frankish king and caliph
Harun ar-Rashid (768–809), and we know that in 801 the
caliph sent ambassadors to respond to Charlemagne's mission.
He even sent a wondrous gift, the elephant Abul Abbas. It was
the first time the emperor had seen one of the huge animals
mentioned so frequently in Roman history, and one can imagine
the depth of Charlemagne's sorrow when, several years later,
Abul Abbas died from the Rhineland's cold climate.[42] The
Frankish chronicles describe two additional missions to and
from Baghdad in 802 and 807.[43]

On all these occasions and more,[44] Christian rulers initiated
diplomatic relations with Muslim sovereigns. The latter thought
these embassies demonstrated their superiority over European
monarchs and treated the Christian envoys as tributes from
lands that accepted the suzerainty of the leaders of Islam. Sometimes, however, Muslim rulers sought contacts with Christendom in order to bolster their influence locally and generally
in the Muslim world, and to aggrandize the splendor of their

courts by borrowing cultural achievements from a people whom they otherwise considered inferior.

Arabs knew and respected, for example, ancient Greek civilization and its Christian heirs in Constantinople. Conquered and occupied by Muslim conquerors, Byzantium nevertheless remained the acme of the civilized world. In splendor and prestige the Byzantine emperor's court outshined the most prosperous capitals in the Arab world. Masterpieces in Constantinople substantiated the genius of Greek architects, decorators, sculptors, and artists, and attracted the attention not only of conquerors but of rulers who could profit from peaceful relations with the Byzantine Empire.

One of these was Abd al-Rahman III (912–961), who proclaimed his possessions in Spain's caliphate and bestowed upon the Umayyad dynasty in Cordoba its greatest glory. Desiring to free his state from Baghdad's influence—if not in politics then culturally—Abd al-Rahman sent envoys to Constantinople in 949 and again in 955 in order to resume relations between the two states (an emissary of Emperor Theophile's had attempted this almost a century earlier, unsuccessfully). Although relations between the Byzantine emperor and the Spanish caliph remained obscure, Byzantine art in Abd al-Rahman's palace (Madinat al Zahra) testifies to Byzantium's growing influence in the caliphate of Cordoba, and to the caliph's attempt to build closer ties with the Byzantine Empire.[45]

Intensified commercial and political ties, as well as war, multiplied relations between Christian and Muslim states. As wars abated and forces regrouped, truces were negotiated and new alliances formed. Following Koranic prescriptions, Muslim rulers preferred to receive Christian envoys rather than to send their own missions to Europe. Gradually, however, their scrupulosity eroded: Europe's superior economic development persuaded Islamic leaders to adopt European techniques, and they began sending representatives to the courts of European monarchs. From the sixteenth century onward the Ottoman Empire, Iran, and Morocco sent envoys and merchants with increasing frequency to European countries. Initially envoys were local non-Muslims, renegades, or new converts to Islam who were familiar with Europe, its languages and habits. Sometimes Muslim rulers even enlisted the help of foreigners to communicate with their European counterparts. Over time, however, sultans and emirs sent envoys whose rank was low enough to endure the humiliation of traveling through the lands of unbelievers. Representatives became more numerous as Europe extended its dominance, particularly on the battlefield, and as Muslim rulers came to feel that amicable relations with the Christian world were in their best interest.

Upon entering European capitals in their colorful clothes and turbans, Muslim envoys were often consternated by the sensation they caused. When the first Ottoman envoy to Paris, Mehmed Efendi (1720–1721), made his way to the city along canals, he observed crowds gathered on the banks to observe him. Some of the precipitously curious fell into the water, and some were even shot by guards.[46] Whereas Europe was already familiar with the practice of sending ambassadors to foreign countries and establishing permanent diplomatic missions, Muslim emissaries were a rarity. Permanent missions were out of the question because, according to the Islamic canon, permanent peace was impossible with the *Dar al-Harb*. Only after Muslim rulers abandoned all hopes of conquering and converting Europe, and had relinquished territories to European expansion, did they consider sending diplomatic missions. In 1793 at the court of St. James the first permanent Ottoman legation was established. Two years later, in April 1795, Ottoman representation was extended to the courts of Vienna and Berlin. And in the fall of 1795 the sultan decided to add an embassy in Paris to those established in London, Vienna, and Berlin.[47] As early as 1792, in accordance with the Treaty of Jassy, an Ottoman ambassador was sent to St. Petersburg, but deep contradictions between the Ottoman and Russian empires led to his recall in 1794.[48] Each Ottoman ambassador, secretary, or special representative was instructed to learn about the countries of his residence and provide Istanbul with detailed information.[49] This interest reflected a changed relation between Europe and Islam.

CULTURAL INTERACTION

Changed relations between Europe and the Islamic world in the spheres of commerce and diplomacy promoted cultural contacts that made a lasting impression on their respective histories. The consequences of cultural interaction took various forms: from mutual influence in architecture, art, craftsmanship, literature, and even clothing and cuisine to the less obvious domains of administration, habits, traditions, rites, common parlance, and personal perspective. The effect of this interaction varies from the "border areas," where representatives from the two civilizations lived side by side for years and sometimes centuries—as in Spain, southern Italy, the Balkans, and the Trans-Caucasus—and the northern regions of Europe where the influence of Islamic civilization was indirect and diffuse.

It is difficult to measure the influence that Europe and the Arab world had on each other. It requires accounting for not only the long- and short-term consequences of those influences and the ability to appropriate and grow from them, but also for levels of communication with other regions of the world when their mutual influence was strong. European civilization appears to have been more responsive to the influence of Islamic civilization, more impressionable to outside influence, and more enterprising in translating Muslim culture into practical life, particularly when Islam was culturally superior to Europe. But Europe also had a substantial impact on the Muslim world, facilitated by the general advance of communication and travel technology.

It is futile to try to judge whether it was Europe or Islam that exported the most influential ideas. Numerals and a conception of zero, which came to Europe from the Muslim world, propelled developments in mathematics, physics, and astronomy. Without these Europe could not have made its great technological strides nor dominated the world. Ideas of democracy and liberalism, brought to Islam by Napoleon's Egyptian campaign, spread over the whole of Islam and spurred social reform. Can one overestimate the great service of Islamic civilization? It preserved for Europe—when it was rapidly disintegrating under the pressure of the barbaric invasions—ancient Greek philosophy, geography, astronomy, and medicine; and it supplemented these libraries of thought with its own knowledge, which was respected by St. Thomas Aquinas and Bonaventura da Bagnoregio, and praised by the great medieval poet of the *Divine Comedy*, Dante Alighieri.[50] Islam played a key role in the formation of European civilization, though it did so unwittingly. Much depended on the ability of Europe, like that of a pupil, to absorb what was useful and develop it. Islam at first was a willy-nilly tutor, but it became a willy-nilly pupil when Europeans preponderated in science, technology, politics, and culture. Muslims, aware of their backwardness and eager to bridge the widening gap, sought out European civilization as their teacher.

The history of European and Islamic societies demonstrates a combination of deliberate, spontaneous, and unwitting mutual influence. Yet the domain of religion, particularly in Islam, was almost unaffected. Religion formed an integral part of Muslim's cultural and spiritual identity, and it resisted alien intrusion. And since the religion of Islam permeated all social activities, it largely determined Muslims' response to foreign influence. This must be borne in mind when considering Islam of the present day.

Beyond doubt, before the Crusades contact between Europe and Islam was minimal, despite Islam's conquests in Spain, southern Italy, and Byzantium. Islam's impact on these lands was of local character, and continuous warfare with Christians on several frontiers prevented the two cultures from engaging in fruitful dialogues. The muses were drowned out by the clash of arms. Nevertheless Arabs accumulated knowledge elsewhere, and it trickled into Europe as a result of contacts between Europeans and Arabs who had conquered European lands.

Ironically, the first people who enjoyed this knowledge were votaries of the Christian Church, the institution most threatened by Arab conquests and at the forefront of the struggle with Islam. Among the votaries was Gerbert of Aurillac, who became Pope Sylvester II (999–1003). In his early twenties he spent three years in Catalonia and studied mathematics and astronomy under a bishop. He was familiar with the astrolabe and constructed a new form of abacus; his use of Arabic numerals, the first recorded in Europe, was not generally accepted.[51] He was also the first to translate into Latin Arab works on mathematics, astronomy, and medicine.

Islam's cultural influence, however, was not limited to translated treatises or to borrowed devices for calculation and navigation. Poetry, particularly that of the Provençal and troubadour variety, made its way into Europe from the Iberian peninsula. After time it was difficult to say which features were borrowed and which were indigenous; the similarity between the two amounted to a virtual identity.[52]

The most promising cultural exchange began after the first Crusades to the Holy Land. Despite their military failure, the Crusades increased the points of contact between Europe and Islam in number as well as in variety.[53] By the time the Crusades began, the Muslim world possessed numerous translations of the works of ancient Greek philosophers and scientists. These included the ever-popular Plato and Aristotle and other ancient, hermetic, Gnostic, and neo-Platonic philosophers. Arabs took particular interest in the neo-Platonists, whose writings on medicine, astrology and astronomy, alchemy and chemistry, and physics and mathematics could be practically applied. Geographical and political writings also were translated, but in limited numbers. Despite the breadth of interest, no one translated Greek poetry, drama, or history.[54] Europeans then took Arabic translations of the Greek, as well as commentaries by Arab scholars and philosophers, and translated them into Latin.

Europeans completed the bulk of these exceedingly influential translations by the end of the thirteenth century. They not only thus rediscovered their ancient Grecian predecessors, they also discovered Muslim scientists and philosophers who thereafter influenced the development of European thought. Avicenna's (d. 1037) book, the *Canon of Medicine*, translated into Latin in the twelfth century, was for hundreds of years the primary textbook in Europe's medical schools. Avicenna also influenced Europe's philosophical development, which can be explained by the fact that his teaching was "congenial to the platonizing strand in Christian thought."[55] Christian theologians venerated Averroës as the true interpreter of Aristotle.[56] Arabic translations also introduced Europe to Ptolemy's *Almagest*, al-Khwarizmi's writings on algebra, and Alfragan and Albumasar's astrological and astronomical works.

Europeans did not simply receive this body of knowledge; they elaborated and adjusted it to meet their practical needs. Take the case of Arabic numerals. Eased by the publication in 1202 of Leonardo Fibonacci's *Liber abaci*, Arabic numerals introduced Europeans to the concept of zero, which they immediately used for practical purposes. Described by the Arabic term *şifr* (empty), the concept of zero was incorporated into the foundations of Europe's decimal system. Likewise in philosophy, Arabic thought provided European thinkers with fresh perspectives in metaphysics; these were developed by such famous philosophers as Thomas Aquinas and Roger Bacon and taken up by modern European philosophers.[57] Thus the Crusades introduced Christendom to an almost entirely unknown world of thought, science, and culture.

The immediate contribution of the Crusades was more negligible. Knights and peasants were attracted to elements of Islamic life which they tried to imitate upon returning to their homes. They appreciated the *hammām*, or bathhouses, that played a central role in the life of Muslim cities. During the Crusades similar bathhouses were introduced in Europe where they gained considerable popularity, but the church soon forbade them. Crusaders also borrowed tournaments, which combined military exercises with public displays of a knight's virtues.

These tournaments became a characteristic feature of medieval Europe, and even kings participated in them. Finally, Crusaders appropriated from Syria the use of a coat of arms. For instance, the lily in the coat of arms of Louis VII—a leader of the second Crusade—closely resembled the coat of arms of Nur ad-Din, his principal adversary.[58]

After the Crusades, Muslims in Spain and Italy continued to disseminate Arab cultural and intellectual property. Until the *Reconquista* ended in 1492, Spain was the primary exporter of knowledge to Western nations. Comparatively, Sicily and Italy played an insignificant role, yet there too the arts and sciences flourished (laying the foundations for the Italian Renaissance) under the protection and encouragement of the Norman Sicilian kingdom. This hybridization of European and Islamic culture did not stop here but was manifest in other features of Spanish and Italian society.

Much has been written about the splendor of Sicily's royal courts under Roger II, William II, and especially Frederick II Hohenstaufen, who was called by his adversaries the "baptized sultan."[59] Arab influence predominated in the organization and function of these courts as well as in the customs and ceremonies that were practiced and performed within them. Everything from the kings' Arabic titles to their harems and eunuchs and palaces reminiscent of the Andalusian emir reflected this influence. Roger II's documents and decrees were issued in Latin, Greek, and Arabic. Documents that he did not personally sign bore his motto in Arabic, according to the usage of Muslim rulers. William I and William II spoke Arabic fluently, and the latter's concubines and handmaidens were all Muslims or had secretly converted to Islam. Arabian influence also held sway at the court of Frederick II, where it was intensified by political and intellectual relations with the rulers of North Africa and the Near East.[60]

Muslim influence in Spain and Italy was visible not only in the administration, habits, and society of the kings and the nobility but also in architecture and in the poetry, traditions, language, and popular beliefs of the residents. In Sicily this impact was visible in the arabesque decor and interlaced polygons that were worked into the Norman and Byzantine features of its buildings. Arab artists fashioned the mosaics, beautified interiors, and painted ceilings and walls. Arab architectural influences could also be found on the Italian mainland, in Amalfi, Pisa, Genoa, Bari, Salerno, Siena, and other cities.[61] This cannot be solely explained by the transmission of Arab culture from Sicily to other parts of the country. Strong trade relations between these cities and regions of Islam, as well as the Muslim population resettled in Italy by Frederick around 1125 (as part of his policy to suppress rebellious Muslim subjects), must also be taken into account. With respect to language, the Sicilian dialect of Italian contained about two hundred Arabic words that pertained mostly to rural objects, urban industry, clothing, diet, and law and order.[62]

Spanish culture was similarly influenced by the Arab world. In Muslim Spain there was gradually formed a homogeneous Hispano-Arabic culture which spread to areas in the northwest under Christian rule.[63] This explains the Muslim architectural features of the Iberian peninsula, the numerous words of Arabic origin in Spanish dealing with municipal administration and commercial activity, and peculiarities in Christian rites and traditions, such as images of Muhammad (*la Mahoma*) and the Virgin Mary at commemorations of the *Reconquista*.[64] Furthermore the gender of *la Mahoma* was changed to feminine, and it became the center of a cult in some localities in Valencia.

North of Italy and Spain, Islamic culture was less visible but still absorbed, particularly by the upper classes. French and German nobility had participated in the Crusades and were uncomfortably familiar with Europe's cultural inferiority to the Muslim world. They adopted bathhouses, tournaments, and coats of arms, and organized their feudal courts after those belonging to the Umayyads of Spain and the Normans of Sicily. Members of the royal courts of Christian Europe, for example, borrowed their titles from the court of Abd al-Rahman III. The Spanish caliph had his chief of cuisine; grand master of the horse; grand falconer (who superintended couriers); and other officials whose titles resembled those in the Arab world. These titles could also be found at the courts of French and German kings.[65]

Russia also felt the influence of Muslim culture. After the khans of the Golden Horde adopted Islam, the Tatars directly communicated with the principal concentrations of Islamic civilization and diffused Muslim culture among their Russian subjects. Russia's administration adjusted in order to cooperate with the Tatars; Russian folklore adopted "Tatar" (Mongol and Turkish) poetic patterns and themes, and the Russian language incorporated words and phrases borrowed from Mongol, Turkish, Persian, and Arabic. These borrowed words, as in Spanish and Italian, dealt primarily with administration, finance, trade, clothing, and cattle breeding. In addition to this "unwitting" influence, which spread gradually and almost unnoticed, the Tatars' habits, language, and ceremonies were sometimes deliberately copied. In the court of the Grand Duke Vasilii II of Moscow (1425–1462) the language of the Tatars was spoken and their clothing considered fashionable, and Vasilii invited many Tatar nobles into his service.[66]

Without fads, Islamic influence would never have reached the remotest parts of Europe. Almost anything related to the Muslim world became fashionable and was imitated on the continent at one time or another. This was evident in paintings, sculpture, ornaments, house interiors, and even in clothing and habits. By and large these were not well-informed imitations and distorted the civilization they purported to represent. Individuals were caught by some striking detail, like the Turk's turbans or wide trousers, or quality of character, like ferociousness or choler, and constructed fabulous creatures out of these impressions. This tendency could take its cue from the outward appearance of Muslim representatives in Europe (for example, the envoys of the Ottoman sultan or Persian shah) or a new product from Asia, such as a fruit or a drink, which became indissolubly associated with the Arab world. As Franco Gardini notes, the "dreams of European dreamers were filled with magic carpets and Aladdin's lamps (albeit heavily disguised) long before Galland adapted the *Thousand and One Nights* to suit ears more accustomed to the *Contes* of Perrault, and before Irving and Doré translated the courtyards, gardens, and fountains of Granada into words and images that could be grasped by Western minds."[67]

Examples of Europe's infatuation with Asia are numerous. In the fifteenth century Turks wearing huge turbans, flowing robes, or tall white headdresses were frequently included in paintings of northeastern Italy, for example, in the works of Mantegna and Carpaccio and in late Gothic painting and illumination in France, Spain, Germany, and southern Italy.[68] A Moroccan ambassador in London may have inspired Shakespeare's tragic figure of Othello; and Mozart composed his *Così fan tutte* about pseudo-Turkish lovers and included the Moor Monostatos in his most mysterious opera, *The Magic Flute*. A passion for Asia led to a whole trend in European intellectual life known as orientalism, a field devoted to all aspects of the Muslim world.[69]

When the Islamic world was culturally superior to European civilization, intercultural influence was more or less one-sided; what little the Muslims could borrow from Europeans concerned military strategy. After the Crusades, France influenced Muslim weaponry and fortification practices.[70] Europe's influence in Islam increased as it became an economic and political rival in the age of modernization. The Ottoman Empire's Tulip Period (1717–1730) inaugurated new trends in art, architecture, and habits patterned after those in Europe. Chairs and sofas began to replace traditional pillows and divans. French palaces were used as archetypes for buildings and gardens in the Ottoman capital. Turks imitated the lavish entertainments of Versailles and cultivated tulips as in Holland. Islamic architecture was also influenced by the Italian post-Renaissance style.[71]

Other changes followed these first steps toward European culture. Introduced in the 1730s, printing facilitated Muslims' familiarity with life and ideas in Europe. In the nineteenth century the reforms of the *Tanzimat*, initiated by the Ottoman sultan Abdülmejid (1839–1861), standardized European principles not only in administration and economy but also in the intellectual sphere and in the outward appearance of the sultan's subjects. Ottoman officials now visited foreign capitals in European attire. Unfamiliar with their new habiliments, they forgot to fasten their trouser buttons and inadvertently became the object of their "civilized" counterparts' mockery.

This process of Westernization differed by region of Islam. It assumed radical forms in Egypt, Iran, and Turkey under Kemal Atatürk; in other countries the impact of European culture was subtler. Although in some regions this influence penetrated nearly all spheres of society, it did not displace old traditional values based on Islam as a religion and way of life. This survived and existed alongside the new mores, fashions, and habits from the continent; it prescribed the limits of innovation and maintained a sense of communal identity.

SERVANTS, SOLDIERS, WIVES

Over the long history of their relations, Europe and Islam cooperated more than just politically, economically, and culturally, in ways that can be difficult to categorize according to the principal fields of human activity. As already noted, Christian and Muslim rulers were alike open to forming military and political alliances with the infidel, even in times of acute armed conflict, if it suited their interests. When the Ottomans invaded Europe, some local residents regarded the conquerors as a lesser evil than their oppressive landlords and supported them. And other examples persist.

Muslim rulers used Christian servants whom they regarded as reliable despite their religious affiliation. Emirs of al-Andalus frequently employed *Mozarabes* (Christians in Muslim Spain) and even gave them important appointments in their court, like the position of secretary to the emir, which was once held by

Comes, the son of Antonien. A Muslim retainer of the emir appealed to his sovereign about this violation against the basic prescriptions of Islam: "What extraordinary surprise the Abbasid caliphs in the East would experience," he wrote to the emir, "if they learned that the Umayyads in the West are obliged to confer their grand secretariat and their grand chancellery to a Christian, to Comes, son of Antonien who was himself the son of a Christian [woman] Juliana! I would like to know what has blinded you to the extent that you did not make a choice in favor of someone more noble who would lend splendor to this position and would occupy it by force of his [noble] birth."[72] The resistance of their Muslim subjects, however, did not deter Spanish emirs from using Christians and Jews at their court.

This practice was not unique to the caliphate of Cordoba. To conduct foreign affairs, Ottoman sultans increasingly relied on Greeks concentrated around the Orthodox patriarchate in the Phanar district of Istanbul. Phanariot families consolidated their power in their control of ecclesiastic establishments and their involvement in shipping, commerce, and banking. But they acquired real influence in the Ottoman hierarchy when their knowledge of foreign languages and European culture became indispensable to the Ottomans, who, in the seventeenth century, had increasingly to deal with the Habsburgs, the Poles, and Russia. In 1669 the sultan created the office of grand translator, and those who occupied it became, in reality, foreign ministers of the Ottoman Empire. The first to hold this office was Greek, though not a Phanariot. In 1673 Alexander Mavrocordatos, a young Phanariot, succeeded him and held the office until his death in 1709.[73] With this tenure the Phanariots became junior partners in the Ottoman administration. Several became *hospodars*, princes of Moldavia and Walachia, and their influence was felt across these principalities during the last three decades of the seventeenth century.

In premodern times Christians also called on the assistance of the Muslim world to realize their plans. When Frederick II of Sicily resettled his rebellious Muslim subjects at Lucera on the

Italian mainland, he employed them as advance garrisons in his struggle against the papacy. The Saracens of Lucera remained personally faithful to Frederick and demonstrated their respect for him and his relatives.[74] Likewise on the Iberian peninsula, *Mudejares*[75] (the Muslims who submitted to Christian rule) participated in military campaigns waged by Spanish Christian rulers against their foreign and domestic rivals. When the French invaded in 1285, the Valencian Muslim communities sent six hundred *Mudejar* troops to the defense of Gerona, where their fearlessness and marksmanship made them legendary. The cardinal-legate behind that French crusade complained that the king of Aragon "joined himself with Saracens" against Christendom because he "could not stand alone." This remark points up the significance of cooperation between the Muslims and Christians in Spain in the period before the *Reconquista*.[76]

Among Christians who used Muslim help against their adversaries, the most unscrupulous were the Catalans in Greece. In an attempt to conquer central Greece in 1310, a strategically important region in the eastern Mediterranean, Catalans recruited Turks and deployed them in their wars against Christian states in Thrace and Beotia. From 1312 to 1317 Catalans used Turkish mercenaries to ravage Angevin, Briennist, and Venetian territories in the Morea and on Euboea.[77] Complaints against this "unholy" cooperation reached the papal curia and resulted in the excommunication of "these senseless sons of damnation."[78] The Catalans' use of Turks against Christians led some to suspect them of being un-Christian. Yet they were not unique in employing Turkish mercenaries: the Byzantines used them in 1264 in their campaigns in the Morea, and the Franks too recruited them. Nevertheless contemporaries agreed that the Catalans stimulated the Turks to undertake their later conquests in the Balkans.

Rulers of duchies in Russia occasionally recruited Muslim Tatars to help them beat down their rival coreligionists. Beginning in the middle of the fifteenth century, with the reign of the Grand Duke Vasilii II of Moscow, Russian tsars made a policy of employing Tatars.[79] This policy was rooted in the Tatars' power over Russian lands: Moscow's grand dukes were formally vassals of the khan of the Golden Horde and their possessions were part of the khan's *ulus* or appanage, later independent principalities; consequently representatives of the ruling Mongol house could demand from Moscow territory and a share of the tribute due to the duke. Moscow rulers exploited this requirement to their personal advantage and used their loyal Tatars to deal with Tatar hordes.

As the grand duke's power grew and was consolidated, his authority also increased. This induced a growing number of Tatar nobles to pledge their allegiance to him. In exchange, Moscow's tsar granted them towns and lands from his state. Many towns around Moscow were temporarily transferred to Tatar khans and sultans: Serpukhov, Zvenigorod, Kashira, Yuriev, and others. Among them the most famous town was Kasimov, which was under Tatar authority and inhabited by a Muslim Tatar population until the early nineteenth century. Vasilii II gave Kasimov to Kasim, a rival of the khan of Kazan, who, accompanied by his retinue, entered the grand duke's service sometime before 1446 and assisted Vasilii in his many campaigns against domestic and foreign adversaries.[80]

The Russian tsar even employed his Tatar vassals against the khans of the Golden Horde who sought to retrieve their authority over Muscovy, which was growing increasingly independent. Later, under Ivan the Terrible, the khans of Kasimov became a tool in the Russian tsar's struggle against the khans of Kazan and Astrakhan, the two most powerful khanates remaining after the Golden Horde disintegrated. Before Ivan captured Kazan in 1552, the khans of Kasimov were involved in a struggle for power there as candidates for the throne of this khanate promoted by Moscow.[81] Later the Kasimov Tatars participated in the tsar's military campaigns in Livonia and against the Poles and the Crimean khanate and served as Russia's envoys to the independent Tatar hordes that had migrated to the country's borders.[82] Appreciating their services, Ivan IV made the khans of Kasimov "tsars." This gave them a position in the court above the most noble of Russian boyars.[83]

The cooperation of the Kasimov Tatars gave Muscovy's rulers political and military advantages. A Muslim principality in Russia provided them with considerable leverage in their communications with the Ottoman Empire, especially after the conquest of two khanates in Kazan and Astrakhan and the gradual advance against other Muslim territories in the northern Caucasus and along the coast of the Black Sea. When Ottoman sultans met with Russian envoys in Istanbul and complained about the oppression of the Muslims in Muscovy, the envoys replied: "You complain that the Mohammedan faith is oppressed in Russia, but who is oppressed by us? In the heartlands of Moscow's possessions, in Kasimov, are mosques and Muslim monuments."[84] Foreign travelers observed Kasimov's mosques as late as 1692,[85] and conversions of Kasimov's rulers to Christianity, though not unheard of in the history of this vassal principality,[86] were usually the result of personal choice rather than Russian imposition.

In the second half of the seventeenth century, when Kasimov's khanate was liquidated and the Russian tsars became powerful enough to manage without the assistance of Tatar troops, Russification and conversion (of the local population) became a policy of the Moscow authorities. The possessions of Kasimov's "tsars" became the Russian tsar's, and the estates of Muslim Tatars were conveyed to their Christian relatives.[87] Nevertheless Russia's cooperation with the Tatars during the formative years of the Russian state was long felt in various spheres of life. Some of the best boyar families of Moscow were of Tatar origin. Among them were the Godunovs, the family of King Boris, who occupied the throne of Moscow from 1598 until his death in 1605; the Veliaminov-Zernovs, whose scion wrote a fundamental work on Kasimov and its rulers in the nineteenth century; the Saburovs, the Bakhmetievs, and many others. All in all, according to the Russian historian N. P. Zagoskin's calculations, 156 Russian noble families were of Tatar and other Asian origin.[88] The historian Nikolai Karamzin and the poet Gavriil Derzhavin, the writer Ivan Turgenev and the philosopher Petr Chaadaev were descendants of representatives from the ruling class of the Golden Horde who were assimilated by a process of matrimonial alliances with the Russians. Famous families of Russia's high aristocracy, such as the princely Urusovs and Yusupovs, were direct and proud descendants of Tatar nobility. Such examples are endless.

Russia's history demonstrates that intermarriages were, at least among nobility, relatively widespread and served not only as a means of cementing Russian and Tatar political and military cooperation but as a vehicle of mutual influence. With a wife of different origin—even if she had to convert, which was almost always the case in premodern times—came new habits, traditions, and perspectives which had a good chance of taking root in the husband's social milieu, especially when family alliances had become a common practice. Connections between intermarriages and their impact on other spheres of society are often difficult to establish, because we know about matrimonial alliances primarily in the ruling classes, though a few facts about average people have been preserved. A few cases may show how this phenomenon shaped the relationship between European and Islamic civilizations.

Nowhere was the impact of intermarriage so visible as in Muslim Spain where the preference of Andalusian emirs and caliphs for concubines of European origin—Frankish, Saxon, or Slavic—left its mark on their offspring's appearance. Umayyads born with blue eyes and blond hair looked very different from their subjects who came to Spain from the Middle East and North Africa.[89] The European appearance of Spanish rulers struck travelers from other Muslim lands who described this phenomenon in their books and journals. Andalusian caliphs' choice of concubine-wives was not limited to slaves. Often Christian sovereigns offered their daughters to caliphs in order to cement political or military alliances with the powerful leader of the caliphate of Cordoba. Charlemagne, according to one Arab chronicler, proposed a truce with the emir of Cordoba, Abd al-Rahman I (d. 788), in which he offered a matrimonial alliance between the Carolingians and the Umayyads. Abd al-Rahman, so the chronicle goes, favorably responded to the proposed truce.[90] Spanish emirs were not unique in their preference for Christian wives. At the opposite end of the Mediterranean in the twelfth century, Seljuk Muslim royalty willingly married daughters of Greek Christian aristocracy. Kilidj II Arslan had a Christian wife who mothered the sultan Ghiyath al-Din I Kaykhusraw. Ghiyath himself married a Greek woman of the aristocratic family of Maurozomes. The family's Christian lineage was strengthened in the middle of the thirteenth century when at least two of Ghiyath al-Din II Kaykhusraw's sons had Christian mothers. Although Greek and Georgian mothers bore the Seljuk sultans, the story of their own intermarriage with Christian women remains incomplete.[91] The Byzantine emperors continued to form matrimonial alliances with Muslim rulers in order to secure their power against the pressure of adversaries in Asia Minor and the Balkans. Andronikus III (the grandson of Andronikus II, whom he dethroned in 1328) reached a rapprochement with Özbek, the khan of the Golden Horde, by giving him his daughter in marriage. She became known as Khatun Bayalun and had to accept Islam. Their marriage, however, was brief: around 1333 Bayalun was permitted to visit her father in Constantinople and never returned.[92]

Özbek is related to another inauspicious marriage, this time between his sister and Prince Yuri of Moscow. Following challenges by Prince Michael, Yuri's adversary, for supremacy in Russia, Özbek summoned Yuri to the Horde. Using money he had collected in Novgorod, Yuri was able to shower the khan and his retinue with presents. He spent several years in the Horde, and Özbek gave him his sister Konchak in marriage. She was christened and received her baptismal name Agatha. After Özbek made Yuri grand duke of Vladimir, then the highest title in all of Russia, Yuri went to Tver in order to suppress the resistance of his rival, Prince Michael. But Michael defeated Yuri and captured his Tatar wife Agatha, while Yuri himself was able to escape to Novgorod. Eventually Agatha died in captivity in

Tver, and Michael was tried by the supreme court of the Golden Horde for not taking proper care of the khan's sister.[93]

Evidence of Christian women in the harems of the Ottoman sultans is also substantial. Although their influence on the Ottoman court and on the political and cultural life of the empire remains obscure, one fact testifies to their notable presence: the mother of Sultan Murad III (1574–1595) was of noble Venetian descent. Born in Paros in 1525 where her father was governor, she was captured by Barbarossa in 1537 and offered to the sultan Selim II. She became a devout Muslim and Selim's favorite wife. Despite her distance and conversion, her feelings toward Venice remained warm, and thanks to her influence over her son Murad she foiled the Ottoman's plans against the Serenissima.[94]

More is known about the non-Muslim grand viziers of the Ottoman Empire and their influence on the decisions of the sultan and his court. Although most of them, having converted, became part and parcel of the Islamic world, they did not entirely forget their ancestral lands. Sometimes their actions contradicted the interests of their new home country.

The Christian presence in the Ottoman court was striking. The issue of *devşirme* and the role of Christian renegades in the life of the empire have been previously noted. In the Porte's governing circles, between 1453 and 1623, only five of the forty-seven grand viziers were of Turkish origin.[95] Not one of the sultan's advisers and administrative aides was a native-born Muslim. As one historian put it, "The net result of this remarkable system was that a great Muslim empire was based upon Christian brawn and Christian brain."[96]

Thus the history of the two civilizations provides ample evidence of cooperation, mutual influence, and peaceful coexistence. With the passage of time, points of contact between the two worlds increased, primarily because of technological advances in communication and travel. The history of relations between Europe and Islam provides an instructive backdrop for evaluating their relationship in the final decades of the twentieth century and in the dawn of the twenty-first.

SEVEN

Europe and Islam in the Modern World

In the twentieth century European and Islamic civilizations both experienced substantial, historically unprecedented change. In order to present an objective picture of their current relations, and to anticipate how they may relate in the future, we must understand how their relationship was changed by modernization and globalization.

Economic, political, social, demographic, and other transformations relating to the processes of modernization and globalization have had a strong impact on Europe and Islam; these processes have determined their place in the world and how they interact with it. With respect to relations between these two civilizations, the most important event of the last several decades has been the establishment of Muslim communities in western Europe and the growth of European communities that adhere to the religion of Islam—with inhabitants whose lives are structured by traditions and habits alien to the civilization that flourished on the continent.

As already described, Muslims had for many centuries settled in Europe and had made a cultural and social impact on their surroundings. Yet only in the Balkans and Russia did their communities survive intact until the modern period. Adherents of Islam were either forcibly driven from the continent or went voluntarily into exile to Muslim countries (according to the prescriptions of their faith), or they ceased to be Muslims and were assimilated. Visits by Islamic merchants, ambassadors, and captives who became slaves or were ransomed did not change the overall picture. And Muslims themselves generally avoided settling in Europe's alien environment. Muslim jurists disapproved but did not forbid the faithful from living under a Christian government. But for the most rigorous, an authentic Muslim life was impossible under Christian rule, and strict followers of the Prophet therefore never settled on the continent.[1] Hence for centuries the Muslim world had virtually no presence in Europe.

Small Muslim communities first appeared in Europe in the eighteenth century. About a thousand Muslim soldiers are said to have served in the Prussian cavalry, and it soon became necessary to establish a Muslim cemetery in Berlin, where a mosque was built in 1866.

In the British Isles, Muslims first settled because of British commercial and colonial involvement in India. With the growth of the British Empire, indigenous populations from London's various colonial possessions also increased in England, and this was accelerated in 1869 by the opening of the Suez Canal. By the end of the nineteenth century the first mosque had been built at Woking (1889), and prayer halls, Muslim schools, evening classes, hostels, libraries, and periodicals had been established in various parts of England.[2] Pre-twentieth century Muslim communities in other European countries were likewise an outcome of their respective colonial activities, but nowhere were these communities populous and stable enough to speak of a substantial Muslim population in Europe.

Over the course of the twentieth century this situation changed markedly. Muslim populations steadily increased in countries where knowledge of Islam was largely constrained to the memoirs of European travelers to the "Orient" and to newspaper stories about the exotic mores and habits of those who lived on the opposite side of the Mediterranean and on the remote shores of the South Seas. In the eyes of a European audience, these anecdotes and articles vividly painted the strangeness of the inhabitants of Muslim lands. And now Muslims had settled in their very neighborhoods, startling them by their different appearance and clothes and especially by their odd behavior and customs. The number of Muslims in Europe, rising dramatically throughout the century, shifted the frontier of Islam from the opposite side of the Mediterranean into the heart of Europe. By 1990 between seven and ten million Muslims lived in Europe. And their numbers continue to rise.[3]

The primary cause of this migration was economic. In the twentieth century Europe's growth far exceeded that of the Muslim world, and high living standards in Europe relative to Islam spurred people to pack their belongings and find their way in a foreign land. Despite little promise of more than menial employment, Europe offered a chance to prosper. And Muslims were prepared to sacrifice what little they had in their mother country for prospects of a better life for themselves and their children.

Before World War I, migrant laborers from Islam had already crossed over to the continent. In France, Algerians and Tunisians worked in olive oil businesses around Marseilles and in factories and mines in other parts of the country. Yet the most intensive migrations began after 1945, driven by the postwar industrial boom. In the 1960s Europe entered a decade of the "most concentrated immigration of people seeking work ever seen in its history."[4] Despite Britain's efforts in 1962 to obstruct immigration, and the efforts of other countries in the early 1970s, it continued, albeit at a much lower level.

Economic incentives were not the only cause of the migration. Developments in the Middle East, particularly in Lebanon and Iran, as well as the continuing dislocation of the Palestinians, also led Muslims to migrate to western Europe.

Muslims were not alone in moving to Europe in the twentieth century. Non-Muslims from India, Africa, Indonesia, and the Caribbean islands joined them. Yet Muslims attracted the most attention and became the subject of debates and clashes in European society, particularly in recent years. There are several reasons for this, not least of which is the strong tendency on the part of Muslims to assert and emphasize their distinctiveness from others. To Europeans, their rites, dress, and gender roles seemed strange, and their pride may have nurtured an anti-Muslim environment.

A growing Muslim presence in Europe was most visibly demonstrated by the growing number of mosques built with the approval of European governments in their respective countries. In 1963, 13 mosques were registered with the registrar general of Great Britain; between 1966 and the mid-1970s new mosques were registered at a rate of 7 per year; 1975 was marked by the appearance of 18 new mosques; and in succeeding years never fewer than 17 were registered, and sometimes as many as 30. When 1985 drew to a close, 338 mosques had been registered.[5] Other countries evidenced a similar tendency. Paris's first mosque was built in 1926; by 1994 Paris held 5 "mosquées cathedrale"[6] and more were scattered around the country. Italy now has 60 mosques and 100 to 120 halls of prayer, though their actual number is supposed to be greater because new ones are built more quickly than censuses can track them.[7] Mosques became the center of Muslim communities, and many Islamic organizations rose up around them.

In European countries with significant Muslim populations, organizations were established to defend the rights of those of the Islamic faith; to represent their interests in national affairs; to involve them constructively in the social and political life of their new country; and to coordinate the activities of different and ethnically heterogeneous Muslim communities. Over half the Muslims in Britain came from the Indian subcontinent; of these, half came from Pakistan. Muslims also emigrated from West Africa, Arabia, Malaysia, Cyprus, and Turkey.[8]

Immigrant Muslims in France also had diverse national origins, and the history of the composition of French Muslim communities reflects different phases of twentieth-century immigration.[9] These communities comprised young Franco-Maghrebians and Maghrebians of Algeria, Tunisia, and Morocco; Black Africans, Turks, French Muslims (harkis), Pakistanis, and other nationalities. And in recent years more than fifty thousand French have converted to Islam.[10]

Other countries in the European Union also have heterogeneous Muslim populations. In 1990 Switzerland had 65,149 Muslims of Turkish nationality and 55,453 Muslims of ex-Yugoslavian nationality; together they made up about 80 percent of Switzerland's total Muslim population. In the same year 8,172 Muslims of various Middle Eastern nationalities, as well as groups from Asian countries and south Saharan Africa immigrated to Switzerland.[11]

The interests of these different populations were not uniform. Among individuals of differing educational backgrounds and expectations, Islam was the only factor that united them. Muslim organizations sought to represent these divergent interests at various levels: communal, regional, and national. In Britain in 1970, a national organization, the Union of Muslim Organizations of the UK and Eire (UMO), was established. Although its founding seemed premature—most British Muslims were preoccupied with their immediate environment, their communal or professional needs—the countrywide coordination was gradually recognized.[12] The same process took place in France, where many national associations were established in the 1980s, such as the FNMF (Fédération Nationale des Musulmans de France) and the UOIF (Union des Organisations Islamiques de France).[13] In Belgium, which in 1974 became the first western European country formally to recognize Islam, a committee organized by Islamic students and Albanian refugees in the late 1950s consolidated its powers and became the first national organization for Muslims, the Islamic Cultural Center (ICC). In 1976 a nonprofit corporation called Islamic Culture and Religion was established to challenge the ICC's monopoly on relations between the Belgian Muslim community and the government.[14]

Mosques and Muslim associations established in the latter half of the twentieth century have increased Islam's visibility across Europe, in culture and architecture (the emergence of minarets, Islamic cemeteries, and markets and boutiques selling specialties from the Arab world) but also in economic and political life. In France in the 1980s the question of Islam moved to the center of political debates: conflicts in the car industry (1983–1984); protests against Salman Rushdie's *Satanic Verses* (1988), which Muslim authorities charged profaned Islam and derided its Prophet; the Scarf ("foulard") affair (1989), involving demonstrations in support of the right of Muslim girls to wear veils in schools and colleges; and the Gulf War (1991) punctuated these disputes. The Gulf War in particular inspired Muslims to protest, and they demonstrated their allegiance to Islam with actions that bordered on terrorism and nearly led to civil war (for example, the Folembray affair in August 1994, when twenty "Islamists" were expelled from France; the new Scarf affairs of September 1994 and Muslim demonstrations with placards stating "Vive la France musulmane"—All Hail Muslim France).[15] These and similar events across Europe made the question of Islam a leading political and social priority. And it became clear that a balanced and positive response to Islamic concerns had to be based on an understanding of Muslim life in Europe and of the roots of their grievances and actions.

For Muslim immigrants who came to Europe in search of a better life and who had to adapt to a hostile environment, Islam became a guidepost, providing a sense of shared moral orientation. Despite their ethnic differences, it brought Muslims together in defense of their rights. Their embrace of Islam did not mean a greater religiosity or piety; rather, as authorities have noted, "particular identities often become salient when the members of that group feel collectively threatened."[16] Islam offered Muslims in Europe refuge from rejection, discrimination, and racism, and a sense of shared identity. Rites, dress, and gender roles—among the most visible means of exhibiting the distinctiveness of Islam—became the most apparent features of Europe's Muslim communities.[17] Islam also kept immigrant Muslims connected, socially and spiritually, with their countries of origin and with the whole of the Muslim world. Together a sense of community and contact with the Muslim world made Europe a more familiar and comfortable environment in which to live.

The challenges faced by Muslim newcomers to Europe simply reinforce their need to exhibit the distinctiveness of their identity. Muslims comprise a small minority in a society in which Christian cultural, social, and pedagogic traditions, despite an outward appearance of secularism and tolerance, are strongly held. Muslims must therefore find their way through alien structures.[18] They must choose between succumbing to these influences and being assimilated into a Christian society, or resisting it by embracing their specific ethnic, cultural, and religious heritage, by being involved in a broader community for which Islam is the common social and spiritual denominator. Although some European politicians and thinkers may prefer assimilation to resistance, wanting to preserve European values and traditions against the assault of alien cultures—and, indeed, some Muslims choose assimilation in order to become fully integrated into their new cultural environment—still, many immigrants (not only Muslim) for whom Europe is now home refuse to be assimilated.

The rise of a new generation of children born to immigrant families in Europe, contrary to expectations, has not alleviated this dilemma. In some countries, like Britain, they constitute the majority of the ethnic minority's population.[19] Whereas the first generation of immigrants has often been described as being "between two cultures," those who were (or are) born in Europe, though they live in homes and communities dominated by their parents' culture, are more familiar with European society: they are educated in European schools and interact daily with the outside world. Yet surveys show that the majority of this young generation are reluctant to sever its link with their parents' society. They remain attached to their parents' way of life, accept arranged marriages and gender roles, and adapt themselves to the environing European society only as much as is needed in order to function within it.[20] Their attachment to Muslim tradition is reinforced by the unwillingness of European society to accept ethnic minorities as equal partners in many spheres of life. This tension has led to a growing number of disaffected young people whose expectations of social and political equality in their home countries have been disappointed and who feel estranged by European society. It is precisely these individuals who are targeted by radical activist movements in need of recruits.

Illegal immigrants also provide fundamentalist movements with a source of young radicals. Despite barriers created by European legislation, their number continues to grow. Unlike legal immigrants, illegals have little access to the social and economic privileges of the countries in which they live. Excluded from the processes of integration, they threaten to constitute a social underclass in Europe. With neither family nor friends, nor a legal means of earning an income, illegal immigrants become easy prey for criminal and radical organizations that recruit them for their illicit plans.

Muslim communities are not the only ones in Europe to have developed radical elements. Yet given the "overwhelmingly Muslim character of the non-European immigration,"[21] and the contact Muslim immigrants maintain with the world of Islam—either directly or indirectly through radical organizations acting on the continent—more Muslim immigrants are involved in acts of terrorism than any other ethnic minority.

No European country has been spared from the wave of terror that Europeans associate with Islam. During the 1980s France witnessed a string of violent acts related to Lebanon's civil war: hostages were taken and others attacked in connection with the imprisonment of alleged Muslim terrorists; in the Netherlands a group of Moluccan extremists hijacked a train; Sweden confronted terrorism related to Kurdish exile groups, especially in connection with their involvement in the assassination of Prime Minister Olof Palme; and whatever group(s) orchestrated the Berlin bombings of 1986 and the Lockerbie disaster of 1988, for Europeans they became linked with Muslim terrorism. This association was further confirmed by the tragic events of September 11, 2001: those who hijacked the planes lived in Europe and studied in European universities, and had many accomplices on the continent before moving to the United States. Consequently Europeans now feel threatened by their Muslim neighbors, who defy the established order with their pretension of having a superior role in the life of the society, who despise and seek to replace modern society's foundational values—democracy, liberalism, secularism, freedom of cultural and personal expression—with the norms and requirements of Islam. Not surprisingly, Europeans invoke the idea of a "clash" of civilizations in order to justify their fears.

Scholars and experts have written at length in an effort to dispel the fear of Islam that has been generated by the spread of terrorism. In particular, they have tried to dissociate Islamic fundamentalism from the terrorism practiced by some Muslim radical organizations; the latter neither represent mainstream Islamic tradition nor are approved by most Muslims. Furthermore authorities have persuasively shown that a network of Muslim extremist organizations—with a single center that coordinates their activities and regularly disseminates orders—does not and could not exist. Islam has always been as diverse as Christianity, with many (often competing) schools of thought. Over the course of the last two centuries, this diversity has been further complicated by modern ideas of nationalism and national interests powerfully interjected into the notion of *ummah*, making the ideal of unity even more illusory. Thus the establishment of such a central authority seems entirely implausible. Although Muslim European movements and associations are more than likely connected with their radical and militant counterparts in Middle Eastern and North African countries—the Muslim Brotherhood in Egypt or the Islamic Salvation Front in Algeria—they often pursue their goals by peaceful means, for example by corresponding with government authorities in Europe to resolve problems associated with immigration.

Not the religious or ideological outlook of Islam but rather social and economic factors—such as marginalization, inequality, and racial and other forms of discrimination, which Muslims have suffered acutely—explain their violent protests. This fact should compel governments to find ways of better integrating Muslims into European society, ways that do not reject the distinctive cultural and social features of Islam but cultivate and incorporate them into Europe's multi-cultural environment.

Yet European nations have no consistent policy for integrating Muslims. Governments of different countries experiment with various measures in trying to resolve problems of Islam's representation in society, such as in education and municipal management. A growing young Muslim population underscores the fact that a failure to implement these measures quickly may exacerbate already difficult minority-majority relations. A 1981 British census showed that in households of Pakistani origin, 90,000 of a total of fewer than 300,000 individuals were between the ages of five and fifteen; of all ten-year age groups, this one was the largest. Among Bangladeshis and Indians the situation is similar,[22] and the trend continues. This means that if problems of social and economic discrimination, inequality, and unemployment are not resolved, neither radicalism nor terrorism will flag for want of recruits—for the young are the most sensitive to injustices and most responsive to radical slogans—and Europe's peace will be more seriously threatened than it is today.

One of the chief obstacles to Europe's policy-making process with regard to Islam is the European public's prejudiced, distorted, and historically rooted image of Islam and its adherents. European society, with its strong Christian heritage, still cannot bring itself to incorporate a religion and culture that for centuries was held to be an enemy of Christendom. Referring to Spain, a country well acquainted with and even indebted to Islamic culture and tradition, the scholar Montserrat Abumalham notes: "Nobody raises their voice for the nuns to give up their habits and wimples while they cry out and are shocked by a Muslim woman wearing a veil."[23] Indeed, Christianity is such

an integral part of Europeans' life and conscience that even people who profess to be secular or atheist overlook the fact that
most national holidays in Europe are also religious occasions,
and that while Christmas and Easter are decreed as holidays in
most of western Europe, no such treatment is accorded to Ra-
madan, not even at the municipal level.

ISLAM AFTER THE SOVIET UNION

In eastern Europe the situation is different. The former Soviet
Union happened to have one of the largest Muslim populations
in the world (in the 1980s, forty million Soviet citizens were of
Muslim ancestry). Although vitiated by years of Soviet oppression and propaganda, Islam remained powerful in terms of cultural heritage and tradition. Studying the role of Islam in the Soviet Union, Martha Brill Olcott wrote in the early 1980s: "For
most Soviet Muslims, the identification with Islam is an attenu-
ated one. Almost all the Kazakhs, Kirghiz, Uzbeks, Tatars,
Bashkir, Azeris, Tadzhik, Turkmen, and North Caucasian people would affirm that they were Muslims; this response, however, would not imply that they were either practitioners of the
faith or conversant in the doctrinal beliefs of Islam. In the Soviet Union it is possible to be both an atheist and a 'Muslim,'
because to claim to be a Muslim merely means that one is proud
of having a Muslim heritage."[24]

Religious education ground to a halt when the *medreses*
were closed by Soviet authorities. Their efforts to prevent Soviet
Muslims from making contacts with the outside world led, on
the one hand, to the emergence of a so-called unofficial Islam—
a simplistic faith upheld by Sufi holy men who lacked a religious
education and usually emphasized not dogma but rituals
strongly influenced by local (often pagan) beliefs and traditions.
On the other hand, the Soviet Union's Muslim community was
insulated from the rise of fundamentalism and Islamic radicalism that occurred in other Muslim countries: Soviet society was
a closed society, and there were no economic or social factors to

stimulate an Islamic revivalism. Unlike in Turkey, Iran, or Egypt, one could scarcely talk about the failure of modernization to eliminate the backwardness of Islamic civilization and to lay the foundations for its successful competition with the West. The situation in the Soviet Union was different: Moscow stimulated the development of modern industry and agriculture in Muslim regions and republics (particularly in Central Asia and the Caucasus) where patriarchal and feudal regimes had hitherto allowed only minor innovations and improvements. Although in developing these regions Moscow had to defy local interests in order to satisfy the needs of the Soviet economy, generally the popular reaction was favorable, especially in view of the efforts of Soviet authorities to improve living conditions: health care and education were made accessible, unemployment was minimized, and the necessities of life were more or less satisfied. Therefore some observers concluded that the worldwide Islamic revival would have "little direct impact on Soviet Muslims."[25]

Yet the dissolution of the Soviet Union and the establishment in its place of independent states made these predictions obsolete. Secular authoritarian regimes in the new predominantly Muslim states of Central Asia and the Caucasus were willing to use Islam, the ideological and intellectual mainstay of the local populations after the Soviet system collapsed, to consolidate their power. The new republics established official and unofficial contacts with the rest of the Muslim world, ending their virtual isolation and opening themselves to ideas and tendencies in the contemporary world of Islam. Lastly, contemporary Central Asia has shown that it is highly receptive to religious ideas, including those expounded by radical and extremist movements and organizations.

Why did Islamic radicalism spread across the former Soviet Muslim republics of Central Asia? For one thing, these republics inherited from the Soviet regime a civil society unable to adopt and implement democratic and liberal values; this aided the establishment and consolidation of authoritarian regimes that successfully utilize indigenous tribal and clan traditions to sustain citizens' obedient regard for authorities and patriarchal rules. Moreover poor economic and social conditions, caused by the rupture of economic links between different parts of the Soviet Union, led to widespread unemployment and indigence, and thus to widespread dissatisfaction and resentment. Unemployment is particularly high among young people who are quick to protest, often violently. In Uzbekistan in 2000, for instance, 59 percent of the unemployed were sixteen to thirty years old. But even the employed live on the edge of poverty because their wages seldom exceed thirty U.S. dollars per month.[26]

Ethnic and tribal rivalries and border disputes, another legacy of the past, also exacerbate the situation in the Central Asian republics. No republic in the region is ethnically and nationally homogeneous; instead various nationalities live side by side: a strong proportion of Uzbeks have settled in Tajikistan, Kyrgyzstan, and Turkmenistan; Kazakhs live in Turkmenistan and Uzbekistan; and Turkmens inhabit border areas of Uzbekistan. The situation is further complicated by tribal differences and Soviet nationality policies—with their asymmetrical ethnic and territorial borders, large-scale transfers of nonindigenous peoples, and, in some cases, partiality toward ethnic minorities with political power. Under these circumstances only transnational identities, including religious ones, can serve to consolidate a society.

Finally, the Soviet policy of using Communist and atheistic propaganda to diminish the attraction of Islam has paved the way for the spread of Islamic radicalism in the former Soviet republics. In the post-Soviet era, local clergy who adhere to traditional views on Islam and its role in society cannot block these radical influences because they have discredited themselves as collaborators with Soviet authorities or with those who now rule.

In light of these factors it is no surprise that the population finds Islamist movements that promise a just social and economic order appealing. Local governments' repression of Islamists or their supporters radicalizes Islamic movements and creates conditions favorable to the support of radical ideas. And bitter relations between Central Asian states further complicate the situation, for they make it difficult to implement a comprehensive, coherent set of policies to attack the social and economic sources of Islamic militancy. A 1999 incident in the Batken region of Kyrgyzstan illustrates the failure of Central Asian authorities to overcome their differences in order to contain the spread of terrorism: an Islamic movement of Uzbekistan forces crossed over into Kyrgyz from Tajikistan and kidnaped the commander of troops from the ministry of the interior along with a group of Japanese geologists.[27]

Other powers that pursue their own foreign policy goals in the region have a strong influence on the rise of the Islamic movement. The war in Afghanistan encouraged groups and governments abroad—Pakistan, Iran, Saudi Arabia, and the United Arab Emirates—to consolidate their positions in Central Asia. Since Pakistan and Saudi Arabia lacked ethnic, linguistic, and cultural links to the region, they relied on Islam to advance their policies there. Saudis were especially active in promoting Wahhabism as a weapon against Hanafi—a traditionally strong school of thought in Central Asia which promotes a flexible interpretation of the relation between religious norms and reality. The involvement of these states in the region has helped spread an alien and more militant version of Islam; they have also trained and armed Muslim militants.[28]

Russia also has interests in the region. Moscow perceives instability in Central Asian republics as a threat to its southern borders. After the dissolution of the Soviet Union, a fragmentation occurred among the states and alliance systems in the Islamic crescent that during the cold war served as a barrier between opposing blocs of states in Asia.[29] To prevent this fragmentation from threatening Russian territorial integrity and domestic tranquility, Moscow tried to recover its position as the dominant military power in the Caucasus and Central Asia and formed a Russian-led alliance that included former Soviet republics. On May 15, 1992, the heads of six states—the Russian

Federation, Kazakhstan, Kyrgyzstan, Tajikistan, Uzbekistan, and Armenia—signed the Collective Security Treaty. The pact fulfilled Russia's objective to remain a military leader in Central Asia and the Caucasus. Azerbaijan, though not initially a signatory to the treaty, joined at the prompting of Azerbaijan's newly elected president Heydar Aliev, who also brought the country into the Commonwealth of Independent States (CIS). In July 1992 Turkmenistan also joined the alliance, having settled on a package of military agreements that gave Russia a strong presence in the republic.

Despite these efforts to secure stability, the region has remained volatile, and Moscow has frequently had to reconsider its policy, as in May 1999 when Uzbekistan withdrew from the Collective Security Treaty. Yet Russia has always attempted to retain its military dominance in the region by whatever means. Some conservative circles in Moscow, considering their country's security interests, prefer authoritarian regimes in Central Asia to their unpredictable Islamic opposition. But Russia has not been averse to threatening the use of Islamic extremism and terrorism in order to pressure Uzbekistan and other countries of the region into agreeing to a regional security framework dominated by Moscow. The Taliban's victories in Afghanistan in the latter half of the 1990s served this end: alarmed by the bloodshed in neighboring Afghanistan, Central Asian states heightened military security and agreed on the increased presence of Russian troops in the region.[30]

In light of these political and military maneuverings, Russian authorities may have realized that suppressing Islamic opposition in Central Asia will not solve that region's problems. On the contrary, draconian methods of suppressing Islamic opposition (for that matter, any opposition) may lead to a situation in which, according to one journalist, "religious extremism becomes the only ideology of the opposition, in which all others, such as nationalism and pan-Turkism, would be buried."[31] For evidence of such development one need only look to the effects of policies of extreme secularism and the suppression of Islamic opposition in Central Asia, especially in Uzbekistan under Islam Karimov. Perhaps it was to avoid this that Russia moderated the 1997 peace settlement reached in Moscow between the Tajik government and the Islamic opposition.

Russia's foreign policy is determined not only by geopolitical considerations and its desire to be a superpower. Russia recognizes the danger of spreading radicalism and extremism among its own Muslim population. Russia's Muslim community remains large despite the disintegration of the Soviet Union: in 1992 roughly 12 million citizens of Islamic heritage resided in the Russian Federation; of these nearly 800,000 lived in Moscow.[32] This number continues to grow because Muslim families tend to be large and Muslims continue to immigrate to Russia from former Soviet republics. Muslims form the majority of the population in the Volga district—inhabited by Tatars and Bashkirs, whose Islamic heritage dates to the early second millennium—and in the North Caucasian republics where for centuries Muslims lived side by side with Christians.

As in other former Soviet republics, in Russia Islam filled the vacuum created by the collapse of communism by reuniting people with their historical and cultural roots. Its revival went hand in hand with a growing sense of national self-identity and the desire to carve out a distinct cultural niche in the Russian Federation. Yet Islamic revivals differed from region to region: for Muslim Tatars—who always occupied dominant positions in Russia's Muslim community and exerted a strong religious influence on Islamic populations in other regions—Islam has become one of three fundamental spiritual principles (Turkism and nationalism are the other two) that define the public self-consciousness of the nation.[33] Yet not all Tatars are Muslim; many are Christian (the so-called Kryashens), and though they share a linguistic, historical, and cultural heritage with Muslim Tatars,[34] they are opposed to the privileged position of Islam in Tatarstan and emphasize other elements of Tatar self-identity.

Despite these divisions, Islam continues to dominate the political and cultural life of the Tatar republic, though it is regarded more as an ideology and symbol than as a faith and everyday practice. According to some observers, Islam's revival after the collapse of communism has not substantially altered popular attitudes because it has not led to a better knowledge of Islamic principles and a revised system of child-rearing. The great number of Muslim husbands whose wives have converted them to Christianity also proves that, for the majority, Islam is essential neither to their moral outlook nor to their daily practices. In several towns of Tatarstan (for example, Naberezhnye Chelny) every third family is mixed.[35] In the Tatar republic and neighboring territories, a revival of Islam is only just beginning; for the moment Islam mostly serves as an ideological tool in the hands of the clergy and the political elite by which to mobilize the population. Its use as a tool and an ideology, as well as the flexible policy of Tatarstan's republican authorities inside the republic and in their dealings with Moscow, may account for how little influence fundamentalism and radical movements have there.[36]

In regions of the North Caucasus the situation is different, with respect both to the role of Islam in local life and to the spread of fundamentalism and radicalism. Compared to the Volga region, Islam came very recently to the North Caucasus, yet it has been embraced with more energy owing to local history, traditions, and mentality. Blunders in Moscow's policies toward this stormy region also add to Islam's special role here: Islam is not used to assert a particular identity vis-à-vis other creeds but is treated as a symbol and used to express nationalist feelings.

In the Northern Caucasus, as in other regions and countries, Islam is not monolithic. Traditional movements continue to play an important role there. Nevertheless poor economic and social conditions, which have persisted since the collapse of communism, as well as the Soviet Union's use of ideological pressure and political policies to weaken the grip of Islam, have made the region vulnerable to radical versions of Islam and have made it increasingly possible for foreign Islamic trends to replace other religions that historically have existed there.[37] Policies of the local political elites promote this trend: struggling to obtain power and advantage in their dealings with Moscow, they utilize popular feelings of nationalism and dissatisfaction with the existing situation, as well as religion (especially politicized religions like Wahhabism), to mobilize the masses. As in earlier times, Islam has been used in the Northern Caucasus as a powerful tool for pursuing objectives that have nothing to do with the Islamic faith.

The case of Chechnya well illustrates the use of Islam as a tool to fulfill political ambitions. Here the local Muslim community and the state have been openly armed rivals throughout the last decade of the twentieth century, and there is no sign of waning hostilities. Several factors contribute to this situation: the Chechens' history of war against Russian imperialism; their tradition of "raiding," which Shamil himself called "banditry" and which recently criminalized the war and transformed Chechnya into a haven for organized crime;[38] the fundamentalist and activist Sufi brotherhoods of Naqshbandiiya and Qadiriyya, generally known as "muridism" (followers who give unquestioning support to their religious leaders); Chechen political leaders' inability to create effective state institutions and an army (the military, now overseen by General Dudaev and his successors, is an anarchic gathering of informal groups: they lack a hierarchy of rank and responsibility, formal training, formal commanders, and formal rules); and ineffective and inconsistent Russian policies in the region, which over the last several years preferred armed solutions to ideological, political, and administrative conflicts.[39]

All these factors aggravated the issue of Islam in Chechnya. Neither General Dudaev nor his successor Colonel Maskhadov had been a regularly practicing Muslim before the war. Dudaev initially ruled out the creation of an "Islamic state" as a solution to the problem of Chechnya.[40] Despite the growing insistence on Islam over the course of the conflict, it was a tool for mobilizing and disciplining the Chechen people, and a symbol of opposition rather than a sincere devotion. Very few Chechen "fighters for the faith" possess a considered understanding of the norms of Islam; fewer still can read the Koran in its original form, as the religion of Islam requires. The growing strength of Islam, especially its radical versions in Chechnya and in North Caucasian regions, owes a great deal to the Middle East's financial support and to the arrival of Wahhabis, radical Islamists with links to the Middle East and Afghanistan.[41] Their influence and involvement in the conflict brought terrorism to southern Russia and to Moscow. Yet they have nothing in common with the needs and expectations of the Chechen people. Their appearance in Chechnya, as in other conflicts and parts of the world, was a consequence of processes and transformations that took place in Islam during the final three decades of the twentieth century.

THE WORLD OF ISLAM: TOWARD NEW PRIORITIES

Between 1970 and 2000, the Muslim world's attempts to meet the challenges of the modern era by imitating European governments and ways of managing the economy proved unsuccessful. Secular nationalist regimes that came to power in the 1950s and early 1960s in countries in the Middle East and North Africa, promising to remedy the ills of Islamic society, fell far short of what the West and the Soviet Union had accomplished. Imitating Western models, adapting them to local peculiarities in the form of a "directed democracy," and experimenting with socialism in order to avoid the long evolution that the West had experienced brought neither progress nor independence from the West. Reforms that solved one group of problems generated others. Consequently modernization brought few positive results, disillusioning the various strata of Muslim society.

The 1967 Arab-Israeli War dealt the most serious blow to secular philosophies of nationalism and socialism. In the words of Shireen Hunter, Israel's defeat of the Arab armies and the conquest of Jerusalem "seemed to indicate that more than a century of modernization, Westernization, and relative de-Islamization had done nothing to restore the unfavorable balance of power between the West and the Islamic world. Rather, it had led to a widening power gap and a greater foreign encroachment."[42] Defeat revealed the internal evils of Muslim nationalist regimes: their corruption and cronyism, and their failure to resolve such pressing problems as poverty, unemployment, a growing encroachment of government on local freedoms and interests, and an uneven distribution of wealth. Islamic society had split in two: the Westernized ruling elites and the majority of the population who felt that Westernization had failed to change their condition for the better.

Failed attempts to modernize and Westernize Muslim society prompted many to question policies that relegated Islam to a private and spiritual domain. It motivated others to defend traditional religious values in various spheres of life in Islamic society. Yet those who championed the expansion of Islam in Muslim society were not unified: one group was willing to work for expansion from within the established order, and promoted hierarchical and patriarchal values that reinforced the status quo; others sought drastic change and advocated violence in order to establish an Islamic state. What principally distinguished these two Islamist schools of thought—moderate and radical—were their respective strategies and modes of actions.[43]

Events that followed the 1967 Arab-Israeli War helped strengthen radical Islamist movements and organizations. Profits from the oil revolution of the 1970s provided fundamentalist movements with the financial means to promote their goals within and beyond Islam. Saudi Arabia was in the vanguard with its effort to propagate its brand of Islam—Wahhabism—and its activism contributed to the overall Islamization of society: the Saudis financed schools, mosques, and charitable organizations. To this day the Saudi capital actively spreads radical ideas and deploys activists not only in the lands of Islam but also in various parts of Europe.[44]

Revolution in Iran and the Soviet invasion of Afghanistan, together with the ensuing war in that country waged to liberate Afghan lands from Soviet infidels, radicalized many religious revivalist movements. Despite the limited and controversial impact of the Iranian revolution on the intellectual and ideological spheres of Islamic society, the success of the Iranian Islamists demonstrated to other Muslims that a force organized and mobilized by faith in Islam could free itself from domestic oppression and foreign domination: "Impetus from the Iranian revolution helped propel Islamic fundamentalism into the most significant new movement of the late twentieth century," Robert Wiebe has written, "challenging the elite's right to rule from Algeria to Egypt and Turkey, pushing south into Nigeria and the Horn of Africa, swallowing pan-Arabism in the Middle East, placing its stamp on governments in Afghanistan and Pakistan, and penetrating through Malaysia into Indonesia, and by way of migration affecting Islamic life in Europe and North America."[45] By the end of the Iranian revolution, Islamic fundamentalism was not constrained to Muslim countries but had spread to the world.

The Afghan War's boost to fundamentalism and the radicalization of the religious movements in the Muslim world was tainted by the cold war rivalry between the Soviet Union and the United States. When the Soviets invaded Afghanistan, the Afghani fight for Islam against Soviet atheism and imperialism invoked widespread sympathy in Islamic countries. Young Muslims willingly joined Afghan *mujahedin* against Soviet troops—as many as 25,000 to 35,000 idealistic young men, of which the lion's share was from the Arab world, went to Afghanistan to participate in the struggle,[46] and the United States and its Western allies (allies of Pakistan and wealthy regimes in the Gulf) materially supported Afghan fighters and their comrades-in-arms. Few in the United States looked ahead to the war's conclusion and the prospect of veterans prepared to use their fervor and martial skills against governments they deemed un-Islamic as well as against Western powers that supported these governments.

During the war in Afghanistan tens of thousands of Muslim radicals from 43 Islamic countries in the Middle East, North and East Africa, Central Asia, and the Far East had been baptized under fire. More foreign Muslim radicals—in the tens of thousands—came to study in the hundreds of new *medreses* established by General Zia ul-Haq's military government in Pakistan and along the Afghan border. Eventually more than 100,000 Muslim radicals had direct contact with Pakistan and Afghanistan and were influenced by the *jihad*.[47] They met one another in training camps near Peshawar and on the other side of the Pakistan-Afghan border, and studied, trained, and fought together. They learned about Islamic movements in other countries and forged tactical and ideological links that would serve them later. In the words of Taliban expert Ahmed Rashid, "The camps became virtual universities for future Islamic radicalism."[48] In these camps, in classrooms where the students were a generation of Islamic militants who would come to be called "Afghan Arabs" in their native countries and financed by the CIA, were the roots of the terrorism that threatens the stability of today's world. Here the phenomenon of Osama bin Laden and his Al Qaeda was born.

In supporting radicals in Afghanistan a little more than a decade ago, U.S. officials were thinking about other priorities: "What was more important in the worldview of history?" asked Zbigniew Brzezinski, the former U.S. national security adviser. "The Taliban or the fall of the Soviet Empire? A few stirred-up Muslims or the liberation of central Europe and the end of the Cold War?"[49] He and other U.S. political experts failed to perceive that Muslim radicals, inspired by their success against one superpower, were considering whether they could defeat another, the United States, as well as their own regimes. Having dismantled the Soviet empire and liberated central and eastern Europe from Communist oppression, Washington was eager to use the Taliban—an Islamic radical movement that emerged as a contestant for power in Afghanistan after the Soviets withdrew—to advance U.S. policy in the region. Between 1994 and 1996 the United States supported the Taliban politically through its allies in Pakistan and Saudi Arabia, because the

Clinton administration viewed them as anti-Iranian, anti-Shia, and pro-Western.[50] The practice of wavering alliances with the Muslim world has been repeated throughout the centuries and continues to this day.

The Persian Gulf War of 1990–1991 and events in the former Yugoslavia—where the West pursued a policy of noninvolvement in the Serbs' attempted genocide of Bosnian Muslims—also contributed to the rise of the fundamentalist movement and its growing radicalization. Many young people critical of regimes in the Arab world denounced Saudi King Fahd's decision in 1990 to admit Western troops into the kingdom after Iraq invaded neighboring Kuwait. They viewed the presence of infidels on Islam's holiest land as an unforgivable sin and were doubly insulted when a contingent of Western troops remained on the peninsula after the war ended. One of these "angry young Muslims" was Osama bin Laden, son of a Yemeni millionaire who made a fortune in Saudi Arabia with his construction company, which became a financial empire and made the family one of the most prominent in the country. Osama was a hero of the war in Afghanistan where he was involved in building guerrilla trails, tunnels, storage depots, and schools and shelters for refugees in Pakistan, and in financing the recruitment and training of future Arab Afghans.[51] The Saudi government's response to his criticism of their policy during the Gulf War led him to flee to Sudan and then to Afghanistan, which became the notorious base of his activity.

The many factors that influenced the development of Islamist movements in the latter half of the twentieth century must be placed in the wider context of the rise of religious revivalism and nationalism across the globe. Toby Lester writes, "The world is today as awash in religious novelty, flux, and dynamism as it has ever been—and religious change is, if anything, likely to intensify in the coming decade."[52] Not only old religions—Christianity, Islam, Judaism, and Buddhism—dramatically transform themselves; new religions are regularly born, creating "broad trans-ethnic and trans-national communities, so that when somebody moves from city to city or country to country there's a sort of surrogate family structure in place."[53] When one talks about the resurgence of Islam, one should not forget about the spread of Christianity in Africa, Asia, and Latin America, which some experts predict will make Christianity and related movements a major social and political force in the coming century.[54]

Other actors from many countries on the political and social scene, especially various protest movements, increasingly resort to religion in order to attract followers and enlarge their constituency. Religious nationalism, for example, has replaced secular nationalism in the Muslim world. Despite the rhetoric of a supernational ideal—a Muslim unity beyond Muslim nation-states, achieved by a series of Islamic revolutions and the establishment of "open" or "soft" frontiers between states—most Muslim activists seem happy to settle for an Islamic nationalism limited to the countries where they reside. This supernational way of thinking results in "the appropriation of many of the most salient elements of modern nationhood into an Islamic frame of reference. Rather than ridding Islam of the nation-state, they too are creating a new synthesis."[55] The objectives and programs of Islamists in Muslim countries are tied to each country's history and culture and to outside developments, and though they may influence processes in other states, they cannot significantly change them. This anchors the assertion that no "central command" orchestrates the actions of Islamic political movements, moderate or radical, in various countries. These movements are united by their rejection of Western secular nationalism and by their employment of religious language, leadership, and organization to alter the secular rule of their countries.

Iran provides an unparalleled example of the dominance of national interests over universal aspirations. Although Islamist movements in other countries initially viewed Iran as an example of a Muslim people taking their destiny into their own hands, twenty years later that revolutionary spirit is hard to find. Since 1985 Iran's regime has increasingly pursued a pragmatic and moderate course in foreign policy, prioritizing its own national security considerations over the ideals of an Islamic world revolution. During the first Gulf War, Iran's president Ali-Akbar Heshemi-Rafsanjani, to the disappointment of the country's conservative clergy, refused to side with Iraq or seriously criticize the United States. After the demise of the Soviet Union, Iran avoided challenging Russian positions in the Caucasus and urged Christian Armenia and Muslim Azerbaijan to use restraint. In this policy Teheran was guided by a purely pragmatic interest: Iran has a large Azeri population (estimates range from 15 to 22 million), and Teheran did not wish to stimulate an Azeri nationalism that could hasten the disintegration of the state's territorial integrity. The Iranian government also responded to pragmatic interests when it welcomed the replacement of nationalist Abulfaz Elchibey with Heydar Aliev as president of Azerbaijan; a former Communist leader, the head of Azerbaijan's KGB, the first secretary of the republic's Communist party, and a full member of the Soviet Politburo was now president of Azerbaijan.[56] The question of Islam has only marginally shaped Iran's approach toward Russia and other former Soviet republics; instead security and economics have been the major forces.[57]

Religious nationalism nevertheless remains a powerful factor in today's conflicts, inasmuch as its opposition to the secular West is regarded as a new cold war. In the words of Mark Juergensmeyer, a proponent of this idea, "A merger of the absolutism of nationalism with the absolutism of religion might create a rule so vaunted and potent that it could destroy itself and its neighbors as well."[58] The frequency with which religious nationalistic movements resort to violence seems to confirm this opinion. Not only Islamists are eager to utilize violence in order to achieve their goals; Sikhs, Sinhalese, Judaists, and representatives of other religious movements also endorse the use of violence, or "terrorism," against their real or imagined adversaries. Terrorist acts are performed dramatically and have a symbolic import: "They are deliberately designed to elicit feelings of revulsion and anger in those who witness them," Juergensmeyer notes.[59] In recent years terrorism has been used with increasing frequency and has aroused great indignation not only in the Muslim world but in Europe and North America. Yet to what degree are these actions informed by the religion and values of Islam? Does Islam justify other worldly interests and motives? What proportion of Islamists or Islamic fundamentalists endorses violent methods of achieving their ideals?

Like all religions, Islam contains a strand of violence, but a strand does not make a quilt.[60] Violence appeals to those who seek a quick solution to the grave and complex problems of real life. Most radical Islamists—especially those among the Afghan Arabs and their comrades-in-arms in the Taliban who are involved in the movement to reform society according to the basic principles of Islam—are only superficially acquainted with the basic tenets of Islam. They have no positive plan of action to complement their desire to demolish everything they believe contravenes Islam. As one author writes about Osama bin Laden's outlook (similar to that of other Afghan veterans), "He knew what he was against: he opposed Israel, its occupation of Palestinian lands and its control over Jerusalem; he loathed American foreign policy and distrusted its intentions, even during the Afghan war; and he despised a Saudi royal family that would rely on tens of thousands of U.S. troops to protect land holy to Muslims. But what did he stand for? Beyond the slogans of Islam as a solution and a return to God's law, even his supporters would be hard-pressed to answer that question."[61]

Afghan Arabs, having lost contact with their native countries and seldom supported by other Islamist groups, became increasingly marginalized. Even Muslim activists who denounce America and seek to reform their countries on the basis of Islam regard Osama bin Laden and his followers as exceptions to the movement that strives to construct an Islam that is a viable social, legal, and economic alternative to the dominant Western paradigm. "He's a *mujahid*, that's quite clear," an activist in the Islamist movement said of Osama bin Laden. "He would assist anyone who is persecuted, whether it's in Bosnia or in the Balkans or in Asia or in Africa or in any place." But he is no visionary.[62]

The Taliban may be characterized in the same way. They have a poor knowledge of Islamic history, of the Sharia and the Koran, and of political and theoretical developments in the Muslim world over the last century. They also lack a clear plan of action after the enemy is destroyed: vague slogans suggest a state based on the Sharia, in which the precepts of Islam are strictly observed. Taliban policies in Afghanistan that alienated most Afghanis, and criticism from other Muslim countries and Islamist movements, demonstrate the Taliban's obscurantism and narrow-mindedness.

Although the Taliban are ideologically rooted in a form of Deobandism—a branch of Sunni Hanafi Islam that originated in British India and had a history in Afghanistan[63]—they differ from other followers of this branch on a number of significant points. The Deobandis trained a new generation of Muslims who, based on intellectual learning, spiritual experience, Sharia law, and Tariqah (observance), would revive Islamic values. Yet the Taliban took these beliefs to an extreme that would be unrecognizable to the original Deobandis. The Taliban also exhibited an aversion to intellectual activity by closing schools rather than promoting the spread of knowledge. Within three months of their capture of Kabul, the Taliban had closed 63 schools in the city, affecting 103,000 girls, 148,000 boys, and 11,200 teachers. They shut down Kabul University, sending home 10,000 students.[64] The Taliban's extreme anti-intellectualism may be explained by whom it recruited be its soldiers—the orphans, the rootless, the lumpenproletariat from the refugee camps. Their obstinacy on some issues, such as the social role of women, conditioned by their upbringing and by a life among men, is alien not only to Afghanistan, where women play an important part in life and culture, but also to Islam: though it allots women a subordinate role to men, it nevertheless recognizes their involvement in various spheres of human activity. Nor does the Taliban's attitude agree with Islamic traditions and history that glorify love and women's beauty in lyrics and folklore.

The Islamic revival represented by Afghan Arabs and the Taliban is far from a dominant trend. It has few intellectual and spiritual connections with Islam's political body, with its long tradition of critical thought and scholarly interpretation and its struggles within a primarily national context. Deprived of a territorial base and indifferent to their own nationalities, wandering from *jihad* to *jihad* mainly on the fringes of the Muslim world,[65] without a coherent ideology or agenda, these movements are losing their ties with other Islamic groups and movements and becoming increasingly marginalized. The violent methods that the Taliban once shared with Muslim radical organizations in other countries now appear almost exclusively theirs. Other forms of protest on the Islamist agenda are gradually replacing violence: social and political activism blended with religious values now holds center stage.

The world outside Islam associates Hamas and Hezbollah with the Intifada's clashes with the Israeli army, bombings of cafés and disco bars, and innocent victims and the capture of hostages. Yet Palestinians and Lebanese upon hearing these names think of the clinics, legal-aid societies, schools, hospitals, dental offices, and orphanages the organizations have established. When a devastating earthquake in 1999 crippled the industrial heartland of Turkey, killing at least seventeen thousand and injuring more than forty thousand,[66] it was the leading Islamist political organization—the Virtue party—that funneled millions of dollars toward relief efforts. Leaders of Islamist movements now think more often about whether the returns on violence are worth the toll they take on their organizations.[67] Gradually Hamas and similar groups have transformed themselves into political and social movements with specific programs designed to attract followers and compete for power.

This transformation has not excluded violence against the repression of local authorities or occupying forces, as in Palestine. In both cases, violence is prompted by an outside influence rather than an inner disposition; it does not spring from Islam. It is a political rather than a religious act, a product of frustration and anger. For Hamas, violence remains part of its complicated nature, and it is not likely to change in the years ahead unless a settlement to the Palestinian problem is reached.

In other countries Islamist movements will likely continue to switch from armed actions to perhaps less impressive but more useful and rewarding work among the masses, in which they can earn their reputation as nascent political parties.[68] If this happens, the emergence of a radical and violent form of Islamism in the final decades of the twentieth century should be regarded as a stage in the development of Islamic civilization, one that manifested itself in the social, economic, political, and cultural transformations of Muslim societies, and which was influenced by its encounter with the non-Muslim world.[69]

Whether this stage will lead to a greater secularization of Muslim societies and "a synthesis of Islamic precepts and Western concepts," as some experts suggest,[70] remains to be seen. The growing involvement of Islamist movements in political and social activities has already resulted in a reappraisal of their conceptions of the West. Muslim activists and groups of new thinkers in many Islamic countries are now prepared to consider what is useful in Western society and to adapt it to the realities of Muslim societies. The most prominent among these thinkers is Seyyed Mohammad Khatami, who in 1997 was elected in a landslide victory as Iran's president. Although devoted to his faith and to his country, he attempts to approach the modern world and prospects for his country's further development realistically. "We must understand the peculiarities of our era and treat Western civilization as our era's ultimate manifestation and symbol," Khatami says. "This means understanding the values and tenets of Western civilization and freeing ourselves from the equally harmful extremes of either hating it or being completely taken in and entranced by it."[71] Suggesting a middle course between extremes, Khatami speaks in favor of a civil society that would borrow Western ideas of political parties, social organizations, and an independent free press without undermining the Islamic identity of Iranians and other Muslims.

Khatami's ideas are consonant with those of Muslim thinkers who seek to create a modern Islamic polity. Although they believe that Islam should inspire this polity, most of them do not advocate a return to a seventh-century golden age of Islamic civilization (which probably never existed). They dismiss Islamic traditionalists who criticize democracy as a Western invention and therefore alien to Muslim societies. Instead they emphasize how political organization reflects the universal will of the people and their sentiments. Former Marxists and Communists are also among the new thinkers; disillusioned with secular nationalist ideologies, they have turned to Islam as the best tool by which to achieve the same goals.[72] Through Islam, Muslims can dismiss those products of Western civilization they find unacceptable—sexual promiscuity, consumerism, materialism, and moral decadence—while borrowing those achievements that can help Islamic civilization meet the challenges of the contemporary world.

The influence of these new thinkers on the political and intellectual life of Islam continues to grow. With Islamist groups and movements who seek constructive activities instead of dismissing whatever they consider non-Islamic, who prefer peaceful to violent methods of realizing a more perfect society, a sustained and fruitful interaction and dialogue between the West and Islam may now be possible. This interaction may portend a decisive departure from a history in which rivalry and competition have often prevailed over understanding and cooperation.

EIGHT

The Great Confrontation

A superficial glance at the history of relations between Europe and Islam sees only war. From the first stirrings of the religion of Muhammad, it would seem that European and Islamic civilizations have found themselves in an acute and irreconcilable confrontation. Even the occasional truce does not alter the picture of a perennial conflict waged along the border that runs through the Mediterranean to the eastern coast of the Black Sea and has divided two worlds—the followers of Jesus Christ to the north, the disciples of Muhammad to the south. This border separated different religions but also different histories, cultures, and ways of life. In short, it separated two civilizations.

Both civilizations sought to prove their superiority and were prepared to use arms. They would spread their values by force if their rival refused to accept them voluntarily. And they waged a series of "holy wars" in which both sides knew the exhilaration of victory and the disgrace of defeat. At the beginning of the Muslim era, Arab armies subjugated most of the Christian lands in the Middle East that belonged to Byzantium, invaded Spain and Italy and established Muslim states there. This was followed by the age of the Crusades aimed at liberating Christian lands from the "yoke" of the infidels and recovering the Holy Land. Then came the Ottoman conquests in southern Europe and the long struggle by Roman popes and European sovereigns against the "Turkish menace." In turn this propelled Europe's expansion and cultural, economic, and political domination, enhancing Europe's presence in the realm of Islam. It coincided with the decline of Islamic civilization and Islam's efforts to bridge the socioeconomic gap that modernization had brought.

Although religion was not always the driving force of this rivalry, it was nevertheless a powerful component of the struggle between the two civilizations and often obscured worldlier motives. For a long time religion gave both civilizations their distinct cultural identities (for Islamic civilization, it still does). Each civilization regarded itself as the highest embodiment of God's will, the sole possessor of His true word; other faiths were deceptions, other sages were false prophets. Although they have common roots and symbolism, Christianity and Islam were clearly antagonists. At times relations between them were characterized by confrontation and enmity rather than coexistence and cooperation.

Yet neither in Islam nor in Christianity has violence played a prominent role. Jesus Christ appealed to tolerance and forgiveness, and praised the word above the sword. Islam likewise advocates tolerance and Muslims spent most of their history peacefully coexisting with people of other faiths. The concept of *jihad*, often treated as proof of Muslim militancy, primarily emphasizes the believer's effort to obtain perfection; only in a secondary sense does it suggest an armed struggle to eliminate or convert adherents of other religions. Even in this latter sense it sanctions the use of the sword only in defense of the faith and lands of Islam against the incursions of an enemy.

Today, after decades in which secularism and toleration have triumphed and religion seems to have lost its hold on people's minds, religions are experiencing revival and various movements in the Muslim world are invoking the old slogans of a "holy war" to express their struggle against an alien influence and a desire to return to the basics of Islam. To justify their violence, these movements depict the long history of relations between Europe and Islam as one of permanent and irreconcilable conflict. They market this conflict to the modern world as truth, appealing to Muslims to rise against "Crusaders" and infidels in order to preserve the purity of Islam. For their part, Europeans and Americans have developed theories of the "clash of civilizations" and have reaffirmed that an implacable hostility divides the West and Islam. They insist that democracy, liberalism, and religious tolerance are incompatible with the basic tenets of Islam. They draw attention to border areas between the two civilizations—"fault lines," areas of war. The history of Europe and Islam they see as a chronicle of confrontation, one that continues to influence their relations today.

A close and impartial study of the history of relations between Europe and Islam reveals that the two civilizations have also cooperated and influenced each other in ways that have left an indelible mark on their respective societies. So-called fault lines between the two civilizations have often been not battlefields but markets and meeting points, and merchants and thinkers throughout the centuries have played as active a role in the life of the two civilizations as soldiers and proselytizers. The Mediterranean, which some regard as an unabating sea of conflict, has also borne witness to peaceful contacts between the two worlds. For centuries Europe and Islam have traded their material and spiritual achievements, and both sides have found the exchange beneficial. While countries from the respective realms have gone to war, others have developed commercial and cultural relations. Countries that have been at each other's throat on the battlefield have often been friendly trading partners. They have formed political and even military alliances. Clearly the two civilizations have never been hermetically sealed off, bristling with arms, unable to communicate with each other, isolated from the outside world. People from different societies have fought and traded, and borrowed and adapted whatever they have found useful. Between the West and Islam there have never existed barriers that made mutual understanding impossible.

Relations between European and Islamic civilizations tend to be intense owing to their geographic proximity. For more than fourteen centuries the two civilizations have remained close neighbors, and this has strongly influenced their interaction. Contemporary relations between Europe and Islam differ in several important ways from their historical experience. Until relatively late in Europe's history, the continent had only a vague notion of civilizations that lay to the east, in India, China, and Japan; and the contacts it did develop were largely with maritime regions. At the same time there was a flourishing civilization very close to the continent that displayed its religious zeal and desire to conquer Europe. Although such ambitions may also have been expressed by other civilizations, it is hard to imagine any sustained and acute conflict between, for example, Europe and China simply because of the great distance that separates them.

Unlike Europe, the Muslim world was familiar with Indian and Chinese civilizations and maintained close contact with them, enjoying the benefits of trade and cultural exchange. But it never regarded India and China as serious competitors to the preeminence of Islamic civilization and to Islam as a world religion. In Christianity, however, Islam saw another faith with universal aspirations. And common borders, as well as an essentially common history and culture, made religious rivalry a dominant feature of the two societies.

Rivalry, however, never brought interaction between the two civilizations to a halt. Historical evidence amply testifies to the functioning of Christian communities in various Muslim countries; and we know that during the premodern period Muslims lived on the continent, though Europe proved to be a less hospitable host.

Changes in the twentieth century have further strengthened the tendency to coexist peacefully. Processes of economic integration and globalization have made possible a global economy and culture: countries that were fiscal strangers are now interrelated and interdependent; people have a higher degree of

mobility; and demographic shifts have generally made countries more heterogeneous. Consequently more Muslims live in
Europe today than in any other period in history. This makes
the "great confrontation" between Europe and the world of
Islam a thing of the past, a conceptual relic devoid of meaning.
In today's interrelated and interdependent world, lines of division do not run between different civilizations—like European
and Islamic—but between civilization and the challenges that
threaten it: poverty, famine, terrorism, environmental pollu-
tion, and weapons of mass destruction, among others.
Mankind must cope with these challenges and learn how to
prevent them. Attempts to divide up the contemporary world
according to categories of race, culture, religion, and nation,
and to set them against one another, are not merely counter-
productive; they can lead to catastrophe. It is instructive to
find in the history of relations between different societies not
instances of enmity and fanaticism but examples of tolerance
and partnership. These are the more important guiding principles for the future.

Notes

Preface

1. The title of Bernard Lewis's article in the *Atlantic Monthly* (September 1990).
2. See, for example, Ali A. Mazrui, "Islamic and Western Values," *Foreign Affairs* 76 (September/October 1997), 5:118–132.
3. Huntington, in his interview in *l'Express*, on the question of whether the September 11 attacks represented a clash of civilizations, answered "Not yet." He characterized these attacks and the U.S. response to them as rather a war between civilization and barbarism. See "Samuel P. Huntington: 'Le dialogue entre les civilizations doit s'engager,'" *L'Express*, October 25, 2001.
4. Shireen T. Hunter, *The Future of Islam and the West: Clash of Civilizations or Peaceful Coexistence?* (Westport: Praeger, 1998), p. 16.
5. Franco Gardini, *Europe and Islam*, trans. by Caroline Beamish (Oxford: Blackwell, 1999).
6. Bernard Lewis, *Islam and the West* (New York: Oxford University Press, 1993).

Chapter One. Setting the Stage.

1. Daniel Pipes, "Who Is the Enemy?" *Commentary* 113 (January 2002), 1:23.
2. See, for example, Mary Jo White, "Prosecuting Terrorism in New York," *Middle East Quarterly* 8 (Spring 2001), 2:12.
3. Quoted in Bernard Lewis, "License to Kill. Usama bin Ladin's Declaration of Jihad," *Foreign Affairs* 77 (November/December 1998), 6:15.

4. Bernard Lewis, "The Revolt of Islam: When Did the Conflict with the West Begin, and How Could It End?" *New Yorker*, November 19, 2001, p. 50.

5. *Corriere della Sera*, September 25, 2001.

6. Dale F. Eickelman, "Bin Laden, the Arab 'Street,' and the Middle East's Democracy Deficit," *Current History* 101 (January 2002), 651:37.

7. Oriana Fallaci, "La rabbia e l'orgoglio," *Corriere della Sera*, September 29, 2001.

8. *Le Monde*, May 25, 2002.

9. Paola Caro, "L'Occidente è una civiltà superiore," *Corriere della Sera*, September 27, 2001.

10. Paola Caro, "Berlusconi: 'Non criminalizzate l'Islam,'" *Corriere della Sera*, January 30, 2002.

11. See, for example, Leon T. Hadar, "What Green Peril?" *Foreign Affairs* 72 (Spring 1993), 2:29.

12. Ibid., p. 31.

13. Pipes, p. 23.

14. Ibid. Emphasis added.

15. Lewis, "The Revolt of Islam," p.58.

16. See, for example, Ahmed Rashid, *Taliban: Militant Islam, Oil and Fundamentalism in Central Asia* (New Haven: Yale Nota Bene, 2001), p. 39.

17. Bernard Lewis, "The Roots of Muslim Rage," *Atlantic Monthly* 266 (September 1990), 60. Emphasis added.

18. Samuel P. Huntington, "The Clash of Civilizations?" *Foreign Affairs* 72 (Summer 1993), 3:24, 31.

19. Samuel P. Huntington, *The Clash of Civilizations and the Remaking of World Order* (New York: Touchstone, 1997).

20. Ibid., p. 28.

21. Huntington, "The Clash of Civilizations?" p. 32.

22. Idem, *The Clash of Civilizations*, p. 209.

23. Idem, "The Clash of Civilizations?" pp. 34–35.

24. Fernand Braudel, *Écrits sur l'Histoire* (Paris: Flammarion, 1969), pp. 266–267.

25. Huntington, *The Clash of Civilizations*, p. 43.

26. Ibid., p. 46.

27. See Braudel, p. 291.

28. Huntington, *The Clash of Civilizations*, p. 43. As to the final link in this chain, I have never heard anyone from Western Europe, Canada, or the United States call himself a Westerner, except during the cold war in the midst of a debate on the advantages of the capitalist and communist systems.

29. Braudel, p. 290.

30. See Arnold J. Toynbee, *Civilization on Trial* (New York: Oxford University Press, 1948), pp. 186, 187.

31. Such as "Nordic" White, the "Alpine," the "Mediterranean," etc. See the subject arguments by Toynbee: Arnold J. Toynbee, *A Study of History*, vol. 1 (London: Oxford University Press, 1963), pp. 239–240.

32. Braudel, pp. 292–293.

33. "While a civilization is radiating out its material products as exports, its human members as traders, conquerors, colonists, and missionaries, and its culture in the shape of technique, institutions, ideas, and emotions, it is all the time drawing in other commodities and other beings and other techniques, institutions, ideas, and emotions from abroad." Toynbee, *A Study of History*, p. 240.

34. Toynbee, *Civilization on Trial*, p. 9.

35. See P. M. Holt, Ann K. S. Lambton, and Bernard Lewis, eds., *The Cambridge History of Islam*. Vol. 1: *The Central Islamic Lands* (Cambridge: Cambridge University Press, 1970).

36. Bernard Lewis, *Islam and the West* (New York: Oxford University Press, 1993), p. 5.

37. Jørgen S. Nielsen, ed., *The Christian-Muslim Frontier: Chaos, Clash or Dialogue?* (London: I. B. Tauris, 1998), p. 2.

38. Charles Issawi, "The Christian-Muslim Frontier in the Mediterranean: A History of Two Peninsulas," *Political Science Quarterly*, 76 (December 1961), 4:550.

39. Fernand Braudel, *The Mediterranean and the Mediterranean World in the Age of Philip II*, translated from the French by Siân Reynolds, Vol. I (New York: Harper & Row, 1972), p. 187.

40. Issawi, p. 544.

41. Nielsen, *The Christian-Muslim Frontier*, p. 2.

42. Lewis, *Islam and the West*, p. 5.

43. Ibid., p. 50.

44. See Hichem Djaït, *Europe and Islam*, translated by Peter Heinegg (Berkeley: University of California Press, 1985), pp. 106–107. The author emphasizes that Islam helped the Europeans define themselves as a part of the world system of civilizations. But, in the same sense, Europe as an opponent of Islam in various spheres of activity played no less important a role in the formation of Islamic civilization, which from the outset scarcely appeared to be a complete cultural entity.

45. Franco Gardini, *Europe and Islam*, trans. by Caroline Beamish (Oxford: Blackwell, 1999), p. 101.

46. Lewis, *Islam and the West*, p. 15.

47. See Bernard Lewis, *The Muslim Discovery of Europe* (New York: Norton, 2001), p. 68.

48. Lewis, *Islam and the West*, p. 26.
49. John Obert Voll, *Islam: Continuity and Change in the Modern World*, 2nd ed. (Syracuse: Syracuse University Press, 1994), p. 85.
50. Ibid., pp. 290–291.
51. Huntington, *The Clash of Civilizations*, p. 263.

Chapter Two. Islam Confronts Europe.

1. The thesis that "Islam has bloody borders" is Huntington's. See "The Clash of Civilizations?" 3:35. For arguments against this assertion, see Graham E. Fuller and Ian O. Lesser, *A Sense of Siege: The Geopolitics of Islam and the West* (Boulder: Westview Press, 1995), pp. 137–138.
2. Paul Fregosi, *Jihad in the West: Muslim Conquests from the 7th to the 21st Centuries* (Amherst: Prometheus Books, 1998), pp. 20–21.
3. *The Koran*, Sura 4, 91.
4. Sura 8, 12.
5. Sura 9, 5.
6. Sura 4, 92.
7. Sura 2, 173, 186.
8. *The Bible*, Deuteronomy, 20, 10–18.
9. Fregosi, p. 22.
10. *The Koran*, Sura 5, 52.
11. Bernard Lewis, *Islam and the West*, p. 9.
12. Paul Fregosi insists that the "Muslim must accept every word of the Koran as coming from God in person, in fact as being part of God and therefore beyond query," and that "the injunctions, penalties, and admonitions in the Koran and Hadiths (or Traditions), the second Muslim sacred book . . . must be as strictly applied today as they were in 630." See Fregosi, pp. 61, 63.
13. Leone Caetani, *Annali dell'islām compilati da L. Caetani*. Vol. 2: *Dall'anno 7 al 12 H* (Milano: U. Hoepli, 1907), pp. 831–861.
14. O. G. Bol'shakov, *Istoriia khalifata*. Vol. 2: *Epokha velikikh zavoevanii, 633–656* (The History of the Caliphate: The Epoch of Great Conquests) (Moscow: Vostochnaia literature, 2000), p. 14.
15. Ibid.
16. Walter E. Kaegi, *Byzantium and the Early Islamic Conquests* (Cambridge: Cambridge University Press, 1997), p. 46.
17. Bol'shakov, p. 111.
18. Kaegi, pp. 182–183.
19. Ibid., p. 146.
20. See Bol'shakov, pp. 69–74.
21. Franco Gardini, *Europe and Islam*, trans. by Caroline Beamish (Oxford: Blackwell, 1999), p. 54.

22. Amin Maalouf, *The Crusades Through Arab Eyes*, trans. by Jon Rothschild (New York: Schocken Books, 1984), pp. 50–51.

23. Kaegi, p. 286.

24. Ibid., pp. 165, 272.

25. According to some sources, when the Arabs captured the capital of Armenia, Dvin, in 642, 12,000 Armenians were killed and 35,000 taken into captivity. Alain Brissaud, *Islam et Chrétienté: Treize siècle de cohabitation* (Paris: Robert Laffont, 1991), p. 237.

26. Kaegi, pp. 198–199.

27. *Ocherki istorii Gruzii*. Vol. 2: *Gruziia v IV–X vekakh* (Essays on the History of Georgia) (Tbilisi: Metzniereba, 1988), p. 172. See also Ronald Grigor Suny, *The Making of Georgian Nation* (London: I. B. Tauris, 1989), p. 27.

28. É. Lévi-Provençal, *Histoire de l'Espagne musulmane*. Vol. 1: *La Conquête et l'Émirat Hispano-Umayade (710–912)* (Paris, Leiden: Brill, 1950), p. 2.

29. Ibid., p. 15.

30. Brissaud, p. 182.

31. Lévi-Provençal, p. 23.

32. "Musa had another project of conquest already germinating in his mind. To invade Spain, yes, but also to advance north th[r]ough Spain and well beyond it, into the land of Franks beyond the Pyrenees, deep into the Dar-al-Harb, the Land of War; to turn to the right through lands unknown and advance on and on until Constantinople and Damascus were reached; and to perhaps overthrow the pope on the way, take over the Vatican, and form the whole Mediterranean into a closed Muslim lake." Fregosi, p. 92.

33. Lévi-Provençal, p. 56.

34. Fregosi writes about this battle as "one of the most renowned battles of Christendom . . . It changed the course of world history." (p. 114).

35. This argument is put forward by Bernard Lewis, who writes that the Arab historians, "if they mention this engagement at all, present it as minor skirmish." See Lewis, *Islam and the West*, p. 11. But it is well known that the Arab chroniclers tended to exaggerate the successes of Muslim troops against unbelievers while remaining silent about defeats. See Lévi-Provençal's description of *sa'ifas*.

36. Lévi-Provençal, p. 63.

37. Henri Pirenne, *Mohammed and Charlemagne* (New York: Dover Publications, 2001), p. 164: "Islam had shattered the Mediterranean unity which the Germanic invasions had left intact." And further: "This was the most essential event of European history which had occurred since the Punic Wars. It was the end of the classic tradition. It was the beginning of the Middle Ages, and it happened at the very moment

when Europe was on the way to becoming Byzantinized." Then further again: "The old economic unity of the Mediterranean was shattered, and so it remained until the epoch of the Crusades. It had resisted the Germanic invasions; but it gave way before the irresistible advance of Islam." (p. 166)

38. "... We can say without hesitation that we are confronted with a civilization which had retrogressed to the purely agricultural stage; which no longer needed commerce, credit, and regular exchange for the maintenance of the social fabric. ... The essential cause of this transformation was the closing of the Western Mediterranean by Islam." Ibid., p. 242.

39. Ibid., p. 195.

40. "The Merovingian was in every sense a secular king. The Carolingian was crowned only by the intervention of the Church. ... Through the rite of consecration the Church obtained a hold over the king ...."; "... what is known as the Carolingian Renaissance ... But it is important to note that this Renaissance was purely clerical." Ibid., pp. 268, 270, 279.

41. Ibid., p. 285.

42. Ibid., p. 166.

43. Daniel C. Dennett, Jr., "Pirenne and Muhammad," *Speculum* 23 (April 1948), 2:173.

44. Ibid., p. 174.

45. Ibid., pp. 176–177.

46. Richard Hodges and David Whitehouse, *Mohammed, Charlemagne and the Origins of Europe: Archeology and the Pirenne Thesis* (Ithaca: Cornell University Press, 1983), p. 169.

47. Marshall G. S. Hodgson, *The Venture of Islam: Conscience and History in a World Civilization*. Vol. 2: *The Expansion of Islam in the Middle Periods* (Chicago: University of Chicago Press, 1974), pp. 42–43.

48. Speros Vryonis, Jr., *The Decline of Medieval Hellenism in Asia Minor and the Process of Islamization from the Eleventh Through the Fifteenth Century* (Berkeley: University of California Press, 1971), p. 73.

49. Ibid., p. 76.

50. Norman Housley, "King Louis the Great of Hungary and the Crusades, 1342–1382," *Slavonic and East European Review* 62 (April 1984), 2:204, 206.

51. Fregosi, p. 242.

52. Gardini, p. 125.

53. Hodgson, p. 560.

54. Lewis, p. 33.

55. Bernard Lewis refers to the Mongol invasion as a "third Muslim advance into Europe" after those of the Moors and the Turks. Although shortly thereafter he points out that only later Berke Khan, the lord of

the Golden Horde, was converted to Islam, the fact remains blurred that when the Mongols penetrated Europe under Batu as far as Poland and Hungary, they were *not* Muslims. Strictly speaking, therefore, the Mongol onslaught could not be equated with those of the Arabs and the Ottomans. See Lewis, p. 12.

56. George Vernadsky, *The Mongols and Russia* (New Haven: Yale University Press, 1953), p. 13. According to some chroniclers, the whole tribe of Keraits was converted to Nestorianism as early as the eleventh century.

57. F. Sh. Khuzin, *Volzhskaia Bulgaria v domongol'skoe vremya (X–nachalo XIII vekov)* (The Volga Bulgaria in the pre-Mongol Times, the Tenth–Early Thirteenth Centuries) (Kazan: Fest, 1997), pp. 89–90.

58. Ibid., pp. 112–113.

59. Devin DeWeese, *Islamization and Native Religion in the Golden Horde: Baba Tükles and Conversion to Islam in Historical Epic and Tradition* (University Park: Pennsylvania State University Press, 1994), p. 83.

60. L. N. Gumilyov, *Drevniaia Rus' i velikaia step'* (Old Rus' and the Great Steppe) (Moscow: Mysl', 1992), p. 526. See also Gumilyov's overview of discussions on this issue, pp. 539–542.

61. Vernadsky, p. 149.

62. Ibid., pp. 165–166.

63. S. M. Solovyov, *Istoriia Rossii s drevneishikh vremyon* (The History of Russia from Ancient Times), Vol. 3 (Moscow: Mysl', 1988), p. 223.

64. Vernadsky, p. 201.

65. A. A. Novosel'skii, *Bor'ba Moskovskogo gosudarstva s tatarami v pervoi polovine XVII veka* (The Struggle of the Moscow State with the Tatars in the First Half of the Seventeenth Century) (Moscow, Leningrad: USSR Academy of Sciences, 1948), p. 41.

66. Ibid., p. 11.

67. Ibid., p. 17.

68. Ibid., p. 80.

69. Ibid., p. 435.

70. Carl Max Kortepeter, *Ottoman Imperialism During the Reformation: Europe and the Caucasus* (New York: New York University Press, 1972), p. 27.

71. Novosel'skii, p. 25.

72. Ibid., p. 440.

73. Ibid., p. 192.

74. A. A. Gordeev, *Istoriia kazakov.* Vol. 1: *Zolotaia orda i zarozhdeniie kazachestva* (The History of the Cossacks. The Golden Horde and the Birth of the Cossackdom) (Moscow: Strastnoi Bul'var, 1991), pp. 16–17, 72, 79. Gordeev refutes the idea that the Cossacks were either serfs or

criminals who fled Russia for asylum in the wild steppe. He also disputes the view that Cossack troops lived in a liberal atmosphere. Although the Cossack ranks were partly filled by Russians, they expanded mostly by natural increase. See ibid., p. 154. Unlike Gordeev, Albert Seaton draws attention to the mixed character of the Cossack population. According to him, many of those who joined the Cossacks were "would-be brigands. . . . Some were fugitives from the law and readily reinforced the steppe robber bands." These Cossacks "turned their hands to whatever was profitable." See Albert Seaton, *The Horsemen of the Steppes: The Story of the Cossacks* (London: Bodley Head, 1985), p. 48.

75. A. A. Gordeev, *Istoriia kazakov.* Vol. 2: *So vremeni tsarstvovaniia Ioanna Groznogo do tsarstvovaniia Petra I* (The History of the Cossacks. From the Reign of Ivan the Terrible to the Reign of Peter I) (Moscow: Strastnoi Bul'var, 1991), p. 163.

76. Seaton, p. 51.

77. Novosel'skii, pp. 130–131.

Chapter Three. The European Response.

1. Lévi-Provençal, p. 127.

2. Arnold Toynbee clarifies the function of the Habsburg monarchy: it "was not, like a shield, a piece of matter external to and alien from the body which it was its function to protect. It was an excretion from the living substance of our Western society—a special political articulation which was evoked by the need of guarding against a particular external attack. Thus it is strictly comparable not so much to a shield as to the carapace of a tortoise or an armadillo." See Arnold J. Toynbee, *A Study of History,* Vol. 1 (London: Oxford University Press, 1963), p. 156n.

3. Lévi-Provençal accepts that the Muslim Bands joined the Basques and sought to liberate their coreligionists taken as prisoners by the Franks. See Lévi-Provençal, p. 125.

4. Gardini, pp. 45–46.

5. Lévi-Provençal, pp. 65–67.

6. Ibid., p. 68.

7. É. Lévi-Provençal, *Histoire de l'Espagne musulmane,* Vol. 2: *Le Califat umaiyade de Cordue (912–1031)* (Paris, Leiden: Brill, 1950), p. 250.

8. Gardini, p. 41.

9. See Fregosi, p. 159.

10. Gardini, p. 42.

11. Ibid., p. 40.

12. Ibid., p. 67.

13. Jean Flori, "L'église et la guerre sainte de la 'paix de Dieu' à la 'croisade'" *Annales* 47 (March–April 1992), 2:458–459.

14. Holt, Lambton, and Lewis, *The Cambridge History of Islam*, Vol. 1: *The Central Islamic Lands*, p. 196.

15. Brissaud, p. 79.

16. Maalouf, p. xi.

17. For example, a sect of Assassins, the Ismailis, were violent and irreconcilable enemies of Sunni orthodoxy.

18. *The Cambridge History of Islam*, p. 156. See also B. Lewis, Ch. Pellat, and J. Schacht, eds., *The Encyclopedia of Islam*, new edition, Vol. 2 (Leiden: Brill, 1965), p. 64.

19. Lewis, p. 13. According to a multi-volume work on the history of the Crusades written by an international group of scholars, "It must be clearly realized that the crusades did not produce much of an impression on the Islamic world in general. . . . Moreover, at first the crusade was considered as related to those earlier Byzantine expeditions, ephemeral and limited to territories traditionally accustomed to frequent changes of masters, incompletely converted to Islam, distant from Baghdad and Cairo, and negligible since commerce never suffered from the changes. They had supplied the opportunity for worthy exploits and for romantic encounters sung on both sides of the frontiers by the poets in the circle of Saif-ad-Daulah or in the Byzantine Digenis. At most it was deemed necessary to try to reduce the ravages of the unbeliever; his expulsion was hardly imagined. . . . Among the Moslems, even in those of their narratives which have survived—all were compiled considerably later than the crusade and had already undergone fundamental revision—the wars with the Franks were invariably treated like any other wars. In the literatures of Iraq and Egypt these wars were scarcely mentioned, in that of Iran not at all. It was to be the length and nature of the Frankish occupation which would gradually provoke a reaction. At the start the crusaders were merely one more pawn on an already overcrowded political chessboard, a pawn indistinguishable from its fellows. The trend of history in the surrounding region was not at all affected by it." (Marshall W. Baldwin, *A History of the Crusades*. Vol. 1: *The First Hundred Years* [Madison: University of Wisconsin Press, 1969], pp. 166–167.)

20. Edgar Weber and Georges Reynaud, *Croisade d'hier, djihad d'aujourd'hui: Theorie et pratique de la violence dans les rapports entre l'Occident chrétien et l'Orient musulman* (Paris: Les Éditions du Cerf, 1989), pp. 226–227.

21. L. Carl Brown, ed., *Imperial Legacy: The Ottoman Imprint on the Balkans and the Middle East* (New York: Columbia University Press, 1996), p. 21.

22. Dorothy M. Vaughan, *Europe and the Turk: A Pattern of Alliances, 1350–1700* (Liverpool: University Press, 1954), p. 104.

23. Ibid., pp. 110–111.

24. Ibid., p. 120.
25. Frederic C. Lane, *Venice: A Maritime Republic* (Baltimore: Johns Hopkins University Press, 1973), p. 198.
26. Ibid., p. 235.
27. Gardini, pp. 130–131.
28. Ibid., pp. 133–134.
29. Jean Richard, *La papauté et les missions d'Orient au Moyen Age (XIIIe–XVe siècles)* (Palais Farnèse: École française de Rome, 1977), pp. 68–69.
30. Vaughan, p. 208.
31. Ibid., p. 209.
32. Claire Gantet, "La dimension 'sainte' du Saint-Empire romain germanique. Les representations du pouvoir en Allemagne entre paix et guerre" *Revue historique*, 615 (Juillet/Septembre 2000), pp. 648–649.
33. Vaughan, p. 140.
34. For example: The diet of Ratisbon, after two years of deliberations, finally voted in February of 1664 for the levy of an army of 21,000 soldiers and for subsidies sufficient to arm 4,000 cavalry and 20,000 infantrymen for war against the Ottomans. But the actual levy was less than expected, primarily because princes—whose possessions were in the Holy Roman Empire—failed to provide the needed troops: Swabia contributed roughly 551 cavalry and 2,904 infantry soldiers rather than the expected 3,000 and 5,000 respectively. See Claire Gantet, p. 640.
35. It was said that for Henry VIII of England the Turkish peril meant no more than if it had been in the Indies. Vaughan, p. 106.
36. Fernand Braudel, *The Mediterranean and the Mediterranean World in the Age of Philip II*, trans. by Siân Reynolds, Vol. 1 (New York: Harper & Row, 1972), pp. 115, 136.
37. Lane, pp. 236–237.
38. This thesis of the "two Mediterraneans" was put forward by Fernand Braudel in his *Mediterranean World in the Age of Philip II*, pp. 136–137.
39. Fernand Braudel, *The Mediterranean and the Mediterranean World in the Age of Philip II*. Vol. 2 (New York: Harper & Row, 1973), p. 906.
40. Ibid., p. 987.
41. Fregosi, p. 297.
42. Braudel, vol. 2, p. 1091.
43. Fregosi, p. 322.
44. Braudel, vol. 2, p. 1103.
45. Vaughan, p. 162.
46. Braudel, vol. 2, p. 844.
47. Salvatore Bono, *I corsari barbareschi* (Torino: Edizioni RAI, 1964), p. 3.

48. Fregosi, p. 61.
49. É. Lévi-Provençal, vol. 1, p. 18.
50. Ibid., pp. 172–173.
51. Lévi-Provençal, vol. 2, p. 157.
52. Ibid., p. 160.
53. Ibid., p. 155.
54. Although their methods are similar, a pirate is different from a corsair. Unlike a pirate, a corsair acts on the permission of its mother country; his status is valid only during times of war and only against enemy vessels. A pirate, on the other hand, "ravaged the seas of his own accord without precise legal sanction, chose his targets more or less indiscriminately, and amassed his prizes or booty only for his own (or his investors, if they existed) profit." See Irene B. Katele, "Piracy and the Venetian State: The Dilemma of Maritime Defense in the Fourteenth Century" *Speculum*, 63 (October 1988), 4:865–866n. Also Bono, p. 12.
55. The terms "Barbary coast" or "Barbary corsairs" (sometimes Barbaresques) originated from the corrupted name of the region in North Africa inhabited by Berber tribes (the land of Berbers). See Martin Rheinheimer, "Identität und Kulturkonflikt: Selbstzeugnisse schleswigholsteinischer Sklaven in den Barbareskenstaaten." *Historische Zeitschrift* 269 (Oktober 1999), 2:320. Among the principalities in North Africa involved in the privateering, the leaders were Algiers, Tunisia, and Tripoli.
56. Braudel, vol. 2, p. 865.
57. Rheinheimer, p. 323.
58. Braudel, vol. 2, p. 867.
59. Ibid., p. 875.
60. Vaughan, p. 243.
61. For further details on the captain of the gulf and the role of the piracy in the rivalry between Italian states, see Katele, "Piracy and the Venetian State," pp. 865–889.
62. Robert C. Davis, "Counting European Slaves on the Barbary Coast" *Past & Present* 172 (August 2001), 89.
63. Ibid., p. 90.
64. Ibid., p. 94.
65. Ibid., p. 118.
66. Bono, p. 231.
67. Rheinheimer, pp. 324–325.
68. Charles Verlinden, *L'esclavage dans l'Europe médiéval*, Vol. 2 (Gent: Rijksuniversiteit te Gent, 1977), p. 259.
69. From 1400 to 1425, Russian slaves in Genoa amounted to 20 percent of the enslaved population; from 1425 to 1450 their number rose to 41.5 percent. See Verlinden, p. 485.

70. On October 1, 1246, Innocent IV complained to prelates from the kingdom of Jerusalem that the merchants from Genoa, Pisa, and Venice who traveled in Byzantine waters sold slaves at Jerusalem ports—Christian Greeks, Bulgarians, Ruthenians, and Vlachs—who sought refuge in churches and demanded liberty. See ibid., p. 449.

71. Ibid., pp. 1031–1032.

72. Ibid., p. 1029.

Chapter Four. Religion's Role in the Confrontation.

1. Fregosi, p. 237.

2. Nikolai Osokin, *Istoriia albigoitsev i ikh vremeni* (The History of Albigensians and Their Time) (Moscow: AST, 2000), p. 241.

3. See Justo L. González, *The Story of Christianity*, Vol. 1: *The Early Church to the Dawn of the Reformation* (San Francisco: Harper & Row, 1984), Appendix.

4. Osokin, p. 263.

5. Lévi-Provençal, vol. 1, p. 115.

6. Ibid., vol. 2, p. 36.

7. Sidney Nettleton Fisher, "Civil Strife in the Ottoman Empire 1481–1503," *Journal of Modern History* 13 (December 1941), 4:451.

8. Vryonis, p. 157.

9. Apostolos E. Vacalopoulos, *Origins of the Greek Nation: The Byzantine Period, 1204–1461*, trans. by Ian Moles (New Brunswick: Rutgers University Press, 1970), p. 73.

10. Vryonis, p. 271.

11. See Hodgson, pp. 203–204.

12. Vryonis, p. 273.

13. Ibid., pp. 171, 274.

14. Vryonis, p. 184.

15. Peter F. Sugar, *Southeastern Europe Under Ottoman Rule, 1354–1804* (Seattle: University of Washington Press, 1977), p. 96.

16. Ibid., p. 73.

17. Ronald C. Jennings, *Christians and Muslims in Ottoman Cyprus and the Mediterranean World, 1571–1640* (New York: New York University Press, 1993), p. 133.

18. Sugar, p. 45.

19. On the ideas and factors that influenced them, see Vaughan, pp. 24–25, 215.

20. Vacalopoulos, p. 93.

21. A few Roman Catholics in the Ottoman Empire were considered members of the Orthodox *millet*, but generally they fell under the jurisdiction of capitulations granted by the sultan to European powers, pri-

marily to France. Already in 1528 France's King Francis, with the assistance of Venice, corresponded with Suleiman the Magnificent about Christian rights in Jerusalem. See Vaughan, p. 121. On the Roman Catholic members of the Orthodox *millet*, see Sugar, p. 49.

22. Oded Peri, "Ottoman Rule, Islam, and Christian Cult in Seventeenth-Century Jerusalem." *Essays on Ottoman Civilization. Proceedings of the XIIth Congress of the Comité International d'Étude Pré-Ottomanes et Ottomanes, Praha 1996* (Prague: Academy of Sciences of the Czech Republic Oriental Institute, 1998), p. 300.

23. Late in 1645, Constantinople instructed the kadi of Jerusalem to inquire into complaints lodged by the Muslims of Mount Zion against Franciscan monks, and to prevent the latter from publicly exhibiting their heretical faith. Yet the Franciscans had a counter-firman from 1641 that allowed them to celebrate Palm Sunday in the manner and place they normally used. Ibid., pp. 301–302.

24. *Cambridge History of Islam*, pp. 89–91.

25. Vryonis, p. 360.

26. John L. Esposito, ed., *The Oxford Encyclopedia of the Modern Islamic World* (New York: Oxford University Press, 1995), p. 103.

27. Hodgson, pp. 220, 222.

28. Sugar, p. 54. Richard Bulliet shows that preachers revered for their sanctity were particularly effective converters: "The converts to Islam did desire guidance, however, in how to live a good Muslim life. Since the role of exemplar was not filled by a formally invested religious functionary, certain obviously pious individuals came to be informally recognized as exemplars. Recognition might derive from membership in or association with the Prophet's family or the families of other saintly early figures, but more often it went to individuals who simply appeared to be good Muslims, notably to those who were studious and ascetic. Indeed, to some extent the Muslim population of convert origin probably recognized as exemplars of good Muslim life individuals whom they judged to be so qualified not by still-uncertain Islamic social standards but by standards they were accustomed to associate with formally defined religious leaders in the non-Islamic communities. The Muslim ascetic or *zāhid*, for example, may have taken the place in the minds of converts from Christianity filled by the monk." See Richard W. Bulliet, *Conversion to Islam in the Medieval Period: An Essay in Quantitative History* (Cambridge, Mass.: Harvard University Press, 1979), pp. 39–40.

29. Hodgson, p. 538.

30. Vacalopoulos, p. 67.

31. Bono, p. 256.

32. Speros Vryonis, Jr., "Isidore Glabas and the Turkish *Devshirme*." *Speculum* 31 (July 1956), 3:437–438.

33. Sugar, p. 56.
34. Ibrahim Pasha of Greek origin, who held the office of grand vizier under Suleiman I for thirteen years befoe his execution in 1536, was accused of many wrongdoings while in office, including the charge that he supported by all means, including obviously financial, his relatives. Mehmed Sokollu, grand vizier from 1564 to 1579, also undertook efforts to promote the interests of the Serbs, toward whom he, being Serb by origin, harbored warm feelings. Ibid., p. 58.
35. Vryonis, "Isidore Glabas," pp. 440–441.
36. This comparison is in David Saville Muzzey, "Medieval Morals," *International Journal of Ethics* 17 (October, 1906), 1:35–36. According to the author, the discrepancy between the romantic air that surrounded public actions and the material and mental poverty and inexperience of the age "makes the Middle Ages so strikingly like the period of childhood in a man's life: generous enthusiasm, immediate world-reformations, unattainable ethical aspirations, inviolable codes of chivalry, uncompromising programs of society on the one hand, as witnessed by the Crusades, the self-chastisement of the ascetics in monasteries, the preaching of Franciscan and Dominican Friars, the vigils of virgin knights, and the visions of macerated saints; on the other hand the violences and crudities of childhood, its ready beliefs and awful fears, its unguarded frankness of expression, its display of emotions, its immediacy of aim, its absorption in moving pictures, its supreme need of restlessness."
37. Norman Daniel, *Islam and the West: The Making of an Image* (Edinburgh: Edinburgh University Press, 1960), p. 116.
38. Aziz Ahmad, *A History of Islamic Sicily* (Edinburgh: Edinburgh University Press, 1975), p. 86. The author notes: "It is an irony of history that this end was brought about by an emperor who was a great admirer of Islamic intellectual and material culture, and was in many ways involved in it personally." (Ibid.)
39. Andrew C. Hess, "The Moriscos: An Ottoman Fifth Column in Sixteenth-Century Spain," *American Historical Review* 74 (October, 1968), 1:24–25.
40. Lewis, *Islam and the West*, p. 128.
41. Ibid., p. 189n.
42. Daniel, pp. 57, 59, 67, 68, 96.
43. Ibid., p. 107.
44. Ibid., p. 145.
45. Ibid., p. 263.
46. Robert I. Burns, S.J., "Christian-Islamic Confrontation in the West: The Thirteenth-Century Dream of Conversion," *American Historical Review* 76 (December, 1971), 5:1390.

47. Ibid.
48. Ibid., pp. 1392–1393.
49. Daniel, p. 120.
50. Ibid., p. 122. Friar Livin burst into the Friday prayer in the presence of the sultan and cried out against Islam. The sultan was initially reluctant to act and tried to quiet the people by saying that poverty and fasting had unbalanced the friar. Over the course of his imprisonment, Livin made himself so objectionable that the sultan gave in and secured to Livin the end he desired.
51. Burns, p. 1408.
52. Robert H. Schwoebel, "Coexistence, Conversion, and the Crusade against the Turks," *Studies in the Renaissance* 12 (1965), 176–177.
53. Ibid., p. 178.

Chapter Five. Europe Ascendant.

1. Ivan Parvev, *Habsburgs and Ottomans between Vienna and Belgrade (1683–1739)* (Boulder: East European Monographs, 1995), p. 28.
2. Ibid., p. 40.
3. This thesis is explored in: Archibald R. Lewis, "The Closing of the Medieval Frontier, 1250–1350," *Speculum* 33 (October 1958), 4:475–483. The author suggests that "the ending or closing of Europe's internal or external frontiers between the years 1250 and 1350" influenced "all segments of life in this period" (p. 479). The external frontiers were closed after the slowing of the process of the *Reconquista* in Spain and the elimination of the Crusaders' conquests in Syria and Anatolia. Thus the prospects for European expansion in the Orient were significantly diminished. When unused land on the European continent itself, which had enriched western European society before 1250, ceased to exist, internal frontiers likewise contracted. "A Western European world which had been steadily expanding internally and externally down to 1250 saw its expansion halted and come to a stop as its frontiers closed" (p. 480). Since the expansion of these frontiers was associated with the rise of the economy, the broadening of intellectual knowledge, and the flourishing of art, their closing led to the stagnation of Europe and its general weakening.
4. Paul Kennedy, *The Rise and Fall of the Great Powers: Economic Change and Military Conflict from 1500 to 2000* (New York: Random House, 1987), pp. 16–17.
5. Ibid., pp. xvi, 19–20.
6. The term is used by Marshall Hodgson in *The Venture of Islam: Conscience and History in a World Civilization*, Vol. 3: *The Gunpowder Empires and Modern Times* (Chicago: University of Chicago Press, 1974).

7. Archibald R. Lewis, "The Islamic World and the Latin West, 1350–1500," *Speculum* 65 (October 1990), 4:839.

8. Hodgson, p. 204.

9. "There was no . . . movement to translate the products of Christian Europe, tainted as they were with a rival and, in Muslim eyes, a superseded religion. With a very few, unnoticed exceptions, no European books were translated into Arabic or Turkish or Persian; apart from some sailors and traders and other men of low estate, who used a kind of pidgin Italian known as the lingua franca, there were few Muslims who could speak or understand a European language, and even fewer who could read a European book." Lewis, *Islam and the West*, p. 34.

10. Hodgson, p. 203.

11. Bernard Lewis, *The Muslim Discovery of Europe* (New York: Norton, 2001), p. 119.

12. Kennedy, pp. 11–12.

13. Stanford J. Shaw, *Between Old and New: The Ottoman Empire under Sultan Selim III, 1789–1807* (Cambridge, Mass.: Harvard University Press, 1971), pp. 211–212.

14. Ibid., p. 212.

15. Lewis, *The Muslim Discovery*, pp. 47–48.

16. Shaw, p. 82.

17. Hodgson, p. 127.

18. Parvev, p. 130. S. M. Solov'ev, *Istoriia Rossii s drevneishikh vremyon* (The History of Russia Since Ancient Times), kniga 7, vol. 14 (Moscow: Mysl', 1991), pp. 589–590.

19. See Paul Bernard, "Austria's Last Turkish War: Some Further Thoughts," *Austrian History Yearbook*, vol. 19–20, part 1 (Minneapolis: University of Minnesota, 1988), pp. 15–31; and Shaw, pp. 49, 61–68.

20. Kennedy, p. 150.

21. Hodgson, p. 177.

22. Salvatore Bono, *I corsari barbareschi* (Torino: Edizioni RAI, 1964), pp. 75–76; Alain Brissaud, *Islam et chrétienté: Treize siècle de cohabitation* (Paris: Robert Laffont, 1991), p. 155.

23. Alexander Bennigsen and Chantal Lemercier-Quelquejay, *Islam in the Soviet Union* (New York: Praeger, 1967), pp. 10–11.

24. Editorial comment, "England and Russia in Central Asia," *American Journal of International Law* 3 (January 1909), 1:170–171.

25. Lewis, *Islam and the West*, p. 22; Hodgson, pp. 315–316.

26. Charles and Barbara Jelavich, *The Establishment of the Balkan National States, 1804–1920* (Seattle: University of Washington Press, 1977), p. 5.

27. Ibid., p. 11.

28. Charles and Barbara Jelavich, p. 51. Moreover, as a result of this victory the Greeks lost the privileged positions they generally enjoyed in the

Ottoman Empire. They lost the hospodarships of Moldavia and Wallachia. In Constantinople, Armenians replaced Greeks as predominant forces in banking. The special position of the Greek merchant community was also lost. In general, afterward the Greeks were looked upon with suspicion and hostility by the Ottoman authorities. (Ibid.)

29. Ibid., pp. 222–229.
30. On the origins of the Wahhabi movement and the Saudi state, see Shaw, pp. 221–227, 294–298.
31. Hodgson, p. 217; Charles and Barbara Jelavich, p. 19; Shaw, pp. 276, 287–291.
32. Lewis, *Islam and the West*, p. 19.
33. Parvev, p. 272.
34. Halil Inalcık, "The Meaning of Legacy: The Ottoman Case," in L. Carl Brown, ed., *Imperial Legacy: The Ottoman Imprint on the Balkans and the Middle East* (New York: Columbia University Press, 1996), p. 23.
35. Ibid., p. 22.
36. Charles and Barbara Jelavich, p. 22.
37. Until the peace of Küçük Kaynarca (1774), Russian merchants had to transport their goods on Turkish vessels, which were often in poor condition. For the economic aspects of Russian policy toward the Ottoman Empire in the eighteenth century, see Vladimir Ulyanitskii, *Dardanelly, Bosfor i Chernoye more v XVIII veke* (The Dardanelles, Bosporus and the Black Sea in the Eighteenth Century) (Moscow: Tipografia Gatzuaa, 1883).
38. The so-called Greek Project of Count Potemkin, which Catherine the Great hoped to realize in the 1780s with the support of the Austrian Empire, proved to be a dream that contradicted existing realities. The principal goal of this project was the expulsion of the Turks from Europe and the establishment of the "Greek tsardom," with a Russian grand duke at its throne. With this purpose in mind, Catherine's grandson, born in 1779, was baptized as Constantine, in memory of the Roman emperor who had founded Constantinople and as a claim of the Russian tsars to the Byzantine heritage. The Greek Project failed because of disputes between its participants, Russia and Austria. See Sergei Zhigarev, *Russkaia politika v vostochnom voprose (eia istoria v XVI–XIX vekakh, kriticheskaia otsenka i budushchie zadachi): Istoriko-yuridicheskie ocherki* (Russian Policy Toward the Eastern Question, Its History in the Sixteenth to Nineteenth Centuries, Critical Appraisal, and Future Tasks: Historical-Juridical Essays) (Moscow: Moscow University, 1896), pp. 208–214.
39. S. S. Tatishchev, *Vneshniaia politika imperatora Nikolaia Pervago: vvedenie v istoriiu vneshnikh snoshenii Rossii v epokhu Sevastopol'skoi voiny* (The Foreign Policy of the Emperor Nicholas I: An Introduction

to the History of Russia's Foreign Relations in the Epoch of the Sebastopol War) (St. Petersburg: I. N. Skorokhodov's Typography, 1887), pp. 202–203.

40. Ibid., p. 205.

41. The concept of Moscow as the Third Rome was first expressed in the famous letter of the monk Philotheos to Grand Prince Basil III early in the sixteenth century. Regarding Muscovite Russia as the only orthodox land in the world, the monk solemnly declared: "Listen and attend, pious tsar, that all Christian empires are gathered in your single one, that two Romes have fallen, and the third one stands, and a fourth one there shall not be; your empire will not fall to others, according to the great Evangelist." See Michael Cherniavsky, "'Holy Russia': A Study in the History of an Idea," *American Historical Review* 63 (April 1958), 3:617–637. Quotation on p. 619.

42. Barbara Jelavich draws attention to this aspect in her book on Russian policy toward the Balkans from the nineteenth century to World War I. See Barbara Jelavich, *Russia's Balkan Entanglements, 1806–1914* (Cambridge: Cambridge University Press, 1991), p. 33.

43. According to the words of one Austrian diplomat. See Tatishchev, p. 307.

44. On August 2, 1914, the Turkish grand vizier signed a secret treaty of alliance with Germany. Under Article II the Ottoman Empire undertook to side with Germany and Austria-Hungary if the latter powers became involved in a war with Russia. Despite Istanbul's initial reluctance to commit to immediate intervention on the side of the Central Powers, the policy of "uneasy neutrality" was overcome by the combined efforts of Turkish "interventionists," such as Enver Pasha, and of German officers and diplomats in the Ottoman capital, and the empire entered the war at the beginning of November 1914. For German-Turkish cooperation in the initial months of World War I, see Ulrich Trumpener, "German Military Aid to Turkey in 1914: An Historical Re-Evaluation," *Journal of Modern History* 32 (January 1960), 2:145–149.

45. Kennedy, p. 149.

46. Hodgson, p. 244.

47. Brissaud, pp. 159–160.

48. Hodgson, p. 299.

49. Between 1738 and 1755, 418 of the 536 mosques in the governorate-general of Kazan were closed while special schools were opened under the direction of Russian missionaries for the children of the converts. See Bennigsen-Quelquejay, p. 12.

50. Heinz-Dietrich Löwe, "Poles, Jews, and Tatars: Religion, Ethnicity, and Social Structure in Tsarist Nationality Policies," *Jewish Social Studies* 6 (Spring/Summer 2000), 3:56.

51. Ibid., p. 67.

52. Bennigsen and Lemercier-Quelquejay, p. 15; Hodgson, p. 320.

53. Löwe, p. 73; see also Galina M. Yemelianova, "Volga Tatars, Russians and the Russian States at the Turn of the Nineteenth Century: Relationships and Perceptions," *Slavonic and East European Review* 77 (July 1999), 3:474–475.

54. For example, by the close of the nineteenth century, among two million Muslim Tatars there were eight thousand who possessed the hereditary rights of Russia's nobility. More than five hundred had been elevated to the position of nobleman for life and about two thousand had special privileges as merchants. See R. G. Landa, "Rossiia i Vostok. Rossiia i islam: vzaimodeistviie dvukh kul'tur" (Russia and the Orient. Russia and Islam: The Interaction of the Two Cultures) *Vostok* 5 (September 1, 2000), 26. See also Bennigsen-Quelquejay, p. 17.

55. "The Bolshevik leaders considered themselves committed by their doctrine to a ceaseless fight against all religions—'false ideologies in the service of the exploiting classes.' For them, Islam was like any other religion: a 'superstructural' phenomenon of capitalist or pre-capitalist society. . . ." See Bennigsen-Quelquejay, p. 139.

56. Baymirza Hayit, *Islam and Turkestan Under Russian Rule* (Istanbul: Can Matbaa, 1987), pp. 87, 121.

57. ". . . Since 1945, perhaps 500 Soviet Muslims have been able to visit the Holy Places of Islam. An absurdly small number, it is true, yet these carefully screened pilgrims, who usually know Arabic well, have by their very presence furnished evidence of the survival and traditional character of Islam in the USSR." Bennigsen-Quelquejay, p. 178.

58. Holt, Lambton, and Lewis, *The Cambridge History of Islam*, Vol. 1: *The Central Islamic Lands*, p. 642.

59. Lewis, *Islam and the West*, p. 20.

60. For example, by Bernard Lewis. See ibid., p. 39.

61. M. M. Bliev and V. V. Degoev, *Kavkazskaiia voina* (The Caucasian War) (Moscow: Roset, 1994), pp. 129–130.

62. Ibid., p. 215.

63. Parvev, p. 202; Shaw, p. 8; Lewis, *The Muslim Discovery of Europe*, pp. 49–50.

64. For a full description and analysis of Selim III's reforms, see Stanford Shaw, *Between Old and New*.

65. On the role of this issue during the period of *Tanzimat*, see Roderic H. Davison, "Turkish Attitudes Concerning Christian-Muslim Equality in the Nineteenth Century," *American Historical Review* 59 (July 1954), 4:844–864.

66. Hodgson, pp. 262, 265.

67. John Obert Voll, *Islam: Continuity and Change in the Modern World*, 2nd ed. (Syracuse: Syracuse University Press, 1994), p. 157.

68. Ibid., p. 165.
69. Ibid., p. 157.
70. Bennigsen and Lemercier-Quelquejay, p. 46.
71. Hodgson, pp. 275, 308; Voll, pp. 91, 95, 163.
72. On *Jadidism*, see D. Ishakov, "Jadidism kak natsiestroitel'stvo" (*Jadidism* as the Building of Nation) *Iman Nuri* 4 (1996), 22; Yemelianova, pp. 450, 458.
73. Voll, p. 53.
74. Ibid., p. 181.

Chapter Six. Cooperation, Coexistence, and Influence.

1. In his book *Mohammed and Charlemagne* (Mineola: Dover Publications, 2001).
2. Daniel C. Dennett, Jr., "Pirenne and Muhammad," *Speculum* 23 (April 1948), 2:165–190; Richard Hodges and David Whitehouse, *Mohammed, Charlemagne and the Origins of Europe: Archaeology and the Pirenne Thesis* (Ithaca: Cornell University Press, 1983).
3. Dennett, p. 173.
4. Adam Mez, *Die Renaissance des Islâms* (Heidelberg, 1922). Only a Russian translation of this book was available to me: Adam Mets, *Musul'manskii Renessans* (Moscow: ViM, 1996), p. 428.
5. M. D. Poluboiarinova, *Rus' i Volzhskaia Bolgaria v X–XV vv.* (Russia and the Volga Bulgaria in the Tenth–Fifteenth centuries) (Moscow: Nauka, 1993), p. 114.
6. Lewis, *The Muslim Discovery of Europe*, p. 187.
7. Dennett, pp. 175–176.
8. Lewis, p. 189.
9. Dennett, p. 175.
10. Armand O. Citarella, "The Relations of Amalfi with the Arab World before the Crusades," *Speculum* 42 (April 1967), 2:301–302.
11. Ibid., p. 307.
12. Ibid., p. 311.
13. Lewis, p. 24.
14. Frederic C. Lane, *Venice: A Maritime Republic* (Baltimore: Johns Hopkins University Press, 1973), p. 72.
15. Eliyahu Ashtor, *Levant Trade in the Later Middle Ages* (Princeton: Princeton University Press, 1983), p. 23.
16. Ibid., pp. 24–25. Egypt and Syria also exported alkali needed for the European soap and glass industries.
17. Ibid., p. 23.
18. Lewis, p. 194.
19. Ashtor, p. 428.

20. Ibid., p. 199.
21. Ibid., p. 511.
22. Ibid., p. 57.
23. Michel Balard, "Gênes et la mer Noire (XIIIe–XVe siècles)," *Revue historique* 547 (Juillet–Septembre 1983), 36.
24. Ashtor, p. 58.
25. Papal prohibitions against trade with the Muslim world, as well as trade embargoes imposed by the Holy See, generally ceased in the fifteenth century. "The supplications submitted to the Holy See by some Genoese merchants in 1418–1423 to obtain absolution for having carried on such trade in the past and for permission to engage in it in the future were no more than an expression of personal devoutness." (Ibid., pp. 215–216).
26. Peter W. Edbury, *The Kingdom of Cyprus and the Crusades, 1191–1374* (Cambridge: Cambridge University Press, 1991), p. 165.
27. Ibid., p. 171.
28. Ashtor, p. 88.
29. See Chapter 2 above.
30. Peter Lock, *The Franks in the Aegean, 1204–1500* (London: Longman, 1995), pp. 104, 106, 116.
31. Ashtor, pp. 223, 287.
32. Ibid., p. 287.
33. Arthur Leon Horniker, "Anglo-French Rivalry in the Levant from 1583 to 1612," *Journal of Modern History* 18 (December 1946), 4:297–298.
34. Ashtor, pp. 289–290.
35. Lewis, p. 48.
36. Dorothy M. Vaughan, *Europe and the Turk: A Pattern of Alliances, 1350–1700* (Liverpool: University Press, 1954), p. 121.
37. Horniker, p. 289.
38. É. Lévi-Provençal, *Histoire de l'Espagne musulmane*, Vol. 1: *La conquête et l'émirat hispano-umaiyade (710–912)* (Paris, Leiden: Brill, 1950), p. 251.
39. Ibid., p. 253.
40. Lewis, p. 93.
41. Among them Bernard Lewis, who referred to the absence of any mention about them in Arab chronicles. See Lewis, p. 92.
42. Franco Gardini, *Europe and Islam*, trans. by Caroline Beamish (Oxford: Blackwell, 1999), p. 14.
43. Lewis, p. 92.
44. For example, the embassy sent by a Frankish queen called Bertha to the Caliph al-Muktafi in the year 906, about which there was a description in an Arab chronicle. See Lewis, pp. 92–93, with a passage from an Arab chronicle on this embassy included.

45. É. Lévi-Provençal, p. 148.
46. Lewis, p. 114.
47. Stanford J. Shaw, *Between Old and New: The Ottoman Empire Under Sultan Selim III 1789–1807* (Cambridge, Mass.: Harvard University Press, 1971), pp. 187–188.
48. Ibid., p. 189.
49. Ibid., p. 190.
50. Dante acknowledges the contributions of the two greatest Arabic philosophers, Avicenna and Averroes, by placing them in Limbo.
51. W. Montgomery Watt, *The Influence of Islam on Medieval Europe* (Edinburgh: University of Edinburgh Press, 1972), pp. 58–59.
52. Ibid., p. 27.
53. Oleg Grabar, "Patterns and Ways of Cultural Exchange," in Vladimir P. Goss, ed., *The Meeting of Two Worlds: Cultural Exchange Between East and West During the Period of the Crusades* (Kalamazoo: Western Michigan University Medieval Institute Publications, 1986), p. 442.
54. Lewis, pp. 74–75.
55. Watt, p. 79.
56. Gardini, p. 92.
57. "Without the Arabs, European science and philosophy would not have developed when they did. The Arabs were no mere transmitters of Greek thought but genuine bearers, who both kept alive the disciplines they had been taught and extended their range. About 1100, Europeans became seriously interested in the sciences and philosophy of their Saracen enemies, these disciplines were at their zenith; and the Europeans had to learn all they could from the Arabs before they themselves could make further advances." (Watt, p. 43).
58. Nikita Elisséeff, "Les échanges culturels entre le monde musulman et les croisés à l'époque de Nūr ad-Dīn b. Zankī (m. 1174)" in Goss, *The Meeting of Two Worlds*, pp. 45, 49.
59. Gardini, p. 94.
60. Aziz Ahmad, *A History of Islamic Sicily* (Edinburgh: Edinburgh University Press, 1975), pp. 63, 64–65, 89.
61. See: Joselita Raspi Serra, "Influenze arabe nella cultura architettonica degli ordini in Italia," in Goss, *The Meeting of Two Worlds*, pp. 277–284; and Christine Verzár Bornstein, "Romanesque Sculpture in Southern Italy and Islam: A Revaluation," ibid., pp. 285–293.
62. Ahmad, p. 92.
63. Watt, p. 26.
64. Marlène Albert-Llorca and Jean-Pierre Albert, "Mahomet, la Vierge et la frontière," *Annales* 4 (July–August 1995), 855–886.
65. É. Lévi-Provençal, vol. 2, p. 129.
66. This excessive love of everything relating to the Tatars, especially their language and traditions, was strongly resented by Vasilii II's opponents

among the Russian nobility, who accused him of selling out Russia to the infidels. The Russian boyars overthrew him and had him blinded and sent into exile. But with the help of his Tatar subjects, Vasilii soon reclaimed the throne. See: S. M. Soloviov, *History of Russia from Ancient Times,* book 2, vol. 4 (Moscow: Mysl', 1988), pp. 394, 396, 399.

67. Gardini, p. 185.

68. Ibid.

69. On orientalism as a branch of scholarship, see Lewis, *Islam and the West* (New York: Oxford University Press, 1993), pp. 99–118.

70. Lewis, p. 223.

71. Shaw, pp. 7–8; Marshall G. S. Hodgson, *The Venture of Islam: Conscience and History in a World Civilization,* Vol. 3: *The Gunpowder Empires and Modern Times* (Chicago: University of Chicago Press, 1974), p. 139.

72. É. Lévi-Provençal, vol. 1, p. 290.

73. Peter F. Sugar, *Southeastern Europe Under Ottoman Rule, 1354–1804* (Seattle: University of Washington Press, 1977), p. 128.

74. Charles Verlinden, *L'esclavage dans l'Europe médiévale,* Vol. 2 (Gent: Rijksuniversiteit te Gent, 1977), p. 284.

75. A word derived from Arabic *al-mudajjan,* meaning "those allowed to remain." See Joseph F. O'Callaghan, "The Mudejars of Castile and Portugal in the Twelfth and Thirteenth Centuries," in James M. Powell, ed., *Muslims Under Latin Rule, 1100–1300* (Princeton: Princeton University Press, 1990), p. 13.

76. Robert I. Burns, S.J., "Muslims in the Thirteenth-Century Realms of Aragon: Interaction and Reaction," in Powell, *Muslims Under Latin Rule,* p. 86.

77. Lock, p. 113.

78. Ibid.

79. George Vernadsky, *The Mongols and Russia* (New Haven: Yale University Press, 1953), p. 320.

80. V. V. Vel'aminov-Zernov, *Izsledovanie o Kasimovskikh tsariakh i tsarevichakh* (Research of the Tsars and Tsarevichs of Kasimov), vol. 1 (St. Petersburg: Academy of Sciences Press, 1863), pp. 15, 26–27.

81. Ibid., p. 251.

82. Ibid., p. 290.

83. Vel'aminov-Zernov, *Izsledovanie,* vol. 2 (St. Petersburg: Academy of Sciences Press, 1864), p. 25.

84. Ibid., pp. 83–84.

85. Vel'aminov-Zernov, *Izsledovanie,* vol. 4 (St. Petersburg, Academy of Sciences Press, 1887), pp. 12–13.

86. See, for instance, on the conversion of Murtaza-Ali, in Vel'aminov-Zernov, vol. 2, p. 86.

87. Ibid., vol. 4, p. 5.

88. Vernadsky, p. 370.
89. É. Lévi-Provençal, vol. 1, p. 331.
90. Ibid., pp. 120–121.
91. Speros Vryonis, Jr., *The Decline of Medieval Hellenism in Asia Minor and the Process of Islamization from the Eleventh Through the Fifteenth Century* (Berkeley: University of California Press, 1971), p. 227.
92. Vernadsky, p. 196.
93. Ibid., p. 198.
94. Vaughan, p. 170.
95. Lewis A. Coser, "The Alien as a Servant of Power: Court Jews and Christian Renegades," *American Sociological Review* 37 (October 1972), 5:578.
96. L. S. Stavrianos, *The Balkans Since 1453* (New York: Rinehart, 1958), p. 85. Cited in Coser, p. 578.

Chapter Seven. Europe and Islam in the Modern World.

1. For a discussion of the attitudes of various schools of Muslim jurisprudence toward the issue of life among unbelievers, see Lewis, *Islam and the West*, pp. 51–53.
2. Jørgen Nielsen, *Towards a European Islam* (New York: St. Martin's Press, 1999), pp. 2–4.
3. W. A. R. Shadid and P. S. van Koningsveld, eds., *Muslims in the Margin: Political Responses to the Presence of Islam in Western Europe* (Kampen: Pharos, 1996), p. 1.
4. Ibid., p. 7.
5. Ibid., pp. 15–16.
6. Catherine Wihtol de Wenden, "Muslims in France," in Shadid and van Koningsveld, *Muslims in the Margin*, p. 59.
7. Stefano Allievi, "Muslim Organizations and Islam-State Relations: The Italian Case," in ibid., p. 187.
8. Nielsen, p. 13.
9. Wihtol, p. 53.
10. Ibid., p. 55. The ratio of different nationalities among Muslims is as follows: the most numerous are young Franco-Maghrebians (1 million); they are followed by Maghrebians of Algeria, Tunisia, and Morocco (1,412,000 at the census of March 1990), Black Africans (178,000, half of whom have a Muslim cultural background), Turks (201,000), harkis (500,000), Pakistanese and others (50,000), and converted French.
11. Jacques Waardenburg, "Muslims as Dhimmis. The Emancipation of Muslim Immigrants in Europe: The Case of Switzerland," in Shadid and van Koningsveld, *Muslims in the Margin*, p. 147.
12. Nielsen, p. 17.

13. Wihtol, p. 58.

14. Johan Leman and Monique Renaerts, "Dialogues at Different Institutional Levels Among Authorities and Muslims in Belgium," in Shadid and van Koningsveld, *Muslims in the Margin*, pp. 165–167.

15. Wihtol, p. 62.

16. Jillian Schwedler, "Islamic Identity: Myth, Menace, or Mobilizer?" *SAIS Review* 21 (Summer–Fall, 2001), 2:6.

17. Nielsen, pp. 20, 34.

18. Ibid., 74.

19. Ibid., p. 30.

20. Ibid., pp. 30–32.

21. Ibid., p. 32.

22. Ibid., pp. 89–90.

23. Montserrat Abumalham, "The Muslim Presence in Spain: Policy and Society," in Shadid and van Koningsveld, *Muslims in the Margin*, p. 85.

24. Martha Brill Olcott, "Soviet Islam and World Revolution," *World Politics* 34 (July 1982), 4:494.

25. Ibid., p. 500.

26. In Kyrgyzstan the average monthly wage in 1999 was only US$22, and 60 percent of the Kyrgyz population lives on the edge of poverty. See Shireen T. Hunter, "Religion, Politics, and Security in Central Asia," in *SAIS Review* 21 (Summer–Fall 2001), 2:78.

27. O. Bibikova, "Blizhnee zarubezh'ie. Tsentral'naia Aziia. Nastupleniie islamskogo ekstremizma" (Near Abroad. Central Asia. Advance of Islamic Extremism), *Asia and Africa Today* (August 15, 2000), 15–16.

28. Hunter, pp. 80–81.

29. Robert V. Barylski, "The Russian Federation and Eurasia's Islamic Crescent," *Europe-Asia Studies* 46 (1994), 3:389–390.

30. Some 3,000 Russian troops on the Uzbekistan-Afghanistan border, 25,000 Russian troops on the Tajikistan-Afghanistan border, Russian border guards in Turkmenistan, and local divisions all went on a high state of alert. Russia offered to send ten battalions to Kyrgyzstan after an appeal by Kyrgyz president Askar Akayev, even though this country has no border with Afghanistan. Ahmed Rashid, *Taliban: Militant Islam, Oil and Fundamentalism in Central Asia* (New Haven: Yale Nota Bene, 2000), p. 60.

31. Bibikova, p. 21.

32. Barylski, p. 410. Among the groups of permanent non-Russian residents in Moscow, Muslims are second in number after Ukrainians. They include Tatars, Azerbaijanis, Uzbeks, Kazakhs, Ossetians, Bashkirs, Kyrgyz, Tajics, Chechens, Turkmens, and Daghestanis. According to the results of the 1989 population census, representatives of different Muslim groups living in Moscow made up 2.6 percent of the total population of

the city. Tatars are the largest group, followed by the Azerbaijanis. See Aida Moseyko, "Muslims in Moscow: An Ethnic and Social Portrait of the Interior of a Russian City," in Jørgen S. Nielsen, ed., *The Christian-Muslim Frontier: Chaos, Clash or Dialogue?* (London: I. B. Tauris, 1998), p. 116.

33. R. M. Amirkhanov, "Islam in Tatar National Ideology and Policy," in ibid., p. 67.

34. R. Baltanov and G. Baltanova, "Islam, Christianity and Religious Trends in Tatarstan: The Issue of Conversion," in ibid., p. 88.

35. Ibid., pp. 84, 89–90.

36. Other factors also cited include the successful secularization of society during the Soviet years; the rising standard of Muslim education; the emancipation of women (at least in urban areas); brutal repression against most sections of the Muslim *ulama*; prohibition of religious literature; and the rupture of tradition due to the replacement of the Arabic script by the Roman and then Cyrillic script in all Muslim languages. See Aleksei Vasiliev, "Russia Destinies and Islam," in ibid., p. 30.

37. I. P. Dobaev, "Severnyi Kavkaz: Traditsionalism i radikalizm v sovremennom islame" (The Northern Caucasus: Traditionalism and Radicalism in Modern Islam), *Mirovaiia ekonomika i mezhdunarodnye otnoshenia* (World Economy and International Relations) 6 (2001), 23.

38. Between 1997 and 1999 some thirteen hundred people claimed to have been victims of kidnaping, banditry, and terrorism. See Anatol Lieven, "Nightmare in the Caucasus," *Washington Quarterly* 23 (2000), 1:148.

39. Dobaev, p. 29.

40. Lieven, p. 156.

41. Ibid., p. 155.

42. Shireen T. Hunter, *The Future of Islam and the West: Clash of Civilizations or Peaceful Coexistence?* (Westport: Praeger, 1998), p. 107.

43. Salwa Ismail, "Confronting the Other: Identity, Culture, Politics, and Conservative Islamism in Egypt," *International Journal of Middle East Studies* 30 (May 1998), 2:200.

44. Saudi Arabia's and the Wahhabis' activities are registered in Central Asia, Russia, and the Balkans. In the Balkans, and especially in the former Yugoslavia, Wahhabis increased the scope of their activities following conflicts around Bosnia-Herzegovina and Kosovo. According to a September 9, 1999, news release by the Saudi Joint Relief Committee for Kosovo, out of 4 million Saudi riyals spent by the committee on the ground in Kosovo, nearly half was spent to sponsor 388 religious "propagators" (missionaries), with the intent of converting Kosovars to Wahhabi fundamentalism. Another 600,000 riyals went to the reconstruction of 37 mosques, and 200,000 riyals were spent on 2 schools. As an

observer notes, "The amount of money involved was fairly modest (four million riyals is little more than a million U.S. dollars), except when one considers that the Saudis had only been on the scene in Kosovo for a little over two months at that point." See Stephen Schwartz, "Islamic Fundamentalism in the Balkans," *Partisan Review* 67 (Summer 2000), 3:423. It is noteworthy, as the same observer points out, that a greater proportion of Saudi aid was spent on fundamentalist "propagators" and on mosque building than on other humanitarian needs.

45. Robert H. Wiebe, *Who We Are: A History of Popular Nationalism* (Princeton: Princeton University Press, 2002), p. 204.

46. Anthony Shadid, *Legacy of the Prophet: Despots, Democrats, and the New Politics of Islam* (Boulder: Westview Press, 2001), p. 82.

47. Rashid, p. 130.

48. Ibid.

49. Ibid.

50. Ibid., p. 176. Diplomats at the U.S. embassy in Islamabad were too eager to believe Taliban leaders' assurances that they disliked Iran; that they would curb poppy cultivation and heroin production which flourished in Afghanistan during the civil war; that they were opposed to all outsiders remaining in Afghanistan including the Arab Afghans; and that they had no desire to seize power or rule the country. U.S. diplomats believed that the Taliban would meet essential U.S. aims in Afghanistan. As Ahmed Rashid noted, "It was a patently naïve hope given the Taliban's social base and because they themselves did not know what they represented nor whether they wanted state power" (ibid., p. 177).

51. See Shadid, pp. 85–87.

52. Toby Lester, "Oh, Gods!" *Atlantic Monthly* 289 (February 2002), 2:37.

53. Ibid., p. 45.

54. Ibid. "One of the most remarkable changes already taking place because of new religious movements is the underreported shift in the center of gravity in the Christian world. There has been a dramatic move from North to South. Christianity is most vital now in Africa, Asia, and Latin America, where independent churches, Pentecostalism, and even major Catholic Charismatic movements are expanding rapidly. The story of Christianity in twentieth-century Africa is particularly noteworthy. There were fewer than 10 million Christians in Africa in 1900; by 2000 there were more than 360 million" (ibid., p. 44).

55. Mark Juergensmeyer, *The New Cold War? Religious Nationalism Confronts the Secular States* (Berkeley: University of California Press, 1993), p. 41.

56. Barylski, pp. 403, 405.

57. Hunter, *The Future of Islam*, p. 147.
58. Juergensmeyer, p. 41.
59. Ibid., p. 155. An illustration of this assertion is the attacks of September 11, 2001. Their targets were what the Islamists consider the symbols of the West's capitalist power—the World Trade Center and the Pentagon.
60. "The savage martyrdom of Husain in Shi'ite Islam, the crucifixion of Jesus in Christianity, the sacrifice of Guru Tegh Bahadur in Sikhism, the bloody conquests detailed in the Hebrew Bible, the terrible battles celebrated in the Hindu epics, and the religious wars described in the Sinhalese Buddhist Pali Chronicles—all these events indicate that in virtually every religious tradition images of violence occupy a central place" (Juergensmeyer, pp. 153–154).
61. Shadid, p. 89.
62. Ibid.
63. Rashid, p. 88.
64. Ibid., p. 108.
65. An expression of Olivier Roy, an expert on Afghanistan. See Olivier Roy, "Fundamentalists Without a Common Cause," *Le Monde Diplomatique*, October 2, 1998, cited in Shadid, p. 90.
66. Shadid, p. 142.
67. Ibid., p. 126.
68. Ibid., p. 112.
69. Hunter, *The Future of Islam*, p. 114.
70. Ibid., p. 115.
71. Cited in Shadid, p. 216.
72. Ibid., p. 237.

Index

Index

A NOTE ON THE AUTHOR

Ilya V. Gaiduk is senior research fellow at the Institute of World History, Russian Academy of Sciences. Born in Krasnovodsk, Turkmenistan, he studied at the Moscow State Pedagogical Institute and the Institute of World History. Mr. Gaiduk has been an exchange scholar at the Kennan Institute for Advanced Russian Studies and a fellow of the Cold War International History Project, both at the Woodrow Wilson Center in Washington, D.C., and a fellow of the Norwegian Nobel Institute. He has also written *The Soviet Union and the Vietnam War* and *Confronting Vietnam: Soviet Policy Toward the Indochina Conflict*. He lives in Moscow.

WITHDRAWN